COMPUTER BOOK SERIES FROM IDG

Ami Pro® For Dummies

C000148545

The Standard SmartIcon Set

Icon	Purpose	Menu Command
	Open a file	File, Open
	Save current file	File, Save
	Print a file	File, Print
	Print an envelope	File, Print Envelope
	Full page/layout view	View, Full page and View, Custom
	Undo last action	Edit, Undo
	Cut to Clipboard	Edit, Cut
	Copy to Clipboard	Edit, Copy
	Paste Clipboard	Edit, Paste
B	Boldface text	Text, Bold
I	Italicize text	Text, Italic
U	Underline text	Text, Underline
	Fast format	Text, Fast Format
	Left align text	Text, Alignment, Left
	Center text	Text, Alignment, Center
	Show or hide ruler	View, Show (or Hide) Ruler
	Add a frame	Frame, Create Frame
	Create a table	Tools, Tables
ABC	Spell check	Tools, Spell check
T	Thesaurus	Tools, Thesaurus
G	Grammar check	Tools, Grammar check
	Create drawing	Tools, Drawing
	Add a chart	Tools, Charting
	Next icon set	Tools, SmartIcons

. . . For Dummies: #1 Computer Book Series for Beginners

COMPUTER
BOOK SERIES
FROM IDG

Ami Pro® For Dummies®

Cheat Sheet

Keyboard Shortcuts for Moving Around a Table

Keystrokes	Action
Shift+Tab	Moves the cursor to the left one cell
Ctrl+up arrow	Moves the cursor up one row
Ctrl+down arrow	Moves the cursor down one row
Home	Puts the cursor at the start of the cell you're in
Home, Home	Puts the cursor at the start of the first column of the row you're in
End	Puts the cursor at the end of the line in the same cell
End, End	Puts the cursor in the last column of the row you're in

Moving Around in Your Ami Pro File

Keys	Where They Take You
PgDn	Down one screen
PgUp	Up one screen
arrow keys	Right one character, left one character, down one line, up one line
Ctrl+arrow key	Right or left one word
Home	To the beginning of the line
Ctrl+Home	To the beginning of the document
Ctrl+.	To the beginning of the next sentence
Ctrl+up arrow	To the beginning of the paragraph

Selecting Text

To select a sentence	Hold down the Ctrl key; then click anywhere inside the sentence.
To select a word	Place the cursor on any word and double-click.
To select more than one word or sentence	Hold down Ctrl when you click or double-click, then drag.
To select a paragraph	Hold down Ctrl and double-click.

Help!

Pressing F1 from a document	F1 is the universal Help key. You can press it when you're using a document, if you don't mind starting with the main Contents screen.
Pressing F1 from a menu or dialog box	Pressing F1 from inside a dialog box does the same thing as clicking the question mark in the top right of a dialog box. You receive context-sensitive help.

IDG
BOOKS

. . . For Dummies: #1 Computer Book Series for Beginners

TM

References for the Rest of Us

COMPUTER BOOK SERIES FROM IDG

Are you intimidated and confused by computers? Do you find that traditional manuals are overloaded with technical details you'll never use? Do your friends and family always call you to fix simple problems on their PCs? Then the . . . *For Dummies* computer book series from IDG is for you.

. . . *For Dummies* books are written for those frustrated computer users who know they aren't really dumb but find that PC hardware, software, and indeed the unique vocabulary of computing make them feel helpless. . . . *For Dummies* books use a lighthearted approach, a down-to-earth style, and even cartoons and humorous icons to diffuse computer novices' fears and build their confidence. Lighthearted but not lightweight, these books are a perfect survival guide for anyone forced to use a computer.

> *"I like my copy so much I told friends; now they bought copies."*
>
> **Irene C., Orwell, Ohio**

> *"Quick, concise, nontechnical, and humorous."*
>
> **Jay A., Elburn, Illinois**

> *"Thanks, I needed this book. Now I can sleep at night."*
>
> **Robin F., British Columbia, Canada**

Already, hundreds of thousands of satisfied readers agree. They have made . . . *For Dummies* books the **#1 introductory level computer book series** and have written asking for more. So, if you're looking for the most fun and easy way to learn about computers, look to . . . *For Dummies* books to give you a helping hand.

IDG BOOKS

AMI PRO®
FOR
DUMMIES®

by Jim Meade
Foreword by Van Wolverton

IDG BOOKS

IDG Books Worldwide, Inc.
An International Data Group Company

Foster City, CA ♦ Chicago, IL ♦ Indianapolis, IN ♦ Braintree, MA ♦ Dallas, TX

Ami Pro® For Dummies®

Published by
IDG Books Worldwide, Inc.
An International Data Group Company
919 E. Hillsdale Blvd.
Suite 400
Foster City, CA 94404

Library of Congress Catalog Card No.: 93-80353

ISBN:1-56884-049-7

Printed in the United States of America

10 9 8 7

1A/QS/QV/ZV

Distributed in the United States by IDG Books Worldwide, Inc.

Distributed by Macmillan Canada for Canada; by Computer and Technical Books for the Caribbean Basin; by Contemporanea de Ediciones for Venezuela; by Distribuidora Cuspide for Argentina; by CITEC for Brazil; by Ediciones ZETA S.C.R. Ltda. for Peru; by Editorial Limusa SA for Mexico; by Transworld Publishers Limited in the United Kingdom and Europe; by Al-Maiman Publishers & Distributors for Saudi Arabia; by Simron Pty. Ltd. for South Africa; by IDG Communications (HK) Ltd. for Hong Kong; by Toppan Company Ltd. for Japan; by Addison Wesley Publishing Company for Korea; by Longman Singapore Publishers Ltd. for Singapore, Malaysia, Thailand, and Indonesia; by Unalis Corporation for Taiwan; by WS Computer Publishing Company, Inc. for the Philippines; by WoodsLane Pty. Ltd. for Australia; by WoodsLane Enterprises Ltd. for New Zealand.

For general information on IDG Books in the U.S., including information on discounts and premiums, contact IDG Books at 800-434-3422 or 415-655-3000.

For information on where to purchase IDG Books outside the U.S., contact IDG Books International at 415-655-3021 or fax 415-655-3295.

For information on translations, contact Marc Jeffrey Mikulich, Director, Foreign & Subsidiary Rights, at IDG Books Worldwide, 415-655-3018 or fax 415-655-3295.

For sales inquiries and special prices for bulk quantities, write to the address above or call IDG Books Worldwide at 415-655-3000.

For information on using IDG Books in the classroom, or ordering examination copies, contact Jim Kelly at 800-434-2086.

For authorization to photocopy items for corporate, personal, or educational use, please contact Copyright Clearance Center, 222 Rosewood Drive, Danvers, MA 01923, or fax 508-750-4470.

About the Author

Though Meade staunchly maintains he's a dummy, not a nerd, there is some evidence to the contrary.

"I coach Little League," he insists. But now he's just an umpire, and that's a nerd thing.

"I watch television a lot." That could go either way. Does he watch PBS? The Discover Channel? American Movie Classics? If he sticks to *Beavis and Butt-head*, fine, he's probably OK.

"I still play sports." Probably mainly golf and tennis, with a game of chess in the clubhouse. Maybe some bicycling.

Meade has written fifteen previous computer books, including *PC Housekeeping* on computer memory (a nerd topic. "But it's funny," he insists.) and books on word processing, spreadsheets, graphics, and (gak!) accounting. He is co-author of two books with Van Wolverton, whose foreword appears here. "Van wears cowboy boots and lives in Montana," Meade insists. Sure, but that's Van.

He worked for DEC for two years in its heyday in the early 1980s. "But I wasn't an engineer," he says, "and I moved into marketing, which is strictly for dummies." Debatable.

He received his B.A. in English from little-known Hamilton College, got a Ph.D. in American Literature from better-known Northwestern, and went on to teaching stints at, among other places, Harvard. ("But I was part-time," he says, "and it was only in the night school.") Hmmm...

He lives in Fairfield, IA, is married, has three children, and wears glasses.

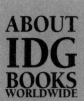
Welcome to the world of IDG Books Worldwide.

IDG Books Worldwide, Inc., is a subsidiary of International Data Group, the world's largest publisher of computer-related information and the leading global provider of information services on information technology. IDG was founded more than 25 years ago and now employs more than 7,200 people worldwide. IDG publishes more than 233 computer publications in 65 countries (see listing below). More than sixty million people read one or more IDG publications each month.

Launched in 1990, IDG Books Worldwide is today the #1 publisher of best-selling computer books in the United States. We are proud to have received 3 awards from the Computer Press Association in recognition of editorial excellence, and our best-selling ...*For Dummies* series has more than 12 million copies in print with translations in 25 languages. IDG Books, through a recent joint venture with IDG's Hi-Tech Beijing, became the first U.S. publisher to publish a computer book in the People's Republic of China. In record time, IDG Books has become the first choice for millions of readers around the world who want to learn how to better manage their businesses.

Our mission is simple: Every IDG book is designed to bring extra value and skill-building instructions to the reader. Our books are written by experts who understand and care about our readers. The knowledge base of our editorial staff comes from years of experience in publishing, education, and journalism — experience which we use to produce books for the '90s. In short, we care about books, so we attract the best people. We devote special attention to details such as audience, interior design, use of icons, and illustrations. And because we use an efficient process of authoring, editing, and desktop publishing our books electronically, we can spend more time ensuring superior content and spend less time on the technicalities of making books.

You can count on our commitment to deliver high-quality books at competitive prices on topics consumers want to read about. At IDG, we value quality, and we have been delivering quality for more than 25 years. You'll find no better book on a subject than an IDG book.

WINNER
Eighth Annual
Computer Press
Awards ≥ 1992

John Kilcullen
President and CEO
IDG Books Worldwide, Inc.

WINNER
Ninth Annual
Computer Press
Awards ≥ 1993

IDG
BOOKS

Dedication

To Aunt Millie, for laughing with me lots of times over really dumb stuff (and for all those birthday and Christmas cards).

Acknowledgments

Thanks to Terrie Solomon, former Acquisitions Editor. It started with you, Terrie. You know the story. Thanks to Janna Custer, the current Acquisitions Editor, who liked my proposal and signed me up. Thanks to tech editor Tom Hirsch, who's a basketball coach and champion athlete on the side. Many thanks also to Kezia Endsley, Barbara Potter, Corbin Collins, Beth Slick, and all the people in production who helped make this book a success.

My wife, Nina, is one of those modern Hillary Clinton types. She's been steering me towards humorous writing all along, because that's all she cares to read. Thanks to Josh, Ben, and Molly, too, who pretty much have those same tastes in reading.

(The publisher would like to give special thanks to Patrick J. McGovern, without whom this book would not have been possible.)

Credits

Contents at a Glance

Cartoons at a Glance

By Rich Tennant

page 205

page 151

page 358

page 255

page 307

page 7

page 339

page 1

page 238

page 81

Table of Contents

Foreword

While it seemed no one was watching, Ami Pro sneaked up on the big guys (let's don't be coy — WordPerfect and Microsoft Word) and transformed itself from "that word processor with the funny name" to, in the words of some recent reviews, "the best Windows word processor around." Although it may seem like an overnight success to some, Ami Pro has been around for quite a few years and has gone through several versions. This one, 3.0, is the best yet.

There's that word again, *best,* a slippery devil when it's used to describe software. Does the best word processor have the most features, or does it run the fastest? Is it easiest to learn (however you measure that) or easiest to use (another measurement problem)? Does it have to be all of these to qualify as best?

The cynic's definition of the best word processor is "the one you already know how to use." But people are putting the lie to that definition by switching to the upstart, Ami Pro, in growing numbers. But this upstart has actually been around longer than either Word for Windows or WordPerfect for Windows. Whatever the definition of best might be, you've made a good choice and you've got a lot of company.

And Jim Meade is a great choice to show you how to use Ami Pro. Jim isn't a computer expert; he's a people expert. Jim isn't interested in dazzling you with how much he knows about computers; he wants you to sit down with this book and, with little sense of time having passed, discover that you're using Ami Pro. When that happens, you won't think "Boy, this guy Meade sure knows a lot about computers!" You might, however, think "Boy, Ami Pro sure is a good word processor!"

Well, take a moment to think "Boy, Jim Meade sure is a good writer!" That would make me feel better. And Jim would probably like it, too.

Van Wolverton
Alberton, Montana
October 1993

Introduction

It's a funny thing about Ami Pro. The whole idea behind it, really, is that you don't need a book to use it. You should be able to just sit down and do stuff with it as if you were sitting down with a pencil and a yellow pad. I mean, nobody after first grade needs many lessons on how to push a pencil around on a pad.

Many times the Nike "just do it" approach does work. But sometimes you need a book to hold close to you while you get Ami Pro to do what it's supposed to — a reliable, accurate, clear, sarcastic, brutal, and twisted book that tells you the real story. A book that doesn't participate in the grand conspiracy maintaining that computers are easy, that whatever program you're using is the greatest breakthrough of human history, and that if you messed up, it's your fault.

The 5th Wave **By Rich Tennant**

Y'KNOW, I DON'T MIND LIVING IN A COMPUTERIZED 'SMART HOUSE', BUT I DO MIND BEING CALLED AN IDIOT BY THE TOASTER.

About This Book

This isn't *Moby Dick* or anything like it, where you sit down and read until the whale kills Ahab. It sounds a bit ponderous even to call it a reference, although that term will do the trick. It's a problem solver. It's the Roto Rooter when your drain gets clogged. You go right for the information you need, grab it, and run.

Each chapter has sections that help you find the Roto Rooter tool you need. Ami Pro (or any other program) is your slave. Don't forget that; this book doesn't. You bought Ami Pro. You own it. It's completely dead and has no human rights or anything for you to worry about. You don't have to be shy around it; it has to be shy around *you*.

Therefore, in this book you don't learn things or memorize stuff. You use the book to get your work done while learning as little as possible. When Ami Pro resists, you have a good laugh at its expense, then go on to get your work done.

How To Use This Book

A good way to use it is to flip through it and look for the Rich Tennant cartoons, the way you'd read a *New Yorker* if someone left one on the train and you didn't have anything else to read. And maybe, as you're flipping forward to the next cartoon, something might strike your eye.

Sometimes you may be really motivated. (I like that word. They use it in real estate — motivated sellers. It means someone who's desperate and will accept almost any lowball offer.) This book is for those occasions, too.

Maybe you just have to know how to get a style sheet to work or how to make an index. Well, don't start just reading through the book to find that out. Go to the index or to the table of contents. You'll be able to find your topics quickly and painlessly.

For everything I discuss, I give you real examples, step-by-step. I actually got all these topics in the book to work the way this book says they do (which isn't always the way the official books say they work). I ran Ami Pro as I wrote for you and didn't just fly by the seat of the pants from memory. You can follow the steps in the example to get your program working (without even understanding it, if you like). You can follow along with the examples too, if you want. When there is something for you to do, you'll see the following icon.

You can type the material exactly as it appears, if you want. You can substitute words of your own. Or you can just read along to get the idea, and ignore all my jocular examples.

Just Who Do I Think You Are?

I'd like you to know where I stand on this "dummy" thing, because the title of the books reads *...For Dummies*. To me, dummy is a term of highest tribute. Being a dummy is something to be proud of — being a nerd is something to be ashamed of.

It has nothing to do with intelligence or learning ability or anything so profound. Some of the most brilliant software engineers in the world are dummies, by my definition, and some of the least informed, incompetent people in software are nerds.

Dummies are simply people who are willing to admit that they don't know everything. They're humans. They don't pretend that they don't make mistakes. That's it. Nerds pretend they're perfect. Nerds are phonies. Dummies are real. Everyone fears learning something new, only dummies admit it.

Also, I'd like to mention that I'm a dummy. I mess up all the time. Things don't work for me. I forget stuff. I'm lazy. Using software isn't my idea of a good time; I'd rather be watching baseball.

It's such a relief to me, when writing to you, to drop the pretense that I'm some omniscient source of infallible information. I think it makes my book much better, because I show you what really happens with Ami Pro, instead of pretending that Ami Pro is always easy and perfect and that if anything goes wrong, it must be your fault.

How This Book Is Organized

Look, I don't think there's anything cosmic about how this book is organized. The publisher makes me put this section in the Introduction. There are parts in here that I hope are logical, that's all, like in any other book from the time when they carved on stone tablets. (I hope people who were word processors back then got paid by the hour, not by the word.)

I start with the simpler stuff and go to the harder stuff, and I break up the sections with many headings, so that it's easier for you to find topics. These are the parts (which it seems to me that you could read just as well by looking over the table of contents).

Part I: Styles: A Gift from Heaven

This section, including Chapters 1–4, covers the supposedly easy stuff you need to get started. I focus on introducing *styles* in this section, which enable you to do much more with Ami Pro. Don't skip this stuff if you are new to Ami Pro.

Part II: Some Tools You'll Love

This part, including Chapters 5–7, covers stuff that enables you to be lazy and not particularly informed while looking like a *know-it-all*. You don't have to read this part to be able to use Ami Pro, but I think you'll want to.

Part III: Some Stuff You'll Hate, and Tools That Help

This part discusses the areas you probably have to use, but never seem to get right. Printing, like love, never runs smoothly. File management can be a nightmare. Chapters 8–10 show you how Ami Pro can help you make it all easier.

Part IV: Do You Have To Be So Graphic about It?

By now, only the curious, the self-torturing, or the stubborn are continuing. You don't *have* to know anything else in this book. But, the stuff is there, you know. There's something tempting about it. In this part, including Chapters 11–13, you find out about the Outliner, frames, drawing, and charting.

Part V: Avoid This Part: Stuff You Don't Want to Know

Wouldn't it have been great, when your chalk-covered history teacher insisted on footnotes, if you could have just pushed a button to insert them? Well, footnoting is still not that great, but this section looks at Ami Pro's honest efforts to make it easier. Also covered here (Chapters 14–16) are creating tables, using document compare and revision marking, creating a table of contents, and adding personal notes to your file.

Part VI: Stuff You Have No Business Touching (Stay Away!)

Listen to these words. Mail Merge. Macros. Try to stay out of this section (Chapters 17–18). But if you have to learn these topics, I have prepared to teach you only what you need to know.

Part VII: The Part of Tens

This section has become a dummies tradition and includes some funny and some particularly useful information for you in easy-to-digest lists. There are three of these.

Appendix A: Installing the Great Beast

Sitting all by its lonesome at the end of book, this appendix shows you how to install Ami Pro for those of you unlucky enough to have to install it yourselves.

Icons Used in This Book

This icon includes useful information that you don't particularly need but that you might like. It describes cool shortcuts and special methods.

Being a dummy, I don't use this one that often, to be honest. It alerts you to the kind of information that computer people talk about with each other.

This icon reminds you of an important fact or action that you might otherwise forget.

You might want to pause over these. Sometimes a natural human action you take causes you to lose information or get lost or wish you were someplace else. This icon points out some of those pitfalls.

This icon signals text that you can actually type in your computer to follow along with the example. Of course, you don't have to type the material to understand the concept.

This icon indicates text that you should pay attention to. It's not quite worthy of a Remember icon, and not as severe as a Warning icon.

Where To Go from Here

That's up to you, pretty much. What do you want to do with Ami Pro? If you have some idea, look the topic up in the index or the table of contents. If you're not sure, flip through and look for cartoons for awhile. Some thoughts will come to you. Or toss the book aside and never come back to it, leaving me trapped inside and neglected. That's OK. I'm used to it.

Part I

Styles: A Gift From Heaven

The 5th Wave   By Rich Tennant

"OH SURE, IT'LL FLOAT ALRIGHT, BUT INTEGRATION'S GONNA BE A KILLER."

In this part...

Getting started is always the hardest part. Have you noticed that? In this part you do the easy (hard?) stuff, like getting Ami Pro running on your computer, making a simple document, making some types look fancy by using style sheets, and creating a basic memo.

Chapter 1
Stirring Up the Ami Pro Batter

• •

In This Chapter

▶ Why styles are important in Ami Pro

▶ How to start your computer, Windows, and Ami Pro

▶ How to get some words into Ami Pro

▶ How to RAM the words onto your hard drive (aka: saving)

▶ How to get words from the screen to boring old paper

▶ How to shut Ami Pro down the safe way

▶ Other stuff, mostly useless, such as why Ami Pro filenames end with .SAM

• •

Stylin' in Ami Pro

Styles. To most people this word refers to hem lines, hair lengths, shirt colors, whether or not it's currently haute couture to wear white socks with a tux, whether wrinkled shirts are in or out, stuff such as that. However, the word does mean something else entirely in word processing, particularly in Ami Pro Professional word processing. You'll find out all about styles in Chapters 3 and 4.

It's a little too soon to talk about styles. You do need them to appreciate Ami Pro, which is why I'm mentioning them first. Using Ami Pro without using styles is like buying a brand new Porsche and then pushing it down the street. Seriously. It's that bad. Or buying a stereo with surround sound and using it to play toneless monophonic Muzak.

But to know what's good about styles, you need to do a few things with Ami Pro. Then, after you do see about styles, it'll be obvious why they're good. In this chapter, you learn how to get started. It's kind of like, you have to know how to open the door of the Porsche before you can drive it (or even push it) down the street.

Kick Starting Ami Pro

Face it. All the books say it's easy; but for you, it seems that starting any program is hard. First of all, you have to turn on the computer. Well, where's the switch? I don't know what ever happened to the ancient principle, established with radios and televisions, of twisting a little knob on the *front* of something to turn it on. Some idiot decided you cannot do that with computers. The switch is always hidden on the side or the back, and it's tough to find. After you do find it, it looks so important that, naturally, you figure it can't be the On switch. It must be the self-destruct switch or something. So you're afraid to flip it, as you should be.

Still, harrowing as it may seem to turn on the computer, it is step one to getting Ami Pro going. Take the plunge, and do so.

After you start the fancy machine, you usually see an almost blank screen with one line of gibberish on it, most commonly C:\>. That means that DOS is running. Just think of DOS as something that has to run after the computer starts, so that Windows can start, so that Ami Pro can start (kind of like a cake, where DOS is the flour and eggs, Windows is the sugar and heat, and Ami Pro is the icing, so to speak).

Starting Windows

Having turned on the computer, you should now start Windows. The letter C and the other gibberish is already there on-screen, so you simply type the following three letters and press Enter:

```
win
```

(It does not matter what case you type the letters in; you can type all caps, a mixture, or all lowercase, as shown here.)

Ninety times out of a hundred, the DOS prompt looks like the one in the example — C:>. However, you might have a different letter, such as D, because someone set up your computer to use drive D rather than drive C. That's fine. You also might not have all the symbols after the C; you might have just a C>. You can read about the various DOS prompts in *DOS For Dummies*. If you aren't splitting hairs about whether or not there's a colon in your DOS prompt, good, you shouldn't be. In the remote chance that you were, I just thought I'd throw in this information to reassure you that your prompt is just fine.

Unless the DOS gods are mad at you today for some reason, the computer purrs and whirs for a little bit; then you have Windows running on-screen, which looks more or less like Figure 1-1 (though not exactly like it, because I've been fiddling with my Windows for a few years and you may have been fiddling with yours, too). Notice all the little pictures with labels under them. These are little energy packets, called *icons,* that you explode by clicking them with your mouse.

If, upon turning your computer on, Windows starts and you see a screen similar to Figure 1-1, you are in luck. This simply means that someone set up your computer to start Windows automatically. You don't have to type WIN at the DOS prompt.

Starting Ami Pro

Having started your computer and Windows, you are now ready to start Ami Pro. You don't have to type anything, but you do have to employ a crafty little technique called the *double-click*.

First, you should double-click the Program Manager if it is minimized. Then, slide your mouse around a little on your desk. Notice that as you slide the mouse, the pointer moves around on the computer screen. Slide the mouse until the pointer is on top of the Ami Pro 3.0 icon, shown in Figure 1-2, and double-click this icon.

Ami Pro icon

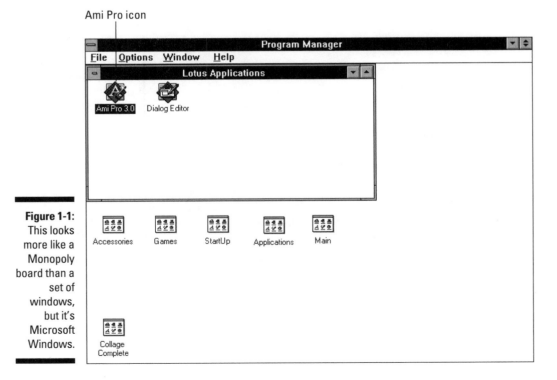

Figure 1-1:
This looks
more like a
Monopoly
board than a
set of
windows,
but it's
Microsoft
Windows.

If your Ami Pro window is not open, look for a folder called *Lotus Applications*. This folder contains Ami Pro, by default. Double-click this folder, then double-click the icon shown in Figure 1-2.

Figure 1-2:
Double-click
this icon to
start Ami
Pro.

You can start Ami Pro without using a mouse, but it's not that easy, and there's a message in that. In Ami Pro, it's often easy to do things the easy way but hard to do them the other way. Pointing and clicking is the easy way. Typing commands is the hard way. You just have to have a mouse with Ami Pro. Not having one is like watching a 3D movie without the weird glasses. Nevertheless, almost every time you read click or double-click in this book, you can either press Enter on the object or find another way to do the same thing with the keyboard.

Here's how to start Ami Pro without using the mouse, if you insist on doing so:

1. **In the Windows Program Manager, open the File menu (Alt+F).**

2. **Choose the Run command.**

3. **Type the command line for Ami Pro, which for most people is C:\AMIPRO\AMIPRO.EXE and then press Enter.**

Double-clicking — a pain in the finger

Double-clicking sometimes takes a few tries to master. If you don't click fast enough between the two clicks, nothing happens; so click twice about as fast as you can — like this: *clickclick*.

The pointer on-screen should turn into the shape of an hourglass for a couple seconds, and then Ami Pro starts — see Figure 1-3.

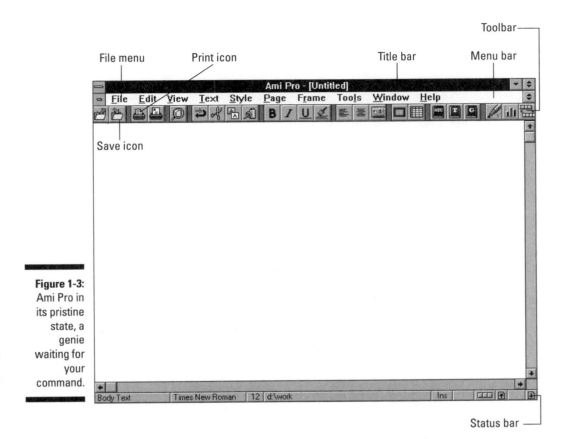

Figure 1-3:
Ami Pro in
its pristine
state, a
genie
waiting for
your
command.

Putting Words on Its Face

You can waste a great deal of your valuable time right now looking over all the different on-screen hieroglyphics that appear after you start Ami Pro. Most books must think you and I want to do that, because they label and talk about everything right away. However, that method doesn't tell you what you need to know to get started, which, in my dumb opinion, is the most essential information.

No, if the force is with you and you've actually managed to get this fancy word processor running, you'd probably like to get right down to processing words and not have to learn anything you don't have to know. If you can pluck keys on the keyboard, you can use Ami Pro without learning much of anything complicated.

Suppose, for example, that you are a terrorist planning to heist a speed boat in Nicaragua, you have Ami Pro running on a battery-powered laptop as you hide in the jungle, and you want to write headquarters for special instructions.

As an example, type the following words. That's right, just type them the way you type anything. Use the backspace key to delete your mistakes and retype.

Don't press Enter at the end of every line the way you do on a typewriter, unless you want to end the line prematurely (like the short date line in the following letter). Ami Pro automatically moves your pointer to the next line when the words begin overflowing.

December 16, 1994

Dear Headquarters:

I have located the speedboat I'm supposed to steal, and I know the owners aren't around. I was just wondering, though — Are you supplying the key, or do I have to try to hot-wire this thing?

Sincerely,

Robert (that's my code name. I'm really Jake.)

Getting started isn't that hard after all, is it? The next thing you need to learn is how to save your letter after you've gone to the trouble of bringing it into existence.

Preserving the Words

Saving in word processing is as important as it is in your savings account — fortunately, it's less painless, because to do it you don't have to give up the new VCR, evenings at the movies, and new golf clubs.

The need to save computer text has nothing special to do with Ami Pro, and you've almost certainly come across the principle somewhere else if you've used other programs. It's one of those things, like locking your car when you park it near Yankee Stadium, that you ignore at your own risk.

Does memory by any other name last as long?

When you type something on-screen, it resides only in the computer's RAM (*random-access memory*), which goes away after you turn off the computer. When you save the information as a file, it resides in the computer's hard disk, which keeps stuff without losing it, sort of a little safety deposit box inside your computer. Most the time, you'll want to keep your writings so that you can edit them later, print them, show them to others, and the like. Therefore, you have to *RAM* the information onto the hard disk, so to speak. You do this by giving the information a filename, thus saving it on the hard disk.

Follow these steps to save your words to the hard disk:

 1. **In the third row of the display, click the icon you see in the margin (a picture of an arrow pointing into a folder).** This is the save SmartIcon.

When you use the SmartIcon, click once instead of double-clicking the way you do to start programs. A box comes up (a *dialog box,* so named because it supposedly allows the computer to have a little conversation with you. Hey, thanks. I've had better talks with my bathroom shower nozzle.). Here you name the file. See Figure 1-4 and notice the File name selection.

2. **Without pressing any other keys or anything, type the name you want to give to your file (it must be eight characters or less).**

Ami Pro adds the .SAM extension for you. In this example, type **SPY** (it doesn't have to be all caps).

3. **Click OK.**

The dialog box closes and the name of the document appears in brackets at the top of your screen (appropriately called the *Title bar*). You've saved this file to the hard disk, and it will last as long as your hard disk does.

 Heed my warning about backing up your work frequently; disk crashes are frequent and you never know when some clumsy coworker is going to walk by, trip over the cord, and pull the cord out of the wall! I suggest saving your work on-screen to a file every 20 minutes or so and saving important files on floppy disks every night before you shut down.

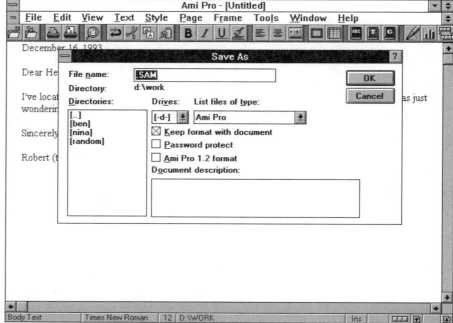

Figure 1-4:
Use the
Save As
dialog box to
name a
document
and put it on
the hard
disk, where
it waits for
you to use it
again.

Printing the Words

When you're a spy working in tough, jungle conditions, you're not going to mail your computer back to headquarters with the letter on it. You need the computer for other things; anyway, the cost of postage is much too high. Besides, then you have to wait until they send your computer back before you can write another letter. Not very efficient.

No. Even the lightest laptops are too heavy to ship frequently. To send your written words to someone else, paper is the way to go. To get the Ami Pro document on to paper, follow these instructions:

 1. Click the printer icon (a little green rectangle with a piece of paper sticking out of it) shown in the margin.

A dialog box comes up with all kinds of options for you to choose. Ignore them.

2. Click OK.

Examining the Save As dialog box

Do you really want to know more about the Save As dialog box? Why, for example, is it called *Save As* rather than just *Save*?

It's because the file doesn't have any name yet, so the box insists that you save it *as* something. The next time you click the icon to save this file, you won't get the dialog box at all. Ami Pro simply saves it with the same name.

"Or," you may wonder, "why am I typing .SAM at the end of this word?" Nobody just automatically types .SAM at.SAM the.SAM end.SAM of.SAM anything.SAM. Right.SAM? Well, the DOS file extension of Ami Pro word processing files is .SAM. You can read about the three letter extensions in *DOS For Dummies*. The reason for these particular three letters? Before it belonged to Lotus, Ami Pro's maker was Samna Corporation. The three letters have stuck around mainly because Lotus hasn't figured out how to get rid of them yet.

"Or," you might wonder, "what the heck does *Keep format with document* mean?" That selection has to do with styles. After you've got a style sheet, you can keep the format of the style sheet with the document without keeping the format, named style sheet with it. Then, if you should change the style sheet later, you wouldn't change the appearance of this document, because it wouldn't actually be using the style sheet any more. I'll come back to this. Surely you aren't curious about it yet.

See the *Password protect* choice? Don't, don't, don't click it. I don't care. Let people steal your stuff. Passwords are the bane of any user's life. We forget them. We lose them. We get them right, and they don't work anyway.

There's more in this dialog box, and I can't even promise I'll ever come back to it. Wait until you need to know it. You may go on forever without it.

The letter comes off the printer in finished form, and you can slide it into an envelope, Federal Express it back to headquarters, wait for the reply to come back, then steal the speedboat. Wow! What a day. (For more details on printing, see Chapter 8.)

Closing Shop

If you don't do anything but use Ami Pro, you can simply close all your files, turn off the monitor on the computer, leave the computer running, and leave Ami Pro running. Then you wouldn't have to start it up each time, and conventional wisdom says that it's easier on the hard drive if you just leave the computer running all the time anyway.

Sometime, though, you'll no doubt want to put Ami Pro away. Instead of using a SmartIcon as you have for saving and printing a document, try using the menus:

1. Click the File menu in the Menu bar (below the Title bar).

The *Title bar* is the bar at the very top of the screen that contains the name of your active file. The *Menu bar* is the bar that appears below the Title bar and contains all the menus. Clicking these menus (File, Edit, View) pulls down all their commands.

A list of commands appears below the word *File*. See Figure 1-5.

2. Click Exit.

Ami Pro closes and you find yourself once again in the Windows Program Manager. (If you have any *open files* — files that are still active in Ami Pro — that have not yet been saved, Ami Pro asks you whether you want to save your file before quitting.)

Now you're ready to exit from Windows and turn off the computer:

1. Double-click the icon in the top corner of the Program Manager (a picture of a file drawer.)

The Exit Windows dialog box appears and cautions, `This will end your Windows session`.

2. Select OK.

Don't turn off the computer immediately. Wait a few moments as Windows puts itself away. After you're back at the `C:>` prompt, it's OK to turn off the computer.

Wow, are those keys hot

Not that you care about such unimportant details, but you may notice that each word in the menu has one letter underlined somewhere, such as the *F* in File. Those underlined letters (called *hot keys*) are for using the keyboard instead of the mouse.

Keyboards aren't as easy as mice. You have to learn and remember stuff to use them. To choose from the main menu with the keyboard, for example, you hold down Alt on the keyboard and then press the letter you want, such as the *F* for

the File menu. Pressing Alt tells the computer to use the letter in its *alternate* way, which is to open the menu. After the submenu drops down, you don't have to use Alt. Just press the letter key for the underlined letter (for example, press *x* to Exit) of the command you want.

Keyboards, in fairness, often are faster than mice. You just type, instead of sliding a pointer around first, and you don't have to take your hands away from the keyboard. The bottom line is to use what works best for you.

Title bar contains description
of highlighted command

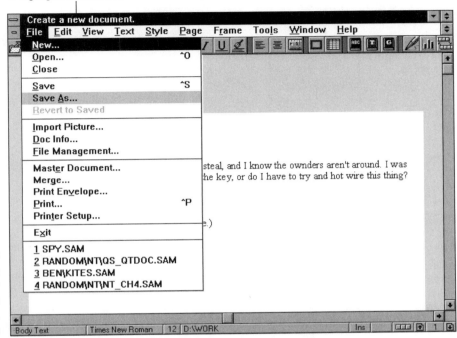

Figure 1-5:
The many
file
commands.

Chapter 2

Cooking on a Wood Stove: Basic Text and Document Maneuvering

The Evolution of Word Processing

There was a time, about 1981, when everybody was thrilled about how much better word processing was than typewriting. (Some literary standouts were convinced that the typewriter was better. Most of them, under the table, use word processors now.)

It was exciting, a long time ago, to see that you could cut text without scissors and paste it without sticky substances, change from Helvetica to Courier typeface without loading a different ball into your IBM Selectric, make text italic just as readily, delete several pages by pressing a couple of keys, make a backup copy (or ten) without a copy machine, and all kinds of neato stuff that seems like nothing any more. It's just word processing. Might as well get excited that your dishwasher has a wash cycle.

Now once in a while you do have the occasion to do some basic selecting text and maneuvering. Once you begin using style sheets in the next chapter, though, you'll do this much less than you might expect. You won't go through your memo, for example, and change all the subheads from bold into bold/italic when your rotten boss says you have to do that (or your rotten assistant or your rotten self. Doesn't matter.) You let a style do it for you.

So in this chapter, you see how to do the word processing basics — selecting text, changing it, organizing it — of a decade ago, just because you might still do things that way occasionally (grin).

Resuscitating a Document

Before you can make a document look fancy, you have to open it. To open a document, follow these instructions:

 1. Click the open SmartIcon (shown in the margin).

The Open dialog box appears. See Figure 2-1.

2. Click the file you want to open, then click OK.

If you are following along with this example, click EXPENSES.SAM. The document opens on-screen.

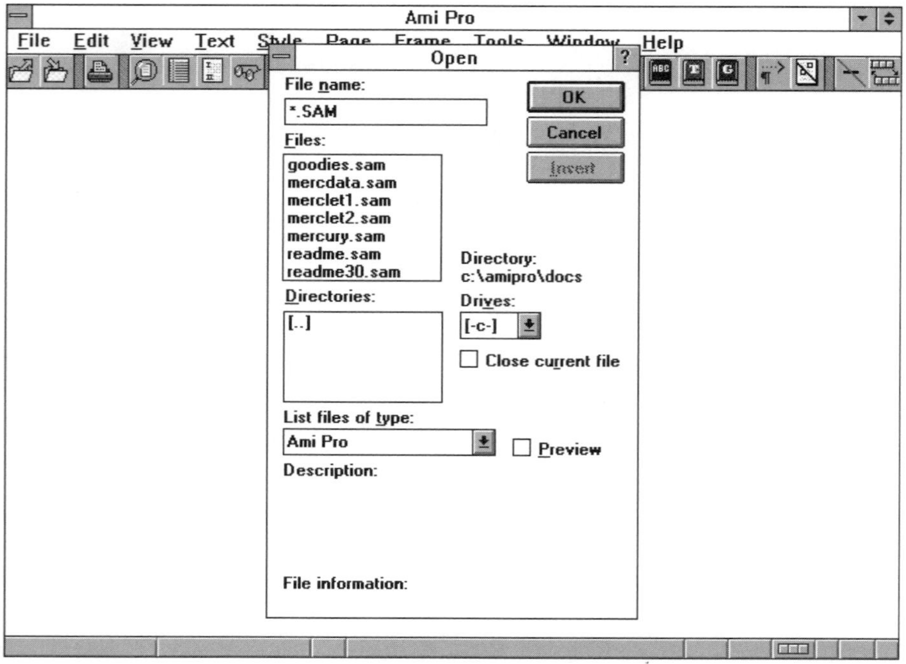

Figure 2-1:
The Open
dialog box.

If you need to open a document you have recently been using, you don't have to go to the Open dialog box, because the last five documents you opened appear at the bottom of the File menu (after the Exit command). You can simply click the File menu and then click the name of the file you want (or press the number next to it). If no files appear at the bottom of your File menu, forget I mentioned it. You can find out how to adjust the number of files in this area in Chapter 9.

When you use the Open and Save dialog boxes, you run smack up against DOS filenames and DOS directory structures. DOS names can be up to eight characters long, and the extensions (the three characters after the period, called a *dot* in computerese) are always three characters long. Standards set by DOS, these file-naming conventions are used by Ami Pro (and all word-processing software) as well.

Creating Directories

To be able to use directories, you have to create them. Ami Pro enables you to move stuff between directories with its File Manager (Chapter 10), but it doesn't enable you to create directories. You must do this in either DOS or Windows.

The easiest way to create directories is with the Windows File Manager (confusingly similar in name to the Ami Pro File Manager, but different). Look it over:

1. **Hold down the Alt key and press Tab a number of times (until you see the Program Manager icon) and then release both keys.**

   How many times you press Tab depends on how many programs you have running. If you have only Ami Pro and Windows running, you have to press Tab only once.

   You can use the Alt+Tab method to switch to any other program you have running, without having to exit from Windows, or from any of your programs. This is one of Windows' great features.

2. **Double-click the File Manager icon (which resides in the Main program group if you have not moved it). See Figure 2-2.**

Figure 2-2:
The File
Manager
icon.

3. In the File Manager, open the File Menu. See Figure 2-3.

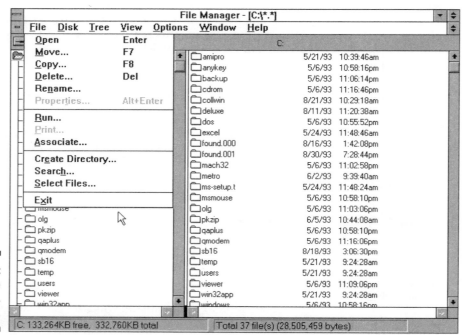

Figure 2-3:
The File
Manager,
File menu.

4. From the File menu, choose Create Directory.

5. In the Create Directory dialog box (Figure 2-4), type c:, then type the name of the new directory, and then choose OK.

Unlike filenames, directories don't have extensions. However, the eight-character maximum does apply to directories.

6. Use Alt+Tab to return to Ami Pro.

Turn to *DOS For Dummies* or *Windows For Dummies* if you want to know more about directories and organizing your files. It is generally a good idea to use subdirectories, though. (I guess that's an understatement.) If you know about subdirectories already, you may have noticed from the illustrations in this book that I use them liberally.

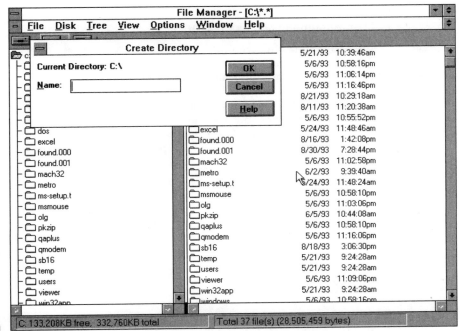

Figure 2-4:
The Create
Directory
dialog box.

Changing Text

Although we give them hoards of credit, word processors are dumb — they cannot learn, unlike you and me. Unless you tell them what text you want to operate on in one way or another, they don't know. They can't tell, so they just sit there and don't do anything. Telling them which text you want to change is called *selecting*.

To select something, you have to have some text. Suppose, for example, that you were the president of Chrysler and were drafting a letter to the board of directors. First you must type your thoughts, then you can select some words and add pizzazz. As an example, type the following text in a new, untitled document. (There's one on-screen when you start Ami Pro.)

> **Memorandum to Members of the Board:**
>
> **I realize that profits are plummeting lately, workers are angry, the Japanese are stealing our market, and the TV networks are always lurking outside our offices looking for exposés.**
>
> **In spite of all that bad news, though, I see a turnaround coming. I've got a great idea for a new car. It's called the Rhinoceros, and it's going to make us all famous. You see, it has a giant rhinoceros horn on the hood. Nobody will ever hit it in a head-on crash. The person would have to be nuts.**

Now you can save the memo. To do so, click the save SmartIcon (the one with the arrow pointing in) and save the letter with the name CARS.SAM.

You might want to do any number of amazing things to the text after you have it in there, but first you have to tell dumb Ami Pro which things to change.

Selecting text

Suppose you wanted to move two sentences from paragraph two to the beginning of the letter (because, as a great marketer, you suddenly realize that you should start your pitch with something rosy). Here's how to select text:

1. **Position the cursor before the first letter of the section you want to select.**

   In this example, click just before the *I* in "I've got a great idea."

2. **Click and hold down the left mouse button and drag the mouse down one line and over a few characters until the section is highlighted. See Figure 2-5.**

3. **Let up on the mouse button.**

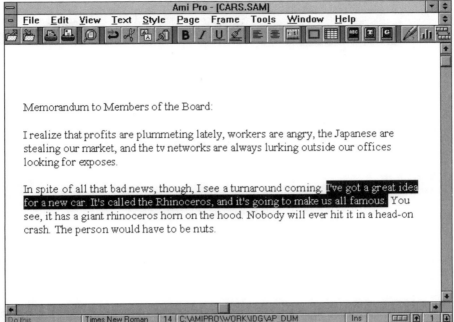

Figure 2-5:
Selected
text.

Cutting and pasting text

After you select text, you can do all kinds of damage using commands from the menus. Just select the text and then choose a command. Cut and Paste is an all-time favorite of editors because they constantly move text to different places. (In this example, you can move two sentences to the front of the Chrysler letter):

1. **Select the text you want to move by using the selection techniques discussed earlier.**

   In this example, select two sentences, beginning with "I've got a great idea...."

2. **Click the Edit menu (see Figure 2-6) and then click Cut.**

   You keyboard lovers can press Ctrl+X.

   The text (yikes!!) disappears. It's a tense moment when anything disappears — but hold on!

3. **Move the cursor to the text's final destination.**

   In this example, move the cursor to the beginning of the first text paragraph.

4. **To paste the text, choose the Paste command from the Edit menu.**

   The mouseaphobics can press Ctrl+V. Either way, the text magically reappears.

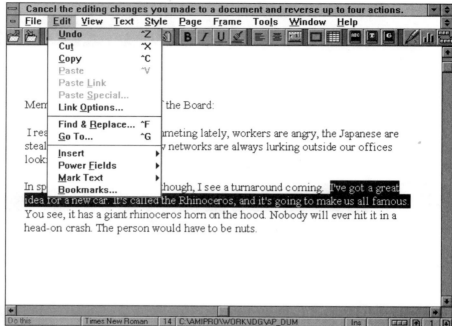

Figure 2-6:
The Edit
menu.

Press the spacebar to put in the space at the end of the sentence if you need to, and that's it. The sentences move to the beginning, where they'll give the board a good feeling right at the outset. (Actually, I hate the way marketers try to get you to say "Yes" at the outset. Some day I hope to strangle a phone sales-person who starts out saying, "Yes, Mr. Meade. Can you hear me OK?" "No, I can't. Now you die. Gurgle. Gurgle. Gurgle.")

When to delete, when to cut?

When you cut something, it goes to a place Windows calls the *Clipboard,* and, like some kind of a clumsy restaurant waiter, the Clipboard can hold only one thing at a time. Cut something else, and you'll realize your worst fears — you lose the first thing you cut. So, if you plan to cut and paste, paste immediately after you cut.

Also be aware that pressing Delete to delete text is not the same thing as cutting it with the Cut command. If you use the Delete key to delete text, you cannot paste it using the Paste command. The only way to retrieve deleted text is to use the Undo command immediately after deleting the text. See the sidebar later in this chapter called "The pains of the Undo command" for more information on the uncertainties of deleting

Drag and drop pasting

Ami Pro also enables you to cut and paste in a fancy way, called *drag and drop pasting* (sounds like the way to dispose of a dead body). Try it:

1. **Select the sentence you want to move (hold down Ctrl and click in the sentence, remember?).**

   In this example, select the sentence that starts "In spite of all the bad news."

2. **While the sentence is selected, point in the sentence again, hold down the left mouse button, and begin to drag. You should no longer be pressing the Ctrl key.**

   The pointer takes the shape of an arrow with a pair of scissors next to it. (If you don't get the scissors, try again.) See Figure 2-7.

3. **Drag the sentence to its new location and then release the mouse button.**

   In this example, drag the sentence to just after the word *nuts*.

When you drag and drop, you can see the sentence as you move the pointer to the new location, so that you don't forget what it is—a problem I often face. And you don't have to worry about copying over it in the Clipboard by mistake, because Ami Pro doesn't leave it in there where you could forget it.

Scissors pointer

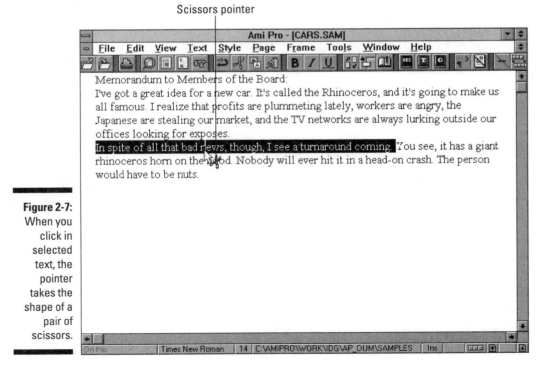

Figure 2-7: When you click in selected text, the pointer takes the shape of a pair of scissors.

Be careful as you drag the sentence that it doesn't kick, squeal, and resist. No sentence truly likes being dragged. I mean, would you like it — being peremptorily picked out of a paragraph, then dragged to some new location without so much as a "how do you do?", then dropped and left in a new location without even a "thank you, sir." Of course you wouldn't. Well, sentences don't like it either.

To *copy* a sentence to another place using drag and drop (that is, you want the sentence to stay in its old location *and* move to its new location), follow these same instructions, with one exception. When you click the sentence a second time to drag it, hold down the Ctrl key while clicking the sentence. You'll get the copy cursor (two boxed *A*s), rather than the scissors cursor. Simply drag the sentence to its new location, as before.

Beaming Around in the Document

After you get a document, you'll want to move around in it in various ways. Back in the keyboard days, this was a daunting activity.

Now that mice have come along, you almost can afford to skip this section. If you want to go somewhere in the document, just put the pointer there and click. Sometimes, though, you cannot see where you want to go. Then, you can use the *scroll bars* to move around.

Scrolling along, singing a song

Scroll bars are supposed to be dummy-proof. Ha ha. I wonder when these software people will realize that nothing is dummy-proof. The *scroll bars,* by the way, are the horizontal and vertical strips that appear at the right and bottom sides of your window. They begin and end with *scroll arrows.* The *scroll box* (often called the *elevator box* — how cute) is the tiny box that appears on the scroll bar. If you are in the middle of the document (page 4 of 8), the scroll box appears in the middle of the scroll bar.

Figure 2-8 shows what happens if you drag the scroll box down a little bit. The figure has arrows pointing to the scroll bars (a horizontal one and a vertical one), the scroll box, and the scroll arrows. Try it.

Drag the scroll box on the right of the screen down an inch or so. When you drag the box, the text moves by about the same proportion as the box in the bar.

Scroll box——
Scroll arrow——

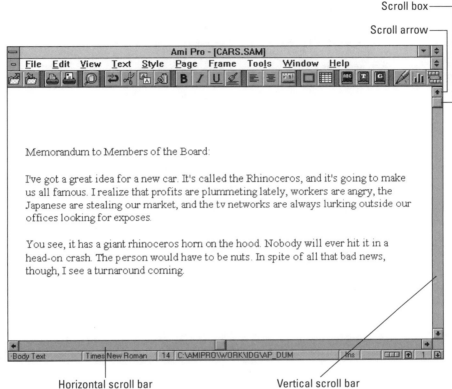

Figure 2-8:
Using the
scroll bars
to move
around.

Horizontal scroll bar   Vertical scroll bar

There are other things you can do with the scroll bars:

- ✔ Click the top scroll arrow to move up one line.

- ✔ Click the bottom-right scroll arrow to move down one line.

- ✔ Click just above the vertical scroll box to move up a page.

- ✔ Click just below the vertical scroll box to move down a page.

- ✔ Click either arrow and hold it to scroll up or down continuously.

Unless you have an extra-wide document (you are using a spreadsheet or something), you probably won't have much use for the horizontal scroll bar. Using the scroll bar isn't much harder than pointing and clicking in the text, and it can get you where you want to go.

Be careful not to confuse the scroll arrows (attached to the scroll bar) with the maximize and minimize arrows (at the top of the screen).

Beaming around by pushbutton

The keyboard sometimes can be handy for moving around, too. The basic idea is that you press the arrow keys on the keyboard to move in the direction the arrows point. Put the cursor at the top of the document and then try moving a word at a time. Table 2-1 lists many of these keyboard shorties. Normal people are not going to sit around and memorize all these keys. They would go dingy. Try them all and use the ones you like.

Table 2-1	Beaming Around Using the Keyboard
Keys	*Where They Take You*
PgDn	Down one screen
PgUp	Up one screen
arrow keys	Right one character, left one character, down one line, up one line
Ctrl+arrow key	Right or left one word
Home	To the beginning of the line
End	To the end of the line
Ctrl+Home	To the beginning of the document
Ctrl+End	To the end of the document
Ctrl+.	To the beginning of the next sentence
Ctrl+up arrow	To the beginning of the paragraph

Vaporizing Text

Being able to delete messy text is essential for any user. To delete something, you simply select it and press the Delete key. What can I say? That's it. Try it. The unwanted words die, and you don't have to worry about them again.

The pains of the <u>U</u>ndo command

Immediately after you delete text, you'll probably want it back. That's just life. People always want what they can't have, even if they just had it. Ami Pro provides a solution with human nature in mind. Try getting back the precious words by putting the cursor where you want the words to appear, then choosing <u>U</u>ndo from the <u>E</u>dit menu.

The deleted text comes back only if you haven't deleted something else since that text. It's a good idea to use <u>U</u>ndo immediately after you've deleted text. And, by the way, you can use it to undo most editing actions, but not all. (If you delete your file from the hard drive, for example, <u>U</u>ndo won't be of any service.)

Whenever you change your mind about a change you've made, try <u>U</u>ndo. Sometimes it works, and sometimes (such as when you've saved the document after making the change), it doesn't. Hey, it's worth a shot any time — well almost any time. If you've just typed something brilliant, haven't saved it yet, and choose <u>U</u>ndo, Ami Pro deletes it. "Wait," you may be inclined to say. "I just wrote that. I didn't want you to undo that." Ami Pro sits there silent, feeling no guilt, maybe even gloating a bit. However, choose <u>U</u>ndo again and Ami Pro undoes your undo (in English that means that you get your text back).

The lesson to learn here, if there is one, is to use the Cut command as often as possible to delete text. That way, you can get it back with the <u>P</u>aste command. Use Delete only when you know you want to kiss that text good-bye.

Getting Fancy with Text

Making your text look fancy is achieved by the same philosophy you use to move or cut text. You simply highlight the word or words and choose the appropriate command. You learn about your formatting options in the following sections.

Making words act really bold

Boldface is a useful character emphasis. As president of Chrysler, you might want to use it on the first line of the memo, just to make it look like the first line of a memo. To make a word or selection bold, use these guidelines:

1. **Select the text.**

   In this example, select the first line of your memo.

 2. **Click the bold SmartIcon (shown in the margin) or press Ctrl+B.**

   The selection turns bold. Figure 2-9 shows the memo after you boldface the first line.

Boldface

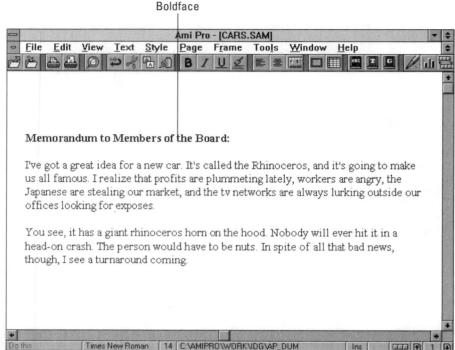

Figure 2-9:
Memo with
boldface on
the first line.

To unbold your text, simply select the text in question (by double-clicking it).
Then you either click the bold SmartIcon again or press Ctrl+B. The text goes
back to normal!

Making words squiggly

You can use the menus to dress up words, too. Try using the menu to make a
word (in this example, Rhinoceros) italic:

1. **Select the word or words by double-clicking or by any other method.**

   In this example, select the word *Rhinoceros* in the first sentence.

2. **Press Ctrl+I or click the italic SmartIcon.**

3. *Note:* **You also can choose the Text menu, shown in Figure 2-10 and then
   click Italic.**

   Now your word of choice (Rhinoceros, Candy Bar, Sex, whatever you
   prefer) is italic.

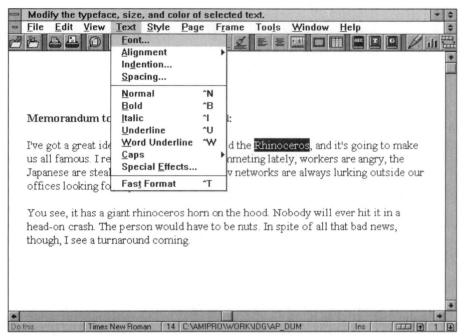

Figure 2-10:
The Text
menu.

Look over all the choices in the Text menu. You can indent stuff, change the spacing, underline it, word underline it (where there's no underline under the spaces between words), and other neat stuff that won't necessarily get explained anywhere in this book. The underlying principle is always the same: Select something, then select something from the menu.

The last example used the menu system, for variety, to apply formatting to a word. Realize that, whenever possible and applicable, using the SmartIcon is much faster. SmartIcons exist for every command you need, and using them is a much faster method.

Making words big using the Status bar

You have used both SmartIcons and the menus to do things. Here's another great way for you to work, though. You can use the Status bar. "The what?" you must be thinking, because I haven't told you what the Status bar is yet. The *Status bar* is the bar across the very bottom of the screen that includes the font, the point size, and the name of your document, among other things.

Suppose you wanted to make a word (in this example, use *nuts*) in a larger type face. You can use the Status bar like so:

1. **Select the word of choice (in this example, *nuts*).**

2. **Click the little box in the Status bar that shows point sizes (it probably has a 10 or a 12 in it now).**

   A column pops up with a listing of all the point sizes. See Figure 2-11.

3. **Click 14.**

The typeface takes on the larger size!

If you click the point size area (or any of these areas, for that matter) and then change your mind and want to cancel, simply click somewhere else on-screen. The point size column disappears.

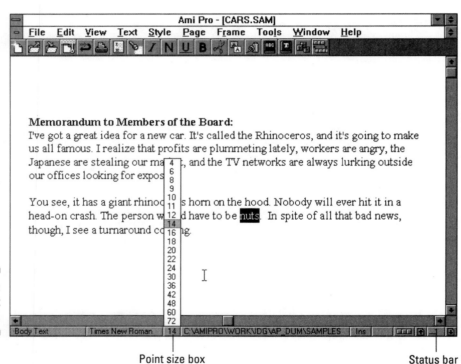

Figure 2-11:
The point size column.

Point size box   Status bar

Your friend the Status bar

You can change myriad things with the Status bar. Click the different areas to see what they do. You can change the page you're on by clicking the arrows in the bottom right. You can change your typeface and point size. You can check the time, date, and the name of your file, in case you need a reality check.

You can change the paragraph style with the rectangle in the very left of the Status bar. This is a quick way to apply a *style* to your paragraph.

You'll learn about styles in Chapters 3 and 4. You can change the SmartIcon set you're using with the blue icon that looks like three boxes. Clicking this shows you the eight sets of SmartIcons that you can use on the toolbar. Don't worry about this for now. The set of SmartIcons you are currently using is fine for now.

The Status bar is right up there with the SmartIcons as a quick way to do things without having to remember anything. Experiment with it!

Making words colorful

Who has a color printer these days? Most the time you don't have any use for making text a color, because you can't print it that way anyway. It looks neat on a color monitor, though. Suppose you wanted to add color to some words:

1. **Select the words you want to change.**

   If you are following along with the example, select *I see a turnaround coming.*

2. **Select the Text menu (Figure 2-10) and then choose Font.**

   The Font dialog box appears. Figure 2-12 shows it in all its glory.

3. **In the Font dialog box, click any color in the color bar and then choose OK.**

   In this example, choose red. The selected text turns red.

Let's examine the Font dialog box for a second (Figure 2-12). Notice that when you click one of the colors in the color bar, the words in the *sample box* turn that color. Now these sample boxes should be called idiot boxes. If you didn't have that idiot box, you'd have to go back to the text to see the results of your change. Then if you didn't like what you saw, you'd have to remember how to get back to the dialog box, then try another one, then go back to the text, and then back to the dialog box. It can be dispiriting. With these idiot boxes, though, you can see the effect of your choice before you ever actually make it. Idiot boxes (aka: *sample boxes*) are a lifesaver.

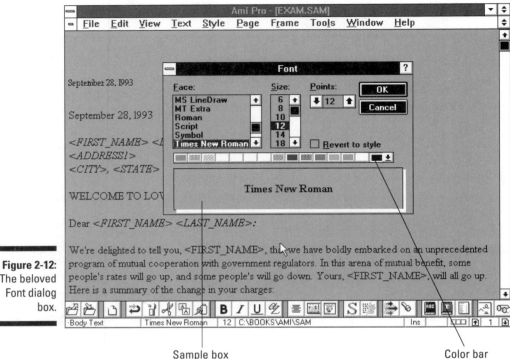

Sample box   Color bar

Marking Your Place in the Text

To quickly find where you were working when you last quit, use the Bookmark feature.

To put a bookmark in a document to mark a specific place in the text, do the following:

1. **Position your cursor at the place in your document where you want to insert the bookmark.**

2. **Choose the Bookmarks command in the Edit menu.**

   The Bookmarks dialog box appears, as in Figure 2-13.

3. **In the Bookmark text box, type a short word that is representative of the contents of that place in your document.**

   I used the word *Engine* for my bookmark.

4. **Click the Add button.**

   The bookmark goes into the document, but it is not visible to you or to anyone but Ami Pro.

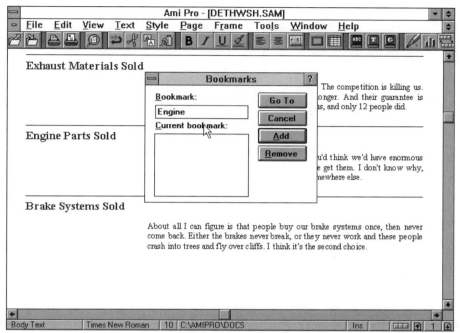

Figure 2-13:
The
Bookmarks
dialog box.

To discover if the bookmark is really in the document, go to the end of the document and choose the Bookmarks command from the Edit menu. Then click the appropriate bookmark in the Current bookmark box (*Engine,* in my example), as illustrated in Figure 2-14. Then click the Go To button, and the pointer goes directly to the place where you inserted the bookmark in the text.

Bookmarks are the opposite of money. Within certain limits, they have their greatest value when there are the fewest of them. After all, when you read a book, you only use one bookmark, right? (Now, nerds may use more than one, but they are nerds!) I, likewise, tend to have no more than one Ami Pro bookmark in a document at one time.

If you want to get rid of a bookmark, simply choose Bookmarks from the Edit menu, click the bookmark you want to remove in the Current bookmark box, and then click the Remove button. Ami Pro takes out the bookmark.

You can do many things in Ami Pro by telling it which words you want to work on (selecting them) and then choosing colors, shapes, sizes, editing choices, and other stuff from the menus or icons. In 1981, doing all this was the cat's meow. People were beside themselves with it — the *paperless office* they called it.

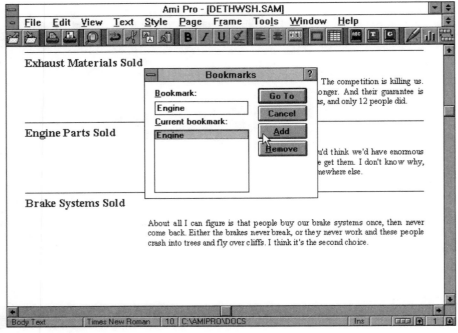

Figure 2-14:
The current
bookmark,
displayed in
the
Bookmarks
dialog box.

This now *old* select and do model, though, has its limitations, the biggest being that if you change your mind after selecting and doing many things, you have to select and do them all over again. The next chapter covers style sheets, a better way to work than selecting and doing.

That's it for this chapter. Get a list of the board members at Chrysler and send them your letter (hee hee).

Chapter 3

Shakin' and Bakin': Basics on Style Sheets and Styles

• •

In This Chapter

▶ Why it's easier to use someone else's style sheet than to make your own

▶ How to look over some of the fancier style sheets you bought with Ami Pro

▶ Why you can't live without a style sheet (though you probably want to)

▶ How to type stuff into a document with a style sheet

▶ How to fire bullets from a style sheet

▶ How to number items from a style sheet

• •

What Is a Style Sheet?

Styles — you put them together and make something called a *style sheet*. A style sheet is a blank template of text formatting and character attributes to which you add your own words. It's like a blank application form in which you fill in your name, address, past jobs, and other vitals. The information is formatted in a set fashion (perhaps numbered and indented, with blank lines for your information), and you simply write in the information needed.

A style sheet, though, includes a compendium of really neat stuff you can choose from after you create a document — everything from boring things, such as margins, to neat memo headers in white on black to stationery with fancy pictures already included.

What Chuck Green has to do with you

Ami Pro, as it turns out, has a good collection of those "styles put together." Somebody put them together. I don't think he's the only one who does it, but a guy called me once who makes style sheets for Ami Pro as a full-time job. His name is Chuck Green. He's a design artist. He's one of these people, good at drawing to begin with, who went to school also to learn all the rules and everything. He's worked at design for a while besides and, on top of that, he knows all kinds of fancy, inside things about Ami Pro that hardly anybody, dumb or not, ever takes the time to learn.

Chuck takes all that skill and knowledge and adds the secret ingredient — time — to come up with all these fancy style sheets that are there when you start Ami Pro. (You see, he gets paid to make style sheets, which, basically, you and I don't. So he will make them, whereas you and I, for the most part, won't.)

Having Chuck's styles is the word processing equivalent of having a warehouse full of Alfa Romeos and Ferraris and Lexuses and stuff. Not using them (which, I'm willing to bet, is exactly the inclination of most busy people) is like choosing to ride a bicycle instead — a one-speed, balloon tire antique that's all rusted and has coaster brakes . . . a totally yuck bicycle.

So, read on to find out how to use these styles that Chuck has spent all his time and energy making. It's the ecologically sound way to use Ami Pro.

You need it, trust me

Any self-respecting person would naturally say, "Hey, I don't want any style sheet. Leave me the heck alone. I just want to type on the screen." I can respect that. I've been there. But the hard truth of the matter is that you can't have a document in Ami Pro without a style sheet. You just don't usually know about it because it's going on behind your back.

Suppose that you were using a typewriter. Could you use it without having some kind of margins, some kind of typeface on the keys, and (most of the time, even for nontechnical people), some kind of tab settings? Fine. Try to do it. You can't do it. WordPerfect and all those other people might let you go along with the blithe impression that you aren't using a style sheet. You always are, though. So why not check out the possibilities?

Choosing a Style Sheet

Ami Pro does its best to get you to notice that garage full of fancy machinery. Every time you create a new document, it tries to wave style sheets in your face (but I just bet, because I was so inclined for so long, you don't want anything to do with whatever it's selling when it waves like that.) Check out a few style sheets.

TIP

Change to Layout mode

You don't have to be in Layout mode to choose a style sheet, but, if you're in Layout mode in this chapter, you'll be able to see all the ingredients in a style sheet. Otherwise, some fancy frames and things don't show up. I talk more about Layout mode in Chapter 8, should you happen to be curious (which, if I were you, I wouldn't be).

To make sure you're in Layout mode, select the View menu and then click Layout mode.

Checking out the available style sheets

Now you can start playing with style sheets. First, get to the list of available style sheets. Follow these steps:

1. **From the File menu, choose New.**

   Instead of just giving you a nice blank document to work with, Ami Pro gives you a dialog box with an explanation of style sheets at the top. Each new Ami Pro document has a style sheet associated with it. The style sheet acts as a template for the document.

   (You have to know what a template is to understand the explanation, which seems to me to be kind of computer jargon as it is. Draftspeople use templates to draw pentagons and stuff, but what does a template have to do with writing?)

2. **The dialog box asks you to choose a style sheet.**

   You can scroll down the list to see how many style sheets Chuck has created just for you — more than you'll ever need! See Figure 3-1.

Style-sheet avoidance

A way to just about forget about style sheets exists — after you're in the New dialog box, click OK and use whatever style sheet is already underlined (usually _DEFAULT.STY unless somebody has changed it). You now are officially diagnosed with *style-sheet avoidance.* This means it is possible some day that they'll be carrying you away from your desk on a stretcher as you bat at invisible insects trying to attack you, all the while mumbling "DEFAULT.STY, DEFAULT.STY, DEFAULT.STY."

It's up to you. Therapy is staring up at you right now. And it's relatively cheap.

Explanation of style sheets

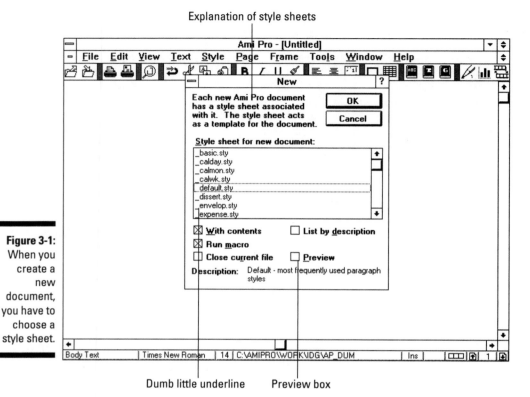

Figure 3-1:
When you
create a
new
document,
you have to
choose a
style sheet.

Dumb little underline   Preview box

To see the names of the style sheets in the New dialog box, be sure that List by description isn't checked (see Figure 3-1). If it is, you see a description of the file rather than the name, which would be confusing, because I talk about the names here.

Previewing the style sheet

While you're still right there in the New dialog box, take a second to cruise around among the possibilities — click Preview.

A display of the style sheet shows up next to the dialog box on-screen (see Figure 3-2.)

For _DEFAULT. STY, the preview isn't much to look at, but try some others, such as _FAX1.STY (Figure 3-3), _LETTER1.STY (Figure 3-4), _MEMO2.STY (Figure 3-5), or _NEWSLT3.STY (Figure 3-6).

The dumb underline in the style name

As far as the names go, if you noticed it there, you probably wonder why the name of the style sheet begins with that underline (_). Hey, I don't know. I hate that underline. I guess it's so that you can tell the Ami Pro style sheets from any you make yourself, because yours don't start with it.

Or, here's another theory. Ami Pro changes the hieroglyphic it uses in different versions of the product, so maybe it's to keep from writing over the old style sheets when you install the new ones (thereby giving you a monster set of style sheets, with two sets of almost identical names except for the character in front).

I know this much. If it didn't put the underline there, you could choose one of the style sheets in the box by typing the first character when you're in the dialog box. I know this because all Windows dialog boxes work like that. You can't though, which, as I say, I hate.

Just from looking at the Preview you can tell that these style sheets ain't no junk. That newsletter one looks like something somebody else did, if you know what I'm saying? No ordinary moron on the street without design training can lay out a newsletter that looks like that. Now try a style sheet to see what it does when you use it.

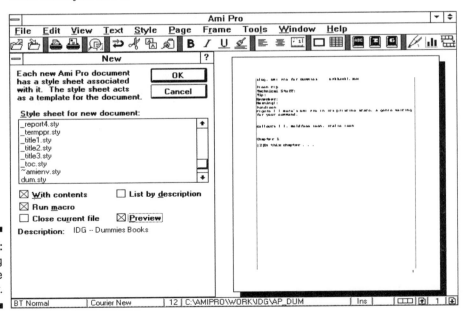

Figure 3-2:
Previewing a style sheet.

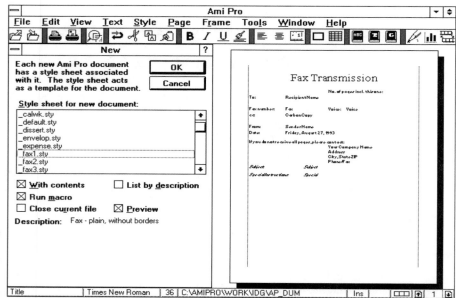

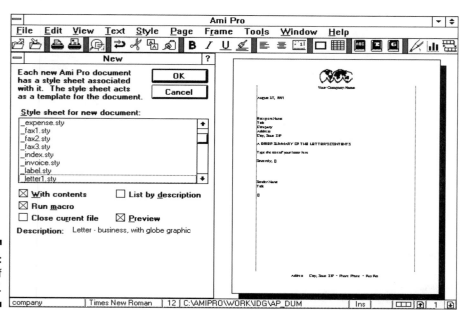

Preview

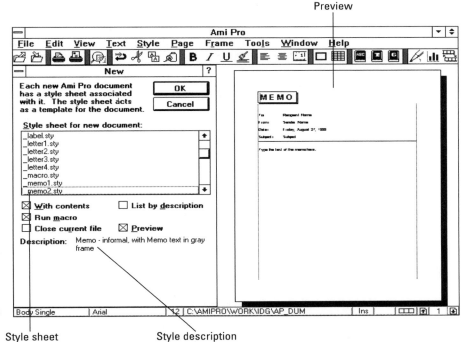

Figure 3-5:
Preview of
_MEMO2.STY.

Style sheet   Style description

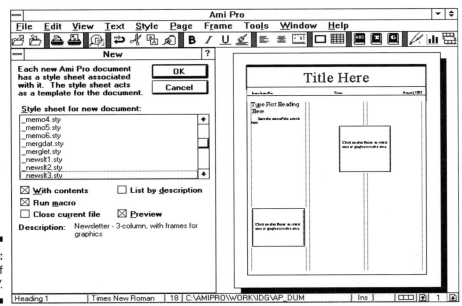

Figure 3-6:
Preview of
_NEWSLT3.STY.

Getting the style sheet on-screen

You can preview to your heart's content. After you know which style sheet you want, though, here's how to choose it:

1. **Highlight the style sheet you want and select OK.**

   In this example, highlight _MEMO2.STY.

   The memo appears on the page. Well, it almost appears there. First there's a personal information box. If you cancel it, a dialog box called the Default Information box appears. This extra box is really fancy. Can you imagine ever doing something like this yourself? After you type in information it asks for, such as your own name, it'll be there every time you start up a memo. That's neat, I think. But for right now, just get around this box.

2. **Press Cancel in the Default Information dialog box.**

   There's the blank memo on your page. Before you even start, it looks like you've bought fancy stationery.

When you're working with styles a great deal, the Styles box is helpful if you need to see the different styles appearing on your style sheet:

1. **In the View menu, click Show Styles Box.**

   A box comes up on-screen showing the available styles. Most people think the box is a pain and don't use it. It takes up too much room on-screen. When you are first learning, though, I think the Styles box comes in handy.

2. **If the box doesn't show all the styles, click and drag the bottom of the box until it does.**

Putting Stuff in the Style Sheet

When you're using a style sheet, you don't have to format text yourself, the way you learned about in the last chapter. You don't have to put things into bold or

The easiest way to apply styles

If it's the easiest, why didn't you tell me before? Well, I suppose it's good to learn all the methods so you can decide which is easiest to you. However, this method involves the fewest clicks and presses.

Recall from Chapter 2 where the Status bar is (bottom of the screen)? If not, check out Figure 3-7. Click the far left block of the Status bar, called the *styles area*. Up pops all the styles on your style sheet. You can select the desired style from this list by clicking it or using the arrows to highlight it. This method has the speed of the Styles box, but without the annoying box taking up room on your screen.

italic or anything. All you do is just choose a style, and the style sheet does all the formatting for you. In other words, you look brilliant, without having to struggle to get that way. Try it once:

1. In the Styles box, click the style you want to use.

In this example, choose the style that reads *To/From/Date.*

Notice that the highlight moves to the style you have chosen in the Styles box and that the Status bar now shows this same style at the left. (See Figure 3-7.)

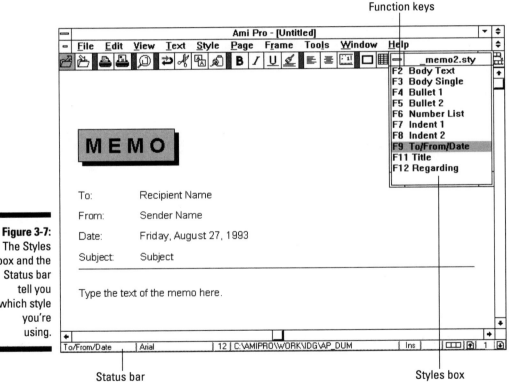

Figure 3-7:
The Styles box and the Status bar tell you which style you're using.

Instead of clicking a style, you can press the function key for a style, such as F2 for Body Text in the memo style sheet you're using here. The Styles box lists the function keys. (See Figure 3-7). Sometimes the function key is quicker than fishing around and clicking the mouse.

Now type some text for your memo (or letter, or whatever). In the memo example, follow these instructions:

1. **Select Recipient Name and type** Travelling Musicians. **(When you type the new text, the selected text disappears, which is what you want.)**

2. **For the From Option, select Sender name and type** Terry, the Band Manager.

3. **For date, don't do anything, because the date comes in automatically. (Make sure it's the right date, though, and change it if it isn't.)**

4. **For Subject, highlight Subject and type** Creative Expense Reports.

5. **Click just below the line drawn across the screen. (Do most people know how to draw such a neat line? No. But you look as if you do, when you use the style that has the line with it.)**

After you click, the highlight moves to Body Text in the two places that show the style you're using — the Styles box and the Status bar. See Figure 3-8.

6. **Save the memo with the name EXPENSES.SAM.**

Remember from Chapter 2 that you save a new file by choosing File, Save As (or clicking the save SmartIcon) and then typing a name for the file.

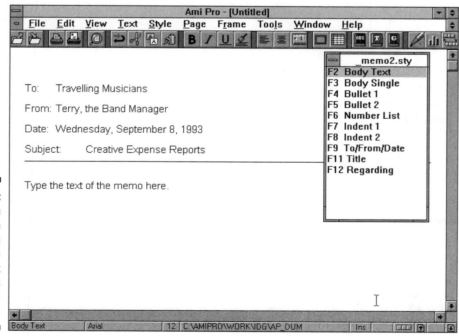

Figure 3-8:
When you click in an existing style, the Styles box highlights the style you are using.

In the Save As dialog box, Figure 3-9, don't select <u>K</u>eep format with document. If you do select it, Ami Pro doesn't identify your style sheet as a separate entity in places like the top of the Styles box. "But I swear I chose a style sheet for this document," you might say. Doesn't matter. Ami Pro treats it as nonexistent, nil, zero, zilch.

Don't click this box

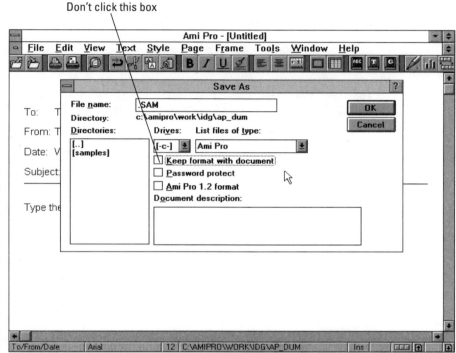

Figure 3-9:
If you select this box, you no longer see your style sheet by name in the Styles box and other places.

Actually, most of the time you're better off keeping the style sheet with the document because, whenever you change a style in a style sheet, you change that style in every document using the style sheet. If you had Ami Pro for a really long time, you could change a style in the style sheet _DEFAULT.STY in, say, 2023, and change the appearance of a document you created in 1993 that used the style sheet.

I often feel a little disappointed when my documents list their style sheets as "none," as if I'm being left out of something important. But I put up with it.

Now you can type the body of the memo:

I appreciate the time and energy you've all been putting into your expense reports lately. NOT. I really thank Tank for trying to put through his new pet bullfrog as a transportation expense. And I truly wonder what Hermie meant by "various amusing and special musical effects." But look, the IRS has no imagination. I need certain things from you if you expect to get reimbursed:

After you've typed the paragraph, press Enter twice. You're ready to create a bulleted list. Figure 3-10 shows the memo with the stuff at the top and the first paragraph.

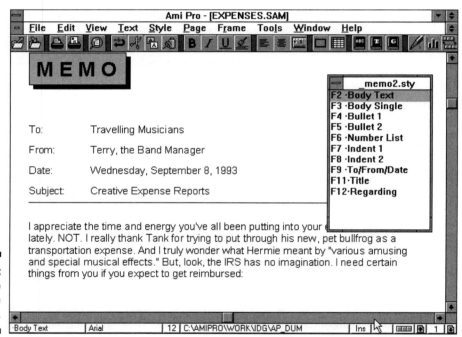

Figure 3-10:
Your memo
using a style
sheet.

Adding bullets

Bulleted lists can be no fun to create. Which bullets do you use? How far do you indent them? These are just a couple of the hard questions you face. When you use the style sheet, though, you don't have to answer them. Just go with the flow.

1. Click the Bullet 1 style in the Styles box.

A fancy check mark appears as a bullet. See Figure 3-11. (Tell me you know how to put one there without help. If you do, you're no dummy.)

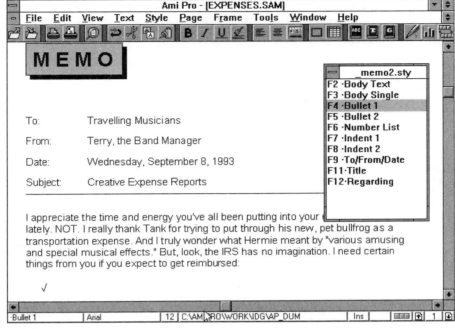

Figure 3-11:
When you
choose the
Bullet 1
style, the
bullet
automatically
appears.

2. **Type this text in the bulleted list, adding a Return after each fragment:**

   Receipts

   Mileage records

   Stubs for your plane tickets

Now you are ready to create a numbered list.

Adding a numbered list

To add a numbered list to the memo, guess what? You choose a style and brainlessly type the text. The style does all the work:

1. **Press F2 (or click the Body Text style) and then type** There are a few simple steps I'd like you to take for future road trips: **and press Enter.**

2. **Press F6 (or click the Number List style). Type each item in the list. Each time you press Enter, the list moves to a fresh line and adds a fresh number to it. Type these items:**

   Get an expense form from me before you go

> **Keep your receipts in an envelope or a purse or an empty cigarette pack**
>
> **Give the form and the receipts to me as soon as you get back**

3. **When you're done with the list, press Enter again; then press F2 to switch to the Body Text style and type** Thanks.

Figure 3-12 shows the bullets and the numbered list, and Figure 3-13 shows a full page view of the whole memo. (I talk about full-page views in Chapter 8. You don't need to move ahead and read about them. I just wanted you to see how great your memo looks.)

If you accidentally click the wrong style in the Styles box, all you have to do is click the correct style. The paragraph in question automatically converts to the style you click.

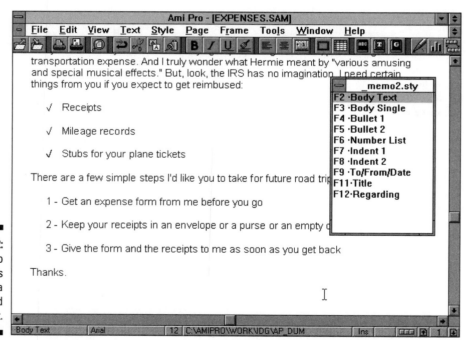

Figure 3-12:
A memo with bullets and a numbered list.

This memo looks professional — like your secretary spent all morning on it. But, as you well know, you didn't do anything professional. You just clicked a few places and typed in a few words. Whoever made that style sheet did something professional. All you had to do to look good was just . . . USE THE STYLE SHEET, right?

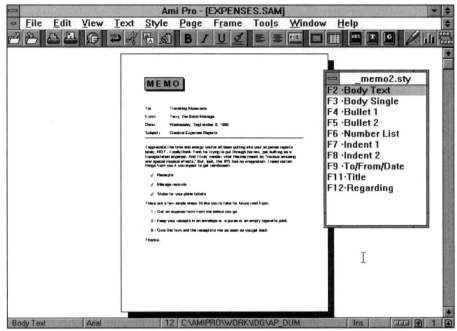

Figure 3-13:
The memo
in full-page
view,
looking
quite
professional.

But look at what's in there — that fancy memo box at the top (which uses an opaque frame with square corners, lines around it, shadow inside, and Arial 24 point bold type), that automatic date field we already admired, the bullets with the correct indention, those artistic check marks (you can't even find those bullets on the keyboard. Do you know how to make them?), and the numbered list. All the type faces go nicely with each other. The spacing is cool.

This puppy looks like it's so important it should be preserved in a scrapbook, and (as you well know) you just tossed it off, without knowing anything about frames, typefaces, bullet styles, conventions for numbered lists . . . or anything.

"Is that all?" I can hear you asking. "You mean, you just click a style sheet, then click a style, and that's all?" Yeah, that's all. I think it's a lot, but, well, I'm probably not going to convince you anyway. Chuck Green spent years on those style sheets and years more learning how to do stuff like that in the first place.

Depending on which style sheet you choose, there are all kinds of styles somebody else has created for you — hordes of them, legions of them. All you have to do to look smart is just click the ones you want. You can create fax pages that look like the company paid some artist $10,000 to design, newsletters that look as if you went to journalism school, letterhead that looks as if some other, grasping design artist took you to the cleaners for it, and on and on. All you have to do is click and type.

Oh, well, I give up. Fine, say "Is that all?" if you want. Fine. Say it. Yes, that's all.

Well, in the next chapter I talk about styles on more advanced topics, such as how you can change something in one instance so it changes in every instance in your document.

Chapter 4

Cooking with Spices: More on Styles

. . . .

. . . .

Being Stylish

Not that many people read *Esquire* or *Vogue*, really, and of those who do, not that many are true clothes horses. I mean, most of the time, except maybe when you were in high school, it's just as well to throw on any old thing and be done with it.

It's tempting to be the same way toward Ami Pro styles — tempting, but not necessarily a good idea. Styles save you work and time, while making you look good at the same time. They are a great boon to distracted people who want to do the latest things in word processing without necessarily learning all the latest things in word processing (in other words, to everybody).

Making Your Change a Global Change

Just suppose that, after you had the memo from the last chapter already typed and everything, Mick Jagger or whoever headed up your band came up and said, "Hey, like, those bullets don't stand out enough. How about if you, like, make 'em darker?"

You can make them darker the way you learned in Chapter 2: Select each bulleted item and click the bold SmartIcon. What if you had a 100 page memo, though, with 1,000 bullets? You'd spend all day selecting and clicking. With styles, you don't have to do all that. Stay tuned to find out how.

Reopening a document

First, open the document named EXPENSES.SAM, unless you already have it open from the last chapter. Recall from Chapter 2 that you click the open icon to open a file (or choose the File, Open command). Use this method to reopen EXPENSES.SAM. If you can't seem to find this file, make sure that the extension listed in the filename box reads *.SAM (if it doesn't, type it in).

Transmogrifying a style

I thought I needed a synonym here, so I came up with *transmogrifying*. You like it? The actual term in Ami Pro is *modifying*, but I thought that lacked a certain panache, so I used my imagination. Transmogrifying speaks more to me about the process of changing a style — oh, is it a magical process.

When you modify a style, you change it once, and then Ami Pro changes the text in every paragraph in the document that uses the style.

To modify (transmogrify) a style, follow these steps:

1. **First, tell Ami Pro which style to modify by selecting text using the style.**

   In this example, put the cursor in one of the bulleted paragraphs so that the Status bar says Bullet 1.

2. **For a shortcut to the Modify Style dialog box, click the right mouse button.**

   This shortcut should tell you something about just how important the Ami Pro gurus think modifying styles is. There aren't many mouse buttons to assign. Whatever those mouse buttons get to do has to be important. Well, the right mouse button, in Ami Pro, modifies styles. That means modifying styles is very important. Anybody who doesn't do it must be missing something great — such as never tasting Ben & Jerry's Rainforest Crunch ice cream bar.

After you right-click the mouse, the Modify Style dialog box pops up. See Figure 4-1. It enables you to change all kinds of elements of the style.

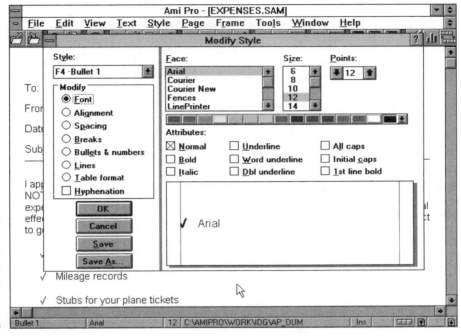

Figure 4-1:
Use this box
to change
just about
anything in
a style.

3. **Select the elements you want to change by experimenting in this dialog box.**

In this example, make sure Font is clicked in the Modify box and then select the Bold check box under Attributes.

Notice that when you click Bold, the word in the little *preview idiot box* (the sample box, you might remember) turns dark, to show you what you get when you accept the change. See Figure 4-2.

4. **Choose OK. Your change should affect all paragraphs with that style attached.**

In this example, all the bulleted items in the document turn bold. See Figure 4-3. You didn't have to go through and select them all. You didn't have to worry about forgetting some of them. They all turn dark. If you changed anything else in that one place — the Modify Style dialog box for bullets — that thing would change for all the bullets in that style, the Bullet 1 bullets. This method is much easier than selecting and clicking, and you don't have to worry about forgetting to change any bullets.

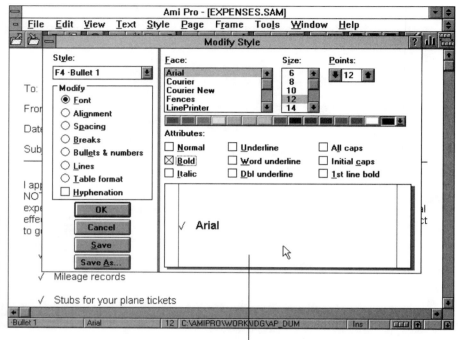

Figure 4-2:
The sample
box shows
the
predicted
change.

Sample box
(aka: idiot box)

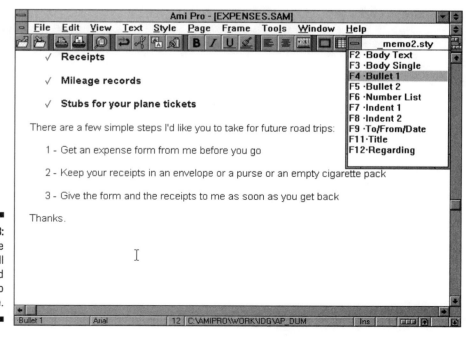

Figure 4-3:
With one
change, all
the bulleted
items turn to
boldface.

When changing elements in the Modify Style dialog box, you change the text only in the same style that you're modifying. If you're modifying Bullet 1, you change all the text in that style. If you haven't used the Bullet 1 style from that style sheet, you might as well go out into the street and shout your modification at a local parking meter. You have to use styles to be able to make these sweeping changes. This obvious point is easy to miss. I even knew a computer smartie once who missed it. Seriously. His name is Jeff, and he runs a computer store. He can build computers, but for a long time he wrote his documents without using styles. So I thought I'd mention it. Just don't tell Jeff I told you.

Remember that you can right-click your mouse to produce the Modify Style dialog box. It's the easiest and fastest way to modify a style!

Transfiguring a Paragraph to a Different Style

Modifying a style is a hot concept, but sometimes you don't even have to do that much tinkering to get your paragraphs to take on one fancy flair or another. It's often handy just to change from one style in your style sheet to another. You can do it just by clicking.

Here's how to change one style to another. In this example, you change the first bulleted item to another form of bullet:

1. **Put the cursor anywhere in the text that has the first style.**

   In this example, put the cursor anywhere in the bullet (many people think you have to select the paragraph, but you don't).

2. **Click the new style you want in the Styles box.**

   In this case, click Bullet 2 in the Styles box (see Figure 4-4).

The old styles now takes on all the characteristics of the new style!

Metamorphosing Several Paragraphs to a Different Style

If you want to change several paragraphs with one click, you select them all:

1. **Select any parts of the paragraphs you want to change.**

   In this case, select the other two bullets (see Figure 4-5).

Click here

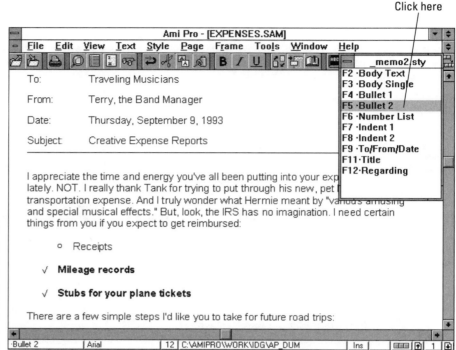

Figure 4-4:
You can
change the
style of a
paragraph
by pointing
and clicking.

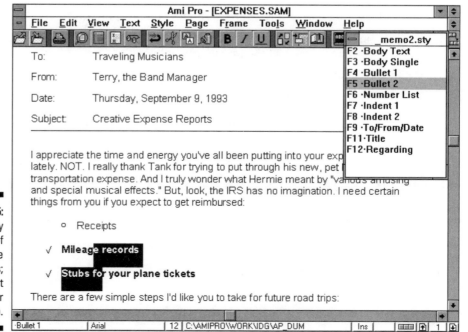

Figure 4-5:
Select any
part of
multiple
paragraphs;
then select
a style for
them.

2. **Click the new Style in the Styles box.**

   Click Bullet 2 if you are following along. The bullets change to the new style.

Eyeballing What You Can Put in a Style

Any time you want to change anything about your document's appearance, use the styles instead of changing it with the Text menu. Get ready to work with a different paragraph:

1. **Put the cursor first into any paragraph in your file.**

   In this example, put the cursor in the main paragraph in this memo, the one that starts "I appreciate."

   You probably didn't think there were so many things you can do to a simple paragraph style, but there are. Look over some of them.

2. **Click the right mouse button.**

   Browse around and check out some of the things you can do. There's a cornucopia of them. Falling into the Modify Style dialog box is like falling through Alice's rabbit hole into Wonderland (well, not really). The next sections cover some of the elements you can use.

Leering at fonts

Fonts (the typefaces you use, also called *faces*) can be fun to play with. In the Modify Style dialog box (Figure 4-6), make sure Font is checked in the Modify box on the left.

1. **In the Face box, select Courier New.**

2. **In the Size box, scroll down and click 24. Figure 4-6 shows the dialog box now.**

   If you chose OK, you would change the look of the paragraph in the document. For now, though, stay in the dialog box and cruise through some of the other things you can change.

3. **Click Arial and 12 to go back to the original sizes.**

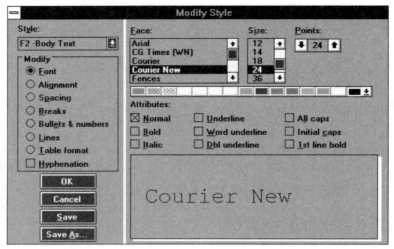

Looking over alignment

In the Modify box, click Alignment. Here (Figure 4-7), you can change everything from how far you indent the lines to, oh, really advanced things such as hanging indents.

Rest box

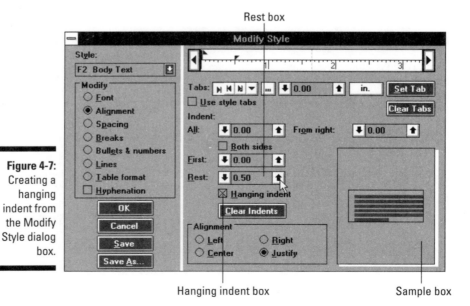

Figure 4-7:
Creating a
hanging
indent from
the Modify
Style dialog
box.

Hanging indent box   Sample box

Suppose that you wanted to hang an indent, which is when you indent every line but the first one:

1. **Click the box that says <u>H</u>anging indent so an × appears in the box.**

2. **Click the up arrow in the <u>R</u>est box until the box shows 0.50.**

You can't have a hanging indent unless you put an amount in the <u>R</u>est box. Ami Pro should do that for you, if you ask me, but it doesn't. You can easily click the hanging indent box over and over, wonder why nothing was happening, and begin to doubt your own knowledge of what a hanging indent even was — all because you didn't know the esoteric fact that you have to put an amount in the <u>R</u>est box if you want to hang an indent.

The sample box shows the effect of the hanging indent. See Figure 4-7.

Taking a gander at spacing

A normal user uses only double space and single space. That's about all anyone needs to do, actually.

1. **Click S<u>p</u>acing in the Modify box (Figure 4-8).**

Try out some of the possibilities. Watch the effect of your choices in the idiot box.

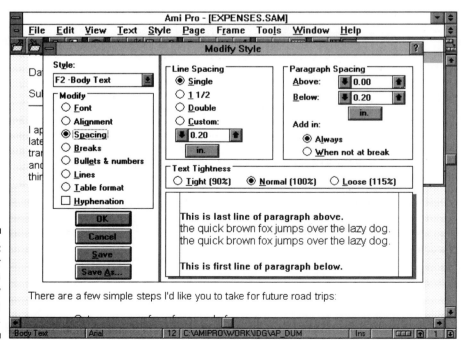

Figure 4-8: Choices for spacing in the Modify Style dialog box.

2. Click Double in the Line Spacing box.

The sample in the sample box shows the double spacing (Figure 4-9).

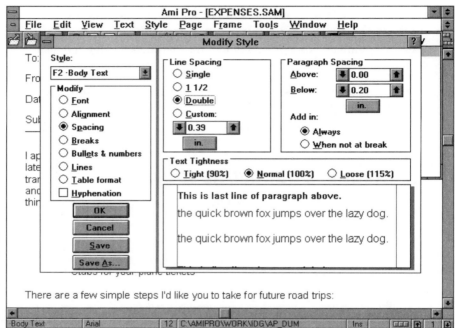

Figure 4-9:
The sample
box shows
double
spacing.

Ogling breaks

Breaks normally have to do with pages, not paragraphs, and not (you hope) bones. Well, they especially have to do with coffee. But when you think about it, a *page break* (an indication to the printer to start printing on a new page) can come in the middle of a paragraph, before it, or after it. In this fancy box (Figure 4-10), you can tell Ami Pro where you want the breaks to appear in your paragraphs.

Try this by clicking Breaks in the Modify box and playing with the options.

I actually use this Breaks choice quite a bit. There are certain types of paragraphs that I hate to see all by themselves, such as high-level subheads in an outline. So I don't allow any breaks in them, and I keep them with the paragraph that follows.

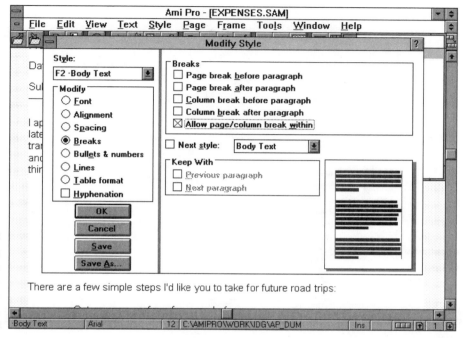

Figure 4-10:
The Breaks
option in the
Modify Style
box.

Examining bullets and numbers

The Bullets & numbers option is more for people who make style sheets for a living than for your average novice. For your on-the-street, nondesign professional, any bullet will do. Still, you may want to fire a few of these bullets into a document:

1. **Click Bullets & numbers.**

2. **In the Before Paragraph box, click Bullet.**

3. **Click an eye-appealing bullet to test.**

    Figure 4-11 shows the flying wedge bullet.

Closely regarding lines

Lines (also called *rules*), too, are more for people who make pages look nice for a living than for rushed modern people with other goals on their minds. However, you can use a line or two if you desire. Whoever created the memo style sheet used in this chapter used a line for the style named *Regarding*.

Click bullet

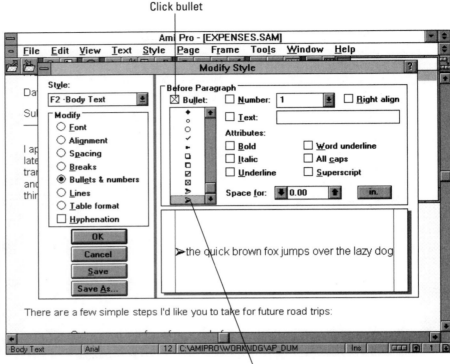

Figure 4-11:
The Bullets
& numbers
option of the
Modify Style
dialog box.

Flying wedge

To add a line to your document, try this:

1. **Choose Lines in the Modify box.**

2. **Check the Line above box.**

3. **Choose a moderately fat line in the box by scrolling and clicking.**

4. **Choose OK to accept your changes or Cancel to ignore any changes.**

   The sample box (aka: *idiot box*) shows what you get if you follow along
   with this example (see Figure 4-12).

You can easily spend your whole summer vacation experimenting with choices
in the Modify Style box. Of course, you don't have to, because you can always
use the styles already in the style sheet and remain happily uninformed and
unburdened by any alternatives. It's up to you.

Line above box   Line sizes box

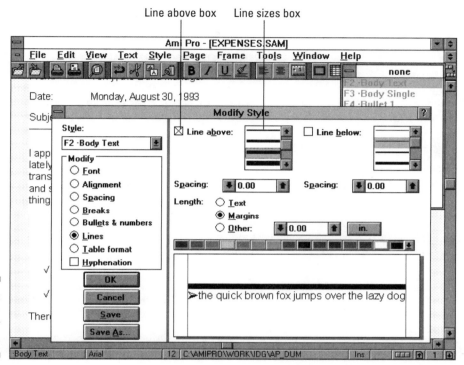

Figure 4-12:
Adding
rules to your
work.

In Windows, when you want to make a choice that Windows can't act on, it stops you from doing it by *graying* the choice. You can click a choice that's grayed as much as you want, and all it does is drive you nuts. (I've tried it many times. I still do it.) When something is grayed, it means you have not met all the requirements necessary to use that command or option. A good example is when you don't have a word highlighted and you attempt to use the Cut or Copy commands. Without a highlighted word, Ami Pro does not know what to cut or copy. Pull down the Edit menu and look at these commands without anything highlighted. These are grayed commands. Another example, closer to home, is in the Create Style dialog box — the Modify button is grayed until you type a name for the new style. Ami Pro just wouldn't feel comfortable going ahead and modifying the style until you tell it a new name. (It seems to me that it should go ahead.) If you ever notice that an option is a lighter color than the rest and you can't seem to use it, it's probably grayed. Try changing something else.

Originating your own style

What does Chuck Green (or any of those people who make style sheets) actually do when he makes a style?

Modifying an existing style is one thing, and you've just seen how to do that. But there's a remote possibility you might decide to come up with a style *on your own.* Maybe you don't like any of the names for the styles in the style sheets you have. Maybe you're just feeling original, and kind of perverse. Maybe (and this is probably about the only time you'd really do it), somebody forces you to do it by saying, "These are the styles we use in this department. Use them or get fired."

Whatever your motivation, you might (but will probably not) decide to create a style. Suppose that you felt nauseous over the choices available for bullets and decided to create one called Bullet 3. You can base your new style on an existing one, just changing what you want but getting the benefit of all the things in the old style you may not have thought of. Here's how to create your own style:

1. **With the cursor anywhere in the document, select the Style menu and then click Create Style.**

   A Create Style dialog box jumps onto the page and invites you to name the new style. See the accompanying figure.

2. **In the New style box, type the name of your new style (you pick it).**

   In this example, type **Square Bullet**.

3. **In the Based On box, click the style in the current style sheet that most closely resembles your new one.**

   This way, you don't have to start from scratch when creating a style. In this example, click the Bullet 1 style.

4. **To set the characteristics of the new style, click the Modify button.**

   The familiar old Modify Style box dialog pops up again. (Feeling a sense of paranoia?)

5. **This is where you modify the old style so it is different from the new. Perhaps you want to add a rule, align the text in a different way, or place the text in a different font.**

   In this example, click the Bullets & numbers option because you want to change the look of the bullet. Under Bullet in the Before Paragraph box, choose the square bullet with an × in the middle (see the accompanying figure).

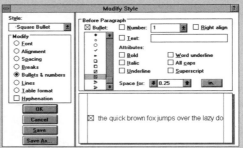

6. **Click OK after you have modified the style to your liking.**

   Ami Pro creates the new style and adds it to the style sheet for your document. You can use it the same way you use any other style in the style sheet (except the new one doesn't have function keys assigned to the styles).

Killing Styles You Don't Like, and Other Gratifying Acts of Violence

I think that what I've said so far in this chapter and the one before it are the main things for any normal, thinking non-nerd to know about styles. "It's good to use styles. You can change them." That's the gist of it. A number of situations exist that can come up in handling styles, though, and they may come up for you someday. The Ami Pro menu has an entire section related to styles; it enables you to modify and create styles. The Style menu is shown in Figure 4-13.

Some of these options you may never use; I don't use them all. Some of the commands may come in handy, however. These options are discussed next.

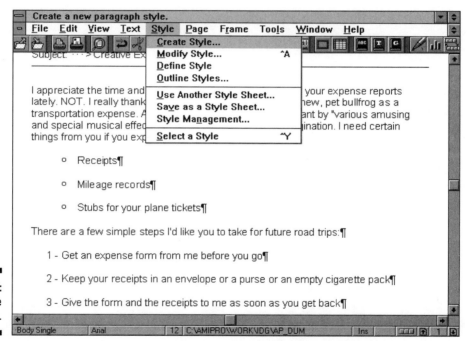

Figure 4-13:
The Style
menu.

Making your own style sheet

Suppose, for example, that you create a style while you're working in a document and want to be able to use it in your own style sheet. You know, the Ami Pro expert who created the style sheet doesn't have the same taste as you, so you want your own style sheet always to have something different, such as a larger typeface.

1. **Create a new document (with the File, New command) and use the style sheet you want to change — _DEFAULT.STY.**

   Figure 4-14 shows the blank document with the style sheet and the Styles box showing (View, Show Styles Box).

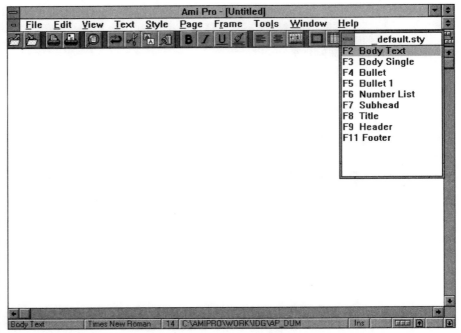

Figure 4-14:
A blank document, before you modify the style sheet.

You can change the styles in the sheet all day long, of course. Try making a couple of changes.

2. **Find the style you want to modify by scrolling through the Styles box or using the styles area on the Status bar.**

   In this example, you don't have to scroll anywhere because the style you are going to modify is Body Text.

3. **Click the right mouse button.**

   The Modify Style dialog box appears. Your selected style should appear in the Style part of this dialog box. In this example, the style listed in the Styles box is Body Text. See Figure 4-15.

4. **Now you can change the characteristics you want by using the familiar dialog box.**

   In this example, change the font in the Size box to 14 points and then choose OK.

OK, you've changed the style to the way you want it. Well, Ami Pro doesn't change the style sheet permanently — that is, next time you use the style sheet, it will act in its old, boring way. Ami Pro doesn't change the style sheet for all of eternity unless you specifically tell it to. How do you do that?

To change a style sheet forever, follow these steps after having changed the styles as you desired:

5. From the S̲tyle menu (Figure 4-13), choose the Sav̲e as a Style Sheet command.

A dialog box comes up where you can either type a new name for the style sheet or use the present one (Figure 4-16).

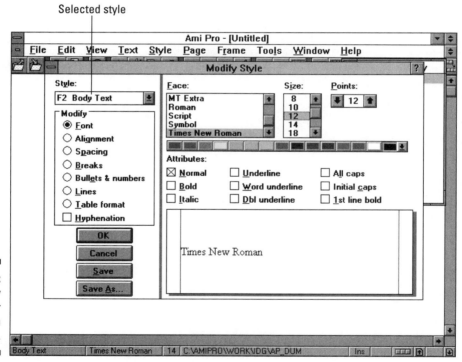

Figure 4-15:
The Modify Style box for body text in _DEFAULT.STY.

6. Type the new name if you want to rename the style sheet or click OK to redefine the old style sheet.

In this example, type **MYSTY.STY** and choose OK.

If you choose to overwrite the original style sheet, a very nice message tells you that the style sheet already exists and asks whether you want to overwrite it — see Figure 4-17. I wouldn't blame you if you wanted to back down at that point. "Well, no, I'm not that sure. Maybe I should just stay with the old way." It's not a bad idea to rename the style sheet so you always have the original in case you need it later.

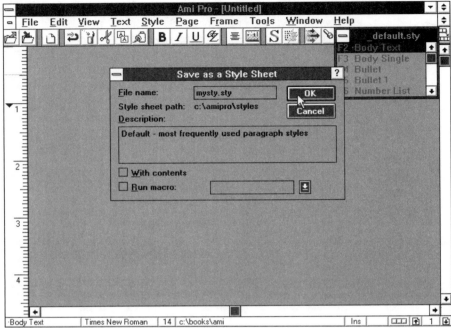

Figure 4-16:
Saving your
changes as
a new style
sheet.

If you want to create a style sheet with a different name or redefine the sheet you're using, you can do so with the Style, Save as a Style Sheet command. Just type a different name for the style sheet (or leave the original name in the box to redefine it) and choose OK. There's nothing obvious or intuitive about saving your new style sheets, and I apologize for this — especially because it's something you're likely to end up doing a great deal.

Figure 4-17:
A very nice
message
box from
Ami Pro.

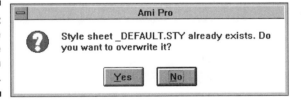

Using a different style sheet with your document

After you've worked with a document and its style sheet for a while, you probably don't want to switch to another one. I think you'd do it only if some overbearing boss insisted that you do so.

Look, don't take my word for it. Try it with EXPENSES.SAM (you created it in Chapter 3) which, you may remember, uses the style sheet _MEMO2.STY.

Suppose that you wanted to use _MEMO3.STY instead. Figure 4-18 shows a blank document using _MEMO3.STY. The word *Memorandum* at the top looks different from the one in _MEMO2.STY.

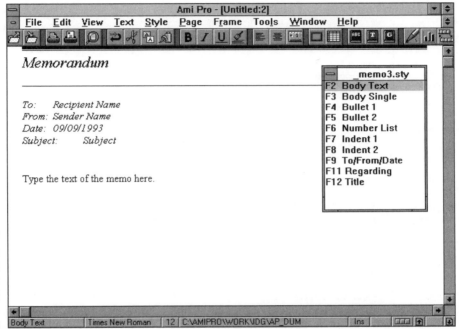

Figure 4-18:
A blank
document
using
_MEMO3.STY.

Now try making the switch:

1. **Open the document that you want to modify.**

   In this example, open EXPENSES.SAM, with its _MEMO2.STY style sheet. (Figure 4-19).

2. **From the Style menu, choose Use Another Style Sheet.**

3. **From the Use Another Style Sheet dialog box (Figure 4-20), scroll through until you find the style sheet you want and then highlight it.**

   In this example, click _MEMO3.STY and choose OK.

Well, the new memo in Figure 4-21 doesn't look as if it's using _MEMO3.STY (the one in Figure 4-18). It looks like it didn't change at all. It even has that Square bullet style that you made yourself and that wasn't even in _MEMO3.STY before. Now, I'm sure a nerd might make a good case that the document did change. But to me, if it doesn't look any different, it really hasn't changed.

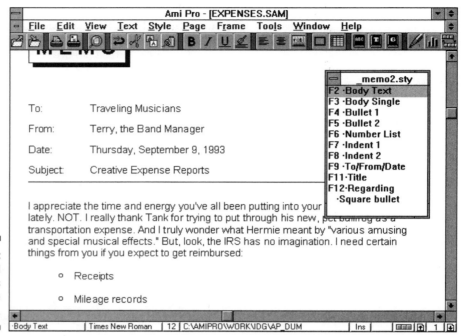

Figure 4-19:
EXPENSES.SAM
with its
original style
sheet.

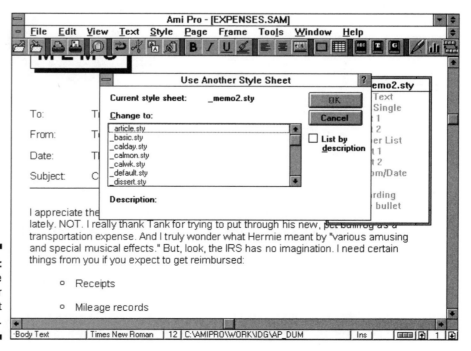

Figure 4-20:
The Use
Another
Style Sheet
dialog box.

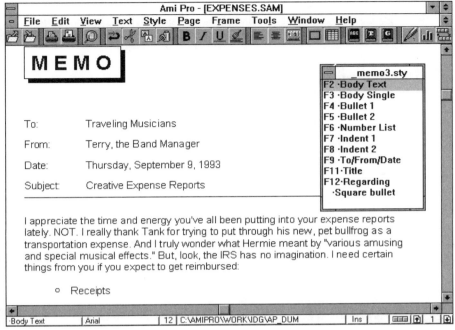

Figure 4-21:
The new
memo.

Sending a style to oblivion

As you begin creating styles, you're no doubt going to hate some of them. It's just natural. Besides, you may get two or three that are identical. Or you may come to hate some of the ones that Ami Pro made for you and want to annihilate them. How would you do it? You can't highlight the style in the Styles box and then press Delete. You can't drag it out of the Styles box with the mouse and then strangle it. What do you do? Either live with it or follow another path:

1. **From the Style menu, choose Style Management.**

   The Style Management dialog box opens. See Figure 4-22.

2. **Select the style you want to dispatch into the ether forever by highlighting it.**

   The styles in the Styles in document box are the ones you created yourself for this style sheet or ones that you modified. The Styles in style sheet box contains the default styles of this style sheet. In this example, let's kill the Square Bullet style, which is listed in the Styles in document box.

3. **Click the Remove button.**

   Ami Pro causes the offending style to drop its mortal coil forever. It's good. And good riddance, too.

4. **Click OK to close the dialog box and return to the document.**

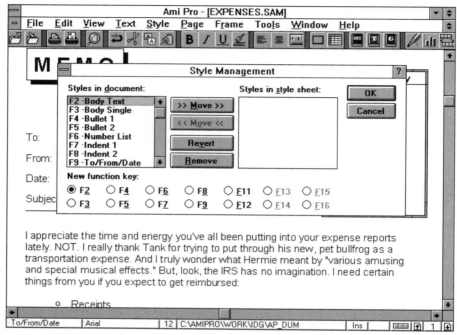

Figure 4-22:
The Style
Management
dialog box.

 ## Sneaking a peak at page styles

If you've had your fill of styles and style sheets, you can stop reading here. This next section is for the more daring readers who crave more knowledge about Ami Pro.

Every style sheet has both paragraph layout and page layouts. You've been working with paragraph styles throughout this chapter and the preceding one, and you'll have much to do with them in the future, I'm willing to venture. Every style sheet has quite a few paragraph styles, and hopefully you're getting a feel for what they are all about.

A style sheet also has one (and only one) *page format.* Now this concept can be confusing because pages and paragraphs share many of the same characteristics, such as margin size and tab settings. But basically, I think it works like this. There's a standard page format for the entire document, but if a paragraph has a different style than the page format, it takes precedence over the page format (which might cause you to forget there was a page format at all).

 It's very possible that you'll never change or manipulate a page style in any way. In fact, fooling with page styles is just asking for trouble. I'm talking about page styles only because they're there and they do have a big influence on your page. Unless somebody tells you to (such as an editor who's paying you great bushels of money), don't change your page styles — meaning your margins for the page, tab settings for the page, things such as that.

The mechanics of changing style sheets

If the styles in the old sheet match style names in the new sheet, Ami Pro makes the substitutions correctly. Any text formatted with a style that isn't on the new style sheet, though, Ami Pro formats as Body Text (its universal style). Yet, Ami Pro still lists the old style name in red in the Status bar. It's perplexing. There's that name in the Status bar, but you don't have the style on the style sheet. You have to assign a different style to get any style at all, other than Body Text.

Also, when you bring in the new style sheet, you can't bring it in with contents. Any neat things you might see in the Preview of the document aren't there when you bring the style sheet into a document that used to have another style sheet.

For these reasons and others, changing style sheets is an elaborate process.

However, just because I like to tempt you (I'm devilish that way), I do include the basic method to use to change your page style:

1. **Open the Page menu (see Figure 4-23).**

2. **Click Modify Page Layout.**

   The Modify Page Layout dialog box (Figure 4-24) enables you to change characteristics of your document — the margins, the size of the page, number of columns, and the like.

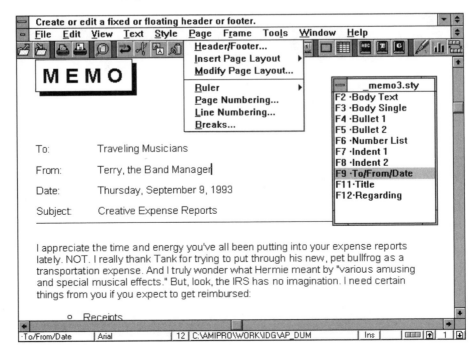

Figure 4-23:
The Page
menu.

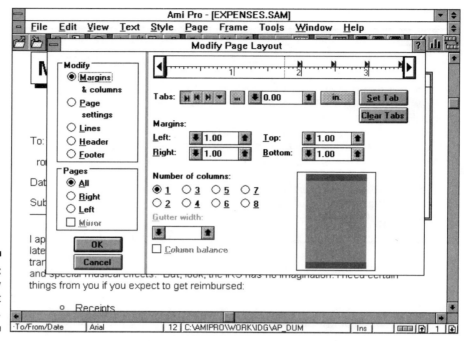

Figure 4-24:
The Modify
Page Layout
dialog box.

There's a pretty good chance that when you go to modify your page layout, the choice isn't available. It is *grayed,* as they call it, on the menu. I hate that. Programmers should be smart enough to know that you want to change the margin for later, even if you're working with a draft at the moment. They pretend, though, that they don't understand that. They force you to change to Layout mode. I talk more about the modes in Chapter 8, but to do it, choose Layout Mode from the View menu.

3. **Under Modify, choose the area you want to change. Adjust the settings to your liking.**

   In this example, click the Lines option. Choices appear for the lines around the page, with option buttons and descriptions such as Inside and Close to inside.

4. **Choose OK.**

   Ami Pro makes your changes. To see them, choose Full Page from the View menu.

Stick to modifying only your paragraph styles if at all possible. When you modify paragraph styles, you can make myriad changes with little effort.

Having said so much about styles, I think I've said enough. In the next chapter I talk about a subject so simple it almost doesn't deserve its own chapter — using SmartIcons. But these icons are a great boon to casual, relaxed, easygoing, or otherwise non-nerdy users.

Part II
Some Tools You'll Love

The 5th Wave   By Rich Tennant

OK—don't use the Spell Checker! We'll just issue a whole line of cards that wish people a "Happy Hollidog," "Seasons Creepings," and "Joy To The Whirled."

Bob's Card Co.

In this part...

This part shows you how to use the SmartIcons, which can help you do something in one step rather than two. The Help program is also covered here. Learn to use the Spell Checker, the Thesaurus, and the Grammar Checker in this part as well.

Chapter 5

Microwaving with Those Cute Little Icons

....

In This Chapter

▶ How to use the SmartIcons in 50 steps or less (hee hee)

▶ How to get a quick translation of an icon hieroglyphic

▶ How to add new icons and eradicate others from the set

▶ Why you can't eradicate a SmartIcon altogether, even if you strike it from a set

▶ How to move the icons toward Communism (or, at least, a little to the left)

▶ How to banish SmartIcons from the page (and how to repent and get them back)

▶ How to make your own SmartIcons

....

SmartIcons are at least as much a gift to the human race as instant coffee is. In a way, it's a shame to have a chapter on them at all, because a chapter is pretentious by its very nature. It creates the unavoidable impression that there is something (probably something really complicated) to explain about SmartIcons. Really, that isn't the case. I mean, there shouldn't be a chapter on these little pictures. If I were here to teach you how to use SmartIcons, the next paragraph should be the entire chapter.

Using SmartIcons

Just click one when you want to use it. You don't have to read this chapter to learn how to use SmartIcons — you just learned how. This chapter explains how to manipulate them in different ways so that they appear just as you want them to appear.

Using SmartIcons: The Sequel

That last section should be the whole chapter, and I don't mind if you just flip on over to some other chapter now. However, since I'm here, I'll dwell a little more on SmartIcons.

What, after all, is a SmartIcon? It's a little picture that you click to do something that otherwise you'd have to do some other way. Usually, it carries out two or three commands that you'd otherwise have to select from the menus. Because it's purely pictorial, you don't have to remember any words or letters or hot keys. You just have to remember which picture means what.

Giving some advice to truckers

There are some SmartIcons on-screen when you first start Ami Pro. Open a document you have previously created or create a new one so you can try the SmartIcons:

1. **Open your document of choice or follow along with this example.**

   Create a new document using the _DEFAULT.STY style sheet.

2. **Type the following (put the first line in a Title style and the list in a Number List style, so that it looks like Figure 5-1):**

   Guidelines for Mack Truck Drivers

   Every Mack truck driver should follow these simple guidelines:

   1. **Drive on the right side of the road.**

   2. **Avoid speeding tickets.**

   3. **Drink hoards of coffee.**

   4. **Avoid truck stops with lousy food.**

   5. **Get gas when the tank gets low.**

The default SmartIcons

Now that there's some text on the page, you can try out a few SmartIcons. Table 5-1 shows the default SmartIcons you see on your screen, their purposes, and the matching menu command. There are other SmartIcon sets available to you, but you'll read about them later.

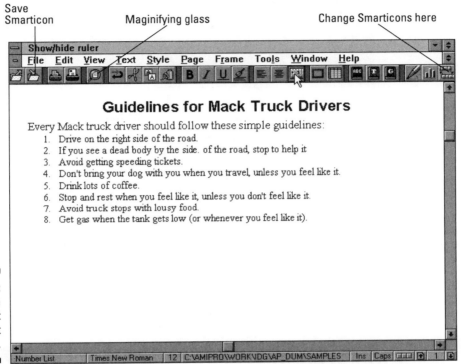

Figure 5-1:
The sample
document
you just
created.

Table 5-1	The Standard SmartIcon Set	
Icon	**Purpose**	**Menu Command**
	Open a file	File, Open
	Save current file	File, Save
	Print a file	File, Print
	Print an envelope	File, Print Envelope
	Full page/layout view	View, Full page or View, Custom
	Undo last action	Edit, Undo
	Cut to Clipboard	Edit, Cut
	Copy to Clipboard	Edit, Copy
	Paste Clipboard	Edit, Paste
B	Boldface text	Text, Bold
I	Italicize text	Text, Italic

(continued)

Table 5-1 (continued)

Icon	Purpose	Menu Command
U	Underline text	Text, Underline
	Fast format	Text, Fast Format
	Left align text	Text, Alignment, Left
	Center text	Text, Alignment, Center
	Show or hide ruler	View, Show (or Hide) Ruler
	Add a frame	Frame, Create Frame
	Create a table	Tools, Tables
ABC	Spell check	Tools, Spell check
T	Thesaurus	Tools, Thesaurus
G	Grammar check	Tools, Grammar check
	Create drawing	Tools, Drawing
	Add a chart	Tools, Charting
	Next icon set	Tools, SmartIcons

Trying out the SmartIcons

Once you have your new file open, click the save SmartIcon to save the file. Click the full page/layout SmartIcon to see what your document will look like on the printed page. Click it again to return to layout mode.

To use a SmartIcon, then, you point and click. It beats remembering which commands to use. Even if you do remember the commands, the SmartIcon is faster — one click rather than two or more.

The magic of the right mouse button

Recall from Chapter 4 that you can right-click anywhere in the document to call up the Modify Style dialog box. Well, the right mouse button serves another nifty purpose. If you ever forget what a SmartIcon does, you can simply right-click it and a description of the icon appears in the Title bar. A very convenient and handy feature of all Lotus products! I really wish Microsoft would adopt this great feature in its products. Figure 5-2 shows the description of the ruler SmartIcon as an example.

Explanation

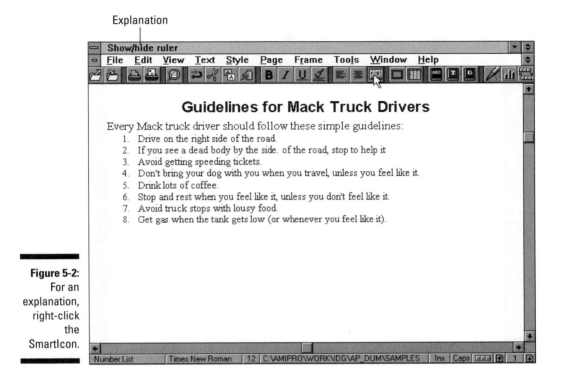

Figure 5-2:
For an
explanation,
right-click
the
SmartIcon.

Rearranging Your SmartIcons

There's a SmartIcon for every command on the menu system. Anything you can do in Ami Pro you can do with a SmartIcon. (I'm sure a nerd can find an exception to that statement. Well, fine.) With so many to choose from, you can't possibly use them all. You're likely to cultivate your favorites and ignore all the others — your pets, so to speak.

Here's how to set up the SmartIcons the way you want them:

1. **Click Tools.**

   The Tools menu opens. See Figure 5-3.

2. **Click SmartIcons.**

   You find yourself in the SmartIcons dialog box. See Figure 5-4.

3. **You can move icons to and from the palette simply by clicking and dragging them.**

   The icons in the left column are the available icons you can add to your *palette* (icon set). The icons on the right are the ones already appearing on your palette.

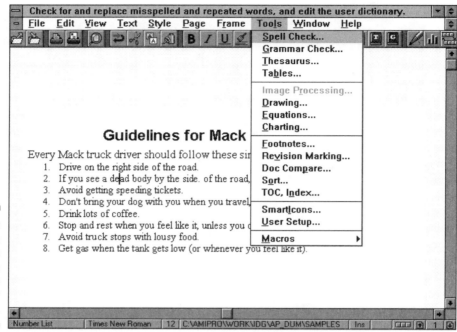

Figure 5-3:
Start with
the Tools
menu to
rearrange
your
SmartIcons.

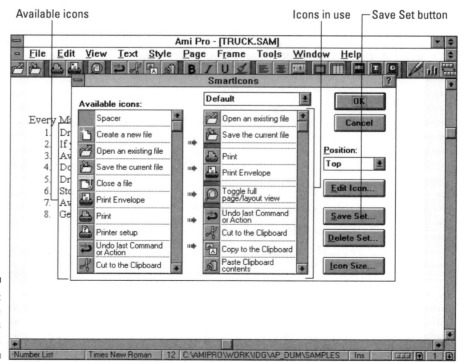

Figure 5-4:
The
SmartIcons
dialog box.

Preserving a set of SmartIcons

Before you change the set, save it with a different name. That way, you don't have to commit forever to this set that you've created. If things get too crazy in your own set, you can go back to the one that the smart engineers set up in the first place.

To save your icon set as a new set, follow these steps:

1. **From the Tools menu, choose SmartIcons to return to the SmartIcons dialog box.**

2. **Click the Save Set button.**

   The Save SmartIcon Set dialog box appears.

3. **In the Name of SmartIcon set box, type your choice of a new name (no extension).**

   In this example, type **My set.** Figure 5-5 shows the dialog box.

DOS name here   Name of set here

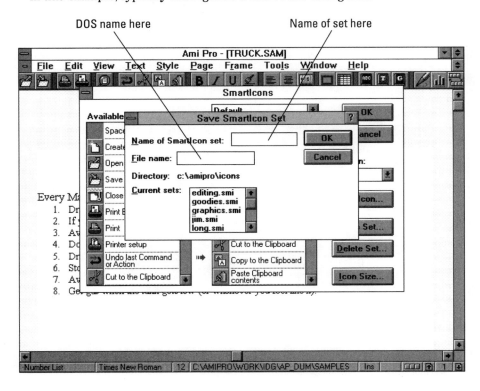

Figure 5-5:
The Save
SmartIcon
Set dialog
box.

4. **In the File name box, type the new name of the file and then choose OK.**

In this example, you should type **MYSET** and then choose OK. Ami Pro automatically adds the .SMI extension.

When Ami Pro saves your SmartIcon set, it automatically adds the DOS extension .SMI and saves the SmartIcons in the C:\AMIPRO\ICONS directory. If you ever decide to install Ami Pro on a new machine, you don't have to build your SmartIcon file from scratch. Instead, simply copy the .SMI files from the C:\AMIPRO\ICONS directory on your original disk to the directory on your new disk.

Transporting a SmartIcon

Now that you've created your own SmartIcon set, you can fiddle with the SmartIcon set and be able to get back to the original setup if you so desire.

Suppose, for example, that you strongly dislike the order in which the icons come. Maybe you want to have the save SmartIcon at the very beginning of all the other SmartIcons. Click the save SmartIcon and drag it to the top of the icons. (See Figure 5-6.) You can move around any of the icons in this manner.

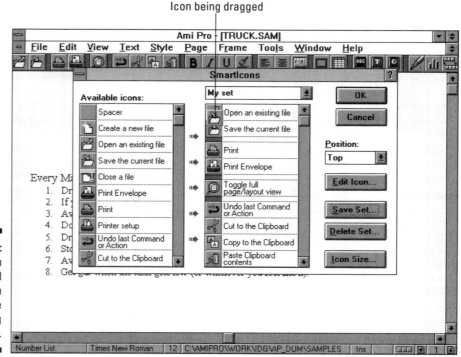

Figure 5-6: You can drag around the icons in your set like a screaming brat.

Adding a new SmartIcon or two

Perfect replicas of all those icons I mentioned earlier (one for every Ami Pro command) live happily in the Available icons box on the left side of the SmartIcons dialog box. You can drag them into your current set if you want. Figure 5-7 shows the *My set* group after dragging a close file icon to it.

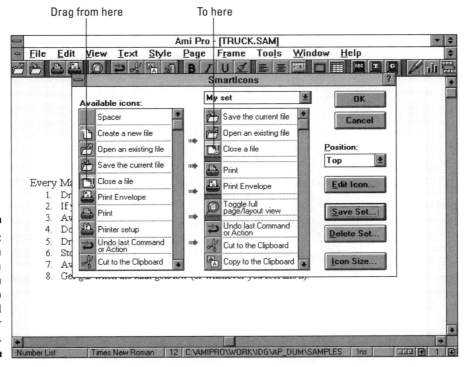

Figure 5-7: You can drag a SmartIcon from here to there to add it to your set.

When you drag an icon from the Available icons column, an original stays in place. You can't accidentally vaporize the original and never have it available when you work with other sets. I wish money in my bank account worked this way!

Expunging a SmartIcon

You can push and pull your icons around like salt water taffy. Of course, as you play around with the possibilities, you may well end up with some icons in your set that you prefer to annihilate utterly. You can do that, too:

1. **From the Tools menu, choose SmartIcons.**

   The SmartIcons dialog box is starting to look familiar, huh?

2. **Scroll down to find the doomed icon and then click and drag it out of the dialog box to delete it.**

   Figure 5-8 shows the deletion of the charting icon in progress.

3. **Click OK to save the set and put it into use.**

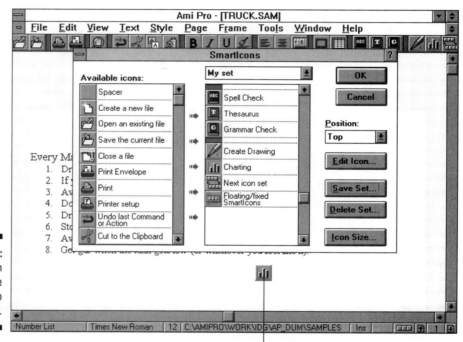

Figure 5-8:
Drag an icon
out of the
box to
delete it.

Deleting this icon

If you change your mind later and want a deleted icon back, you can simply drag it over from the Available icons list.

Choosing a SmartIcon Set

Not all harried modern people with business careers and personal considerations on their minds want to be dedicating their afternoons to designing their own SmartIcon sets. That sounds more like a job for a computer nerd. Well, you get to have some nifty SmartIcon sets without designing your own. Look through the list of SmartIcon sets the smart program engineers have drawn up, and you can just choose to use one of them:

1. Click the SmartIcon with three blue boxes that appears in the Status bar.

Remember, the Status bar is at the bottom of the screen. This icon is on the far right. See Figure 5-9.

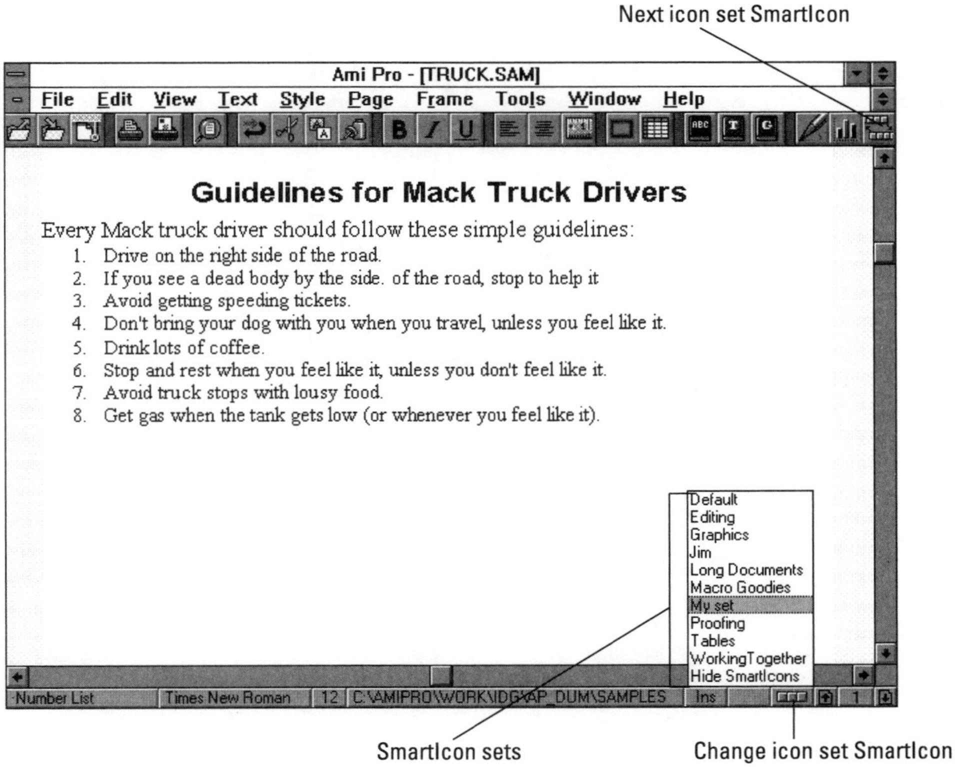

Next icon set SmartIcon

Figure 5-9:
You can
change
your
SmartIcon
set with
these
buttons.

SmartIcon sets   Change icon set SmartIcon

2. Choose the icon set that you want.

In this example, choose *Default* to restore the original icon set.

There are sets for some of the dumb things your boss might force you to do, such as create a chart to illustrate some figures (the Graphics set) or put together a table of a bunch of boring statistics (the Tables set).

There's a quick way to riffle through the icon sets and see what's in them — click the next icon set SmartIcon at the very right of the default set and all the other sets that come with Ami Pro. Keep clicking this icon until you return to your icon set. Review Figure 5-9.

There is only one difference between the next icon set SmartIcon (the very last SmartIcon on the toolbar) and the change icon set icon (bottom of screen on Status bar) — see Figure 5-9. The change icon set icon activates a list of all the icon sets from which you can choose the one you want; the next icon set SmartIcon simply activates the icon set that is next on the list. If you know which icon set you need, the change icon set is the better way to go. The next icon set is helpful if you want to review what icons appear in each set.

Moving the SmartIcons Around on the Page

You don't have to always have your SmartIcons across the top of the screen. That can get pretty boring. You can have them on the left, on the right, on the bottom, even *floating*. (They don't really float off the screen, which would be really cool. Maybe in the next version, Ami Pro will do that. They don't even, exactly, float. I'll come to that in just a second.)

1. **From the Tools menu, select SmartIcons.**

2. **In the SmartIcons dialog box, click the Position box to view the possible positions. See Figure 5-10.**

Position box

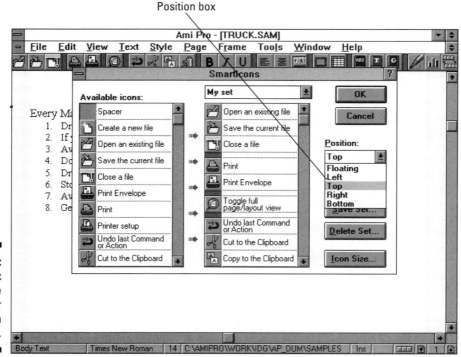

Figure 5-10:
Use this box to move your SmartIcon palette.

3. Click the position of your choice and then choose OK.

Figure 5-11 shows how the SmartIcons appear when you choose Left from the Position box.

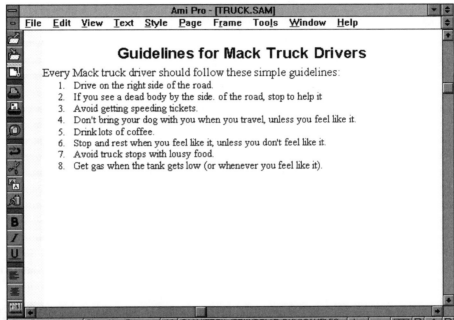

Figure 5-11: SmartIcons on the left.

You can even have so-called *floating icons* that you can drag around on the page as you work. Suppose, for example, that you were doing one of those poems that's in the shape of what it talks about (the words look like a castle or a bridge or something). You can continue dragging the SmartIcons around so that they don't block any of the poem and are convenient for you to use:

1. From the Tools menu, choose SmartIcons.

2. Choose Floating from the Position box (see Figure 5-10).

3. Choose OK.

You work with floating SmartIcons the same way you work with any other window or dialog box item — you click a SmartIcon anywhere and drag it to its location. Figure 5-12 shows the whole set being dragged.

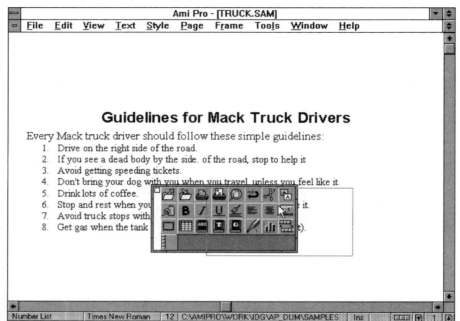

Figure 5-12:
You can
drag your
floating
SmartIcons.

You click and drag the top, bottom, sides, or corners to change the size. Drag the bottom of the floating SmartIcons set to stretch its shape (Figure 5-13).

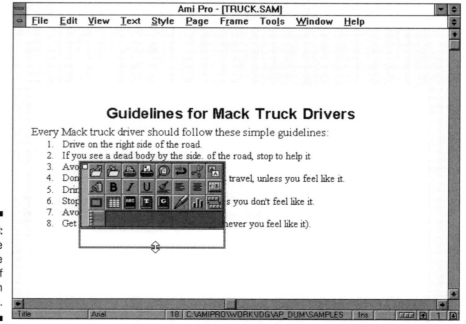

Figure 5-13:
Drag a side
to change
the shape of
the icon
palette.

Annihilating Your SmartIcons

You even can hide your SmartIcons from plain view, although I don't see why you'd want to. Then you'd have to remember the matching commands. Getting rid of the SmartIcons is something nerds do to show off their great memories and brain power. Still, it's always useful to know how to atomize just about anything, if for no other reason, you use it to hide your coworkers' icons and scare them half to death:

1. From the View menu, choose Hide SmartIcons.

Yikes, your SmartIcons are gone. They might as well not exist. Figure 5-14 shows the naked screen. The missing icons render this entire chapter meaningless. If you depend on them to do your work, their absence renders you helpless.

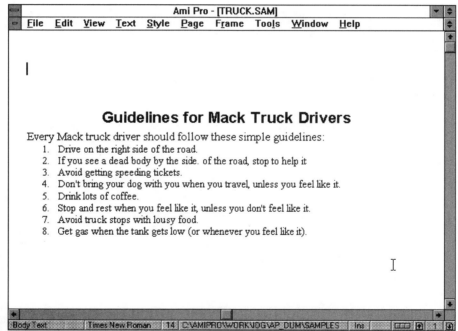

Figure 5-14:
Oh, no.
Where did
my
SmartIcons
go?

Quick, get them back:

1. Click the change icon set icon in the Status bar at the bottom of the screen.

2. Click Show SmartIcons.

The SmartIcons return.

You also can reveal your hidden icons by choosing Show SmartIcons from the View menu. The preceding method is easier, though.

Making your very own SmartIcon

You can even make your own SmartIcon. Now this is getting pretty advanced. Unless you know how to create a bitmap file, copy it to the Clipboard, and assign a macro to it, I suggest you shy away from this sidebar. Unless you've been doing some intensive studying, you don't know what a bitmap is, may not know what the Clipboard is, don't have the foggiest notion what a macro is, and have no inclination to assign one to a SmartIcon that you can supposedly design yourself.

I don't think you should really be doing any of that now either. Like anything, it's not as complicated as it sounds, but it's not a skill needed to use Ami Pro to its full extent. If you need a special SmartIcon for your department or something, let your Ami Pro guru make one for everyone.

If you're curious about how you do it, follow these instructions:

1. **From the Tools menu, choose SmartIcons.**

   The SmartIcons dialog box opens. (Review Figure 5-4, which shows the SmartIcons dialog box.)

2. **Choose Edit Icon.**

   The accompanying figure shows the Edit SmartIcon dialog box.

3. **After you've checked out the dialog box as much as you want (which shouldn't be much), click Cancel and forget about it.**

That's all I'm going to say about making your own SmartIcon right now. Creating your own SmartIcon and assigning a macro to it is a pretty big step. Try learning about macros (Chapter 18) and bitmap files (Chapter 13) first and then return to this dialog box. If your curiosity is aroused, the documentation can give you instructions on creating icons.

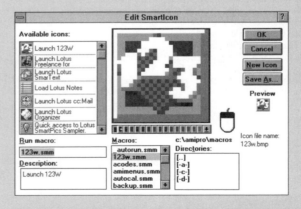

So now I've done it. I've written a whole chapter about SmartIcons. It's not that big a chapter, I'll admit, but it does just what I didn't want to do — inflate the whole topic, as if it were some big deal.

If SmartIcons are a big deal, buying a Coke from a Coke machine is a big deal, tying your shoes is a big deal, changing the channels on the TV is a big deal.

Chapter 6

Help: Like Reading a Cookbook on the Fly

● ●

In This Chapter

▶ How to get Help that's sensitive to your needs and desires

▶ How to jump gleefully from topic to topic

▶ Why the Search button is good but no panacea

▶ How to get Help with one keystroke — F1

▶ How Help is more fun with two keystrokes — Shift+F1

▶ Which types of Help are helpful, which types are not

▶ Why Macro Doc is strictly FNO ("For Nerds Only")

▶ Why I hate "About Ami Pro"

● ●

Standard Ami Pro Help

Unlike Ami Pro SmartIcons, which are a major *paradigm shift* in the entire computer workplace (in other words, SmartIcons kick butt), Ami Pro Help isn't any more scintillating than any other Windows program. Everything can't be a breakthrough, after all.

People might think I'm just jealous because Help is written instruction to go with a program, just as this book is written instruction to go with a program.

Well, that's true. But petty jealousies aside, I don't think Ami Pro Help is any big trendsetter or anything. If you know how to use Windows Help, you know how to use Ami Pro Help. That's all.

Be that as it may, though, Help is probably the most important feature in any program for the on-the-fly users. When you're using something and you're not omniscient, it's easy to get stuck, right? And it's embarrassing and expensive to call up a support line over and over. When you annoy your coworkers with questions over and over, they can get pretty snotty and rude after awhile.

What does that leave? Other than this book (which is the best way to go), it leaves the documentation (ugh) or . . . Help. Help, in the electronic age, comes closer than books ever did to being that imaginary congenial colleague who doesn't mind having you ask the same question a hundred times. It doesn't say, "Look it up in the dictionary." Instead, it nicely answers your questions again and again.

Context-sensitive help

I think that the name *context-sensitive* help is pretentious. It's a nerd name for a non-nerd thing. The term originated somewhere back in the bowels of the minicomputing world, I think, but Ami Pro uses it, too. What context-sensitive help does is not pretentious, though. It's very kind and thoughtful. Context-sensitive help displays on-screen information about the particular command or action that you are performing. That means if you are in the File menu and you press F1 (the Help command), the Help menu appears with information on using the File menu. How convenient!

Figure 6-1 shows the Save As dialog box, a standard dialog box that includes the question mark button in the upper right corner. Every applicable dialog box has this question mark button. You simply click it to obtain help on the dialog box's subject matter (in this case, saving a document).

Question Mark button

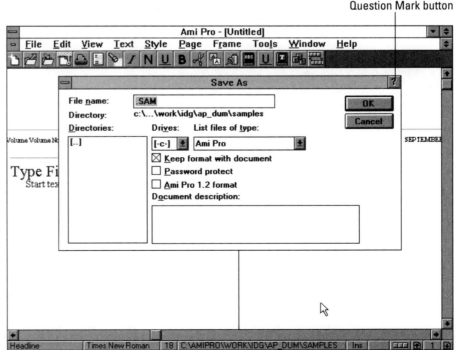

Figure 6-1:
This
question
mark
appears in
the upper
right corner
of every
applicable
dialog box.

After clicking the question mark, a separate window (entitled Ami Pro 3.0) provides help that is indeed sensitive to where you were when you asked for it; in this example, the Save As dialog box help appears. Figure 6-2 shows the Save As Help information.

You use the same techniques to manipulate a Help window as any Windows 3.1 window (which are hardly the techniques I use at home with windows — slamming, propping open with a stick, and wiping with my hand so I can see out of them):

⮕ Click the up arrow to maximize a window (make it take up the full screen).

⮕ Click a down arrow to minimize a window (reduce it to a tiny little icon).

⮕ Click an icon of arrows facing both up and down to restore a window (put it back to the size it was before you maximized it).

The control menu appears in the upper left corner and you can use it to close and resize the window, as you can do for all other Windows windows.

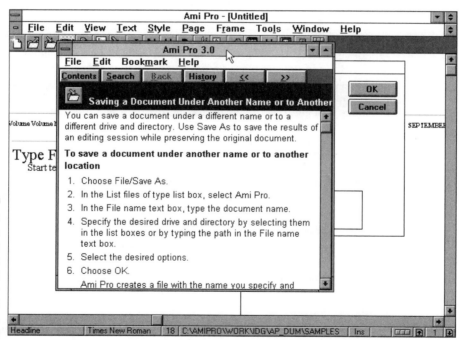

Figure 6-2: Click the question mark button to get caring, to-the-point Help.

Without having to begin with the hard question "What, exactly, do I want help on, anyway?", you can begin getting information. Clicking the question mark may be all you ever need to know about Help. Just remember one phrase you can say to yourself if you get stuck — *Click the question mark.*

There are two ways to quickly access context-sensitive help:

✔ Click the question mark in the dialog box.

✔ Press F1.

Each method works exactly the same way.

Fiddling with the help buttons

Windows Help is like one of those teachers you encountered who graded on class participation. You have to do things — click buttons and stuff. The next few sections talk about those things you do to find the information you want.

Bungee jumping

Whenever there's underlined, colored text in Help, you can click it to jump directly to help on that text. (I refer to it as *bungee jumping* because the cord can break. That is, unless you know about the other buttons, you can get to a place you don't want to be and not be able to get back. In the bungee analogy, the place you get to is the ground, which you hit at a high rate of acceleration. But that's morbid.)

If you were to click the section called *Creating, Saving, and Displaying an Ami Pro Document Contents* from the Save As Help menu (Figure 6-2), you receive a new Help screen. Figure 6-3 shows the new Help screen that you receive. Notice that because all the text doesn't fit on-screen, it also has a vertical scroll bar.

Crawling back

After you are in a new place in Help, you can get back to the one you just left, if you so desire, by clicking the Back button. You can use the Back button repeatedly until you arrive back to the Help window that you started with.

Studying history

As you go through a series of Help screens, you build up a history, just as a person builds a medical history of illnesses or a criminal a history of unlawful behavior. This history is right there for anyone to see. You simply click the History button.

Vertical scroll bar

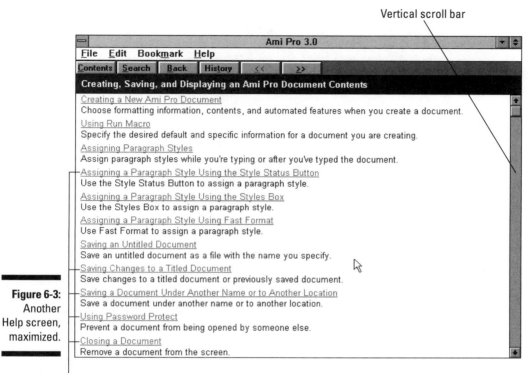

Figure 6-3:
Another
Help screen,
maximized.

Other avenues of help

When you click the History button, the Windows Help History dialog box appears. It lists all the Help topics you viewed during the present Help session. Figure 6-4 shows the history of the example used in this book.

If you double-click an item in the Windows Help History dialog box, you will return to that particular Help window.

The History button is great for distracted people who are lost in thoughts other than Ami Pro Help. You can get thoroughly befuddled as you go bungee jumping through Help. The History button can help you get oriented in time and space and, perhaps, help you find your way back to where you wanted to go after you started taking all those detours.

Figure 6-4:
Clicking the
History
button calls
up this
dialog box.

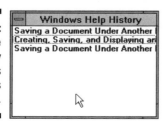

Searching (but not destroying)

The Help Search button is a good thing for people in a hurry, though not as good as you might hope. It searches for what Ami Pro calls *keywords*. Figure 6-5 shows what happens when you click the Search button.

Suppose, for an example, that you wanted to search for help on translating WordPerfect files. If you began typing the word *WordPerfect*, one character at a time, into the empty box, Help tries to anticipate you by listing any matching topics in the Show Topics box. Figure 6-6 shows the topics that appear in the Show Topics box if you were to type **wordp** in the box.

When you see the topic you want in the Show Topics box, you simply click it to select it. Then click Show Topics. A list of the topics you can refer to shows up in the Go To box. Figure 6-7 shows this list of WordPerfect Go To topics.

Show Topics box

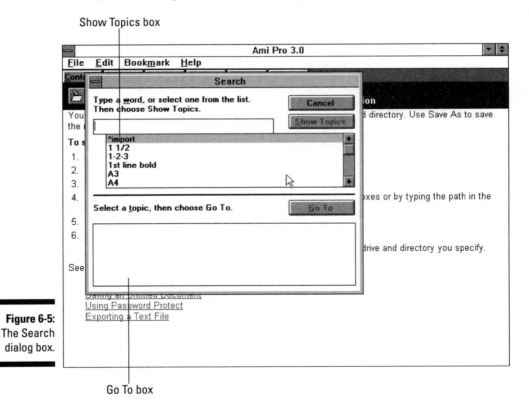

Figure 6-5:
The Search
dialog box.

Go To box

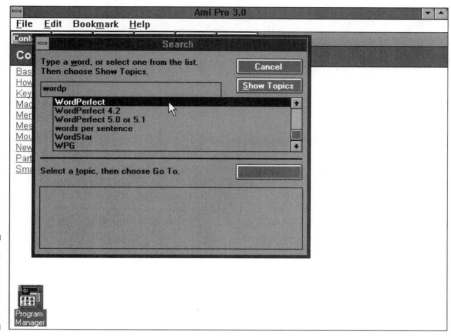

Figure 6-6:
As you type, matches appear in the box.

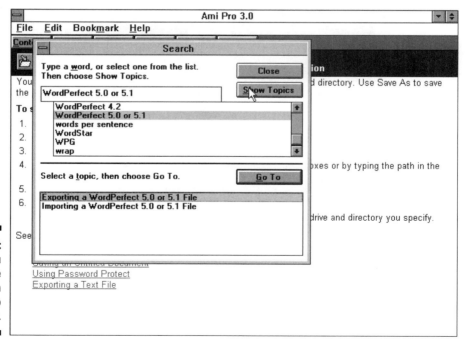

Figure 6-7:
Topics you can explore show up in the Go To box.

Finally, you double-click the topic of your desires (or select it and click the Go To button) to find help on that topic. Figure 6-8 shows what you get if you were to double-click Importing a WordPerfect 5.0 or 5.1 File from the Go To box.

The only trouble with the Search button, from my point of view, is that it can't search for any word or phrase you want. It searches only for a few topics — really, the topics in the Show Topics box. (Well, it'll search for absolutely anything, but it'll only find certain topics.) The topics in the Show Topics box represent only a tiny smidgen of the possible topics an uninformed, fumbling, hurried, mildly desperate person might find to ask about Ami Pro. Suppose that you wanted help on highlighting, for example, which is another word for selecting and not the Ami Pro keyword for it. Do you get a cross reference or anything — no, way, Jack; ain't there. Until you learn to play by the rules, which means that you select words only from the list, you end up searching frequently for words that aren't there. This is particularly frustrating when you don't know quite what you need help on.

Spilling out the contents

The Contents button takes you to the list of main Help topics, which I talk about later in the chapter, so I won't talk about them much now. If you click the Contents button, you receive the screen shown in Figure 6-9.

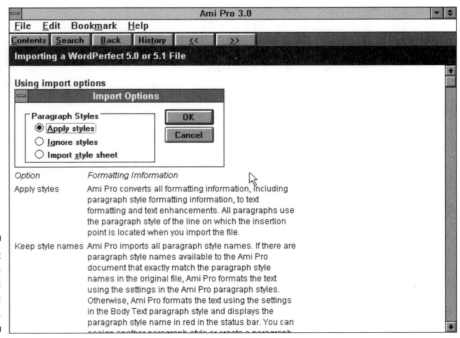

Figure 6-8:
Help on the topic you chose in the Go To box.

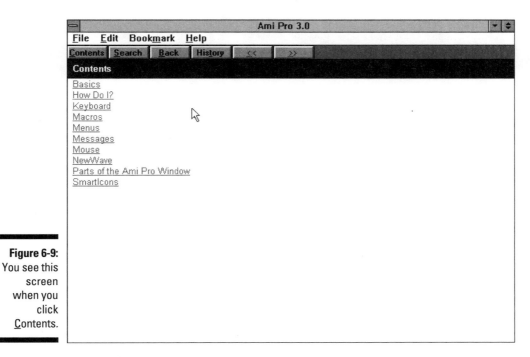

Figure 6-9:
You see this
screen
when you
click
Contents.

Clicking any of the topics on this screen carries you to that type of help. The Contents button is another way to help you become oriented after you get lost by bungee jumping around. It's a fresh start.

Browse-beating someone

The two buttons on the right of the row of buttons are Browse buttons. It's very easy to confuse the button that faces left with the Back button. Very, very easy. The Browse buttons take you backward or forward a screen in a Help topic that happens to have more than one page, so to speak. If there are no additional pages, these buttons are grayed.

Terminating Help

Help is a separate Microsoft Windows program running in its own window, so you actually close the Help program completely when you don't want to use it anymore:

1. **Open the File menu in Help by clicking File.**

   Figure 6-10 shows the Help File menu.

2. **Choose Exit.**

   Help shuts down, and you return to Ami Pro.

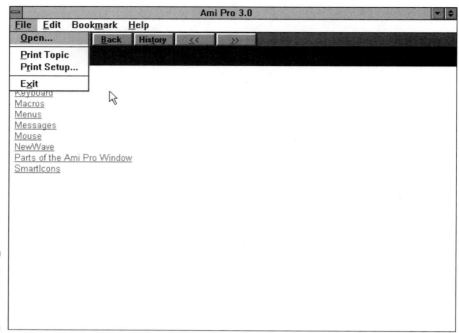

File menu screen showing:

Ami Pro 3.0

File   Edit   Bookmark   Help

Open...   Back   History   <<   >>

Print Topic
Print Setup...

Exit

Keyboard
Macros
Menus
Messages
Mouse
NewWave
Parts of the Ami Pro Window
SmartIcons

Figure 6-10:
The File
menu in
Help.

Pressing Esc also cancels Help, and it's obviously a much faster method.

Shooting from the hip with F1

The F1 key accesses the Help system in two different ways, depending on when and where you press it:

Pressing F1 from a document   F1 is the universal Help key. You can press it when you're using a document, if you don't mind starting with the main Contents screen (review Figure 6-9).

Pressing F1 from a menu or dialog box   Pressing F1 from inside a dialog box does the same thing as clicking the question mark in the top right of a dialog box. You receive context-sensitive help.

When a menu command appears with an *ellipsis* following it (three dots, not to be confused with *ellipses* — the ovals you had to draw in high school), it means Windows calls up a dialog box after you click this command.

Figure 6-11 shows the Help menu you receive when you press F1 in the Text, Special Effects dialog box, for an example.

Getting Help on a menu item

You can get help on a menu item (as well as on a dialog box) by pressing F1 in the following manner:

1. **Open the menu of choice by pressing Alt+the hot key.**

   In this example, open the View menu (Alt+V) and click Enlarged.

   Remember that when you click a menu item, hoping just to select it, you activate the command instead. Now that's a bummer when all you want to do is highlight the command. If you want to select the command to get help on it, you have to use the arrow keys on your keyboard to highlight the command without activating the command.

2. **Select the command you want by pressing the down arrow until the command is highlighted.**

3. **With the command selected, press F1.**

   Figure 6-12 shows the Help box you get when pressing F1 on the View, Enlarged command.

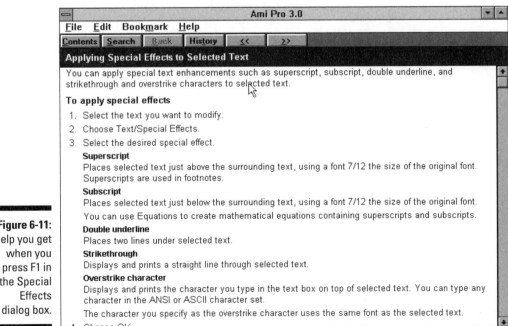

Figure 6-11:
Help you get
when you
press F1 in
the Special
Effects
dialog box.

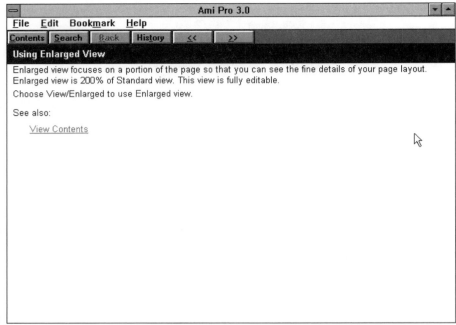

Figure 6-12:
Help comes
up on the
selected
menu item.

4. **After reading the relevant material, close the Help window by double-clicking the control menu button (in the upper left corner, remember?).**

Menus come with Help on them initially. If you select a command or menu, there's a description of the command in the Title bar. If you click the File menu, for example, the words Create a new document. appear in the Title bar. Pay attention to these descriptions if you want to avoid using Help so much.

Pressing Shift+F1

There's a way to avoid the problem of inadvertently implementing menu commands when you click them, intending only to select them. In fact, this form of Help is good in its own right. Pressing Shift+F1 turns the pointer into the neat question mark/pointer deal shown in Figure 6-13.

With this nifty pointer, click the menu and command that you need help on. Figure 6-14 shows the menu you get when you click the Style, Select a Style command with this nifty pointer.

Question mark pointer

Figure 6-13:
Press
Shift+F1 to
get this neat
question
mark
pointer.

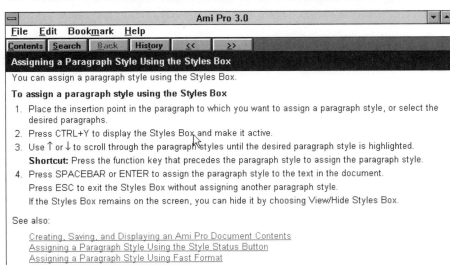

Figure 6-14:
You get this
Help
window
when you
click Select
a Style with
the question
mark
pointer.

Reluctantly scanning the main Help menu

When you're panicked over trying to figure out how to do something, you can forget everything I've told you in this chapter. You can forget whether you want F1 or F11 or an F-11 Fighter Jet. You can forget about buttoning your own buttons, let alone pressing Windows buttons. At such times, you don't mind if it takes a little longer to get help, you just want to get help somewhere.

To start at the beginning of Help, choose Help from the menu. Figure 6-15 shows this main Help menu.

From this menu, you can wind your way through a variety of choices until you find the one that takes you where you need to go.

Opening the contents

The most linear way to proceed is by starting with the Contents command.

If you were to click Contents, you would see the same Help screen you get when you click the Contents button from any Help window, as I wrote about earlier in the chapter. From here, you can pick your avenue of help and eventually narrow your search until you find the subject you desire.

Figure 6-15:
The main
Help menu.

Getting help on Help

The Using Help window tells you much of the same stuff I covered in this chapter, but without the facetiousness, irony, and needless digression. Figure 6-16 shows the Using Help window.

Spotlighting some keyboard stuff

The Help, Keyboard command provides you with many keyboard command shortcuts, which are very helpful if you are just getting used to Ami Pro and feel more comfortable using the keyboard. Figure 6-17 shows this window.

This Keyboard Help window summarizes all those shortcuts that even a nerd has to read at least two or three times to remember. Acknowledging that nobody can remember them all, this screen makes it easy to access them when you can't remember one.

Asking "How do I?"

In this section of Help, you'll find topics arranged by actions — for example, "How Do I Create a Document?" The list is alphabetized, so if you know what you are looking for, it might be helpful. I counted close to 30 topics in this section and didn't get past words starting with *C*. I usually don't use this type of Help because the list is so long. By the time you find the topic you want, you have forgotten what it was. But my reticence shouldn't stop you from doing what works for you.

Figure 6-18 shows the interminable list of activities you get when you choose How Do I? from the Help main menu.

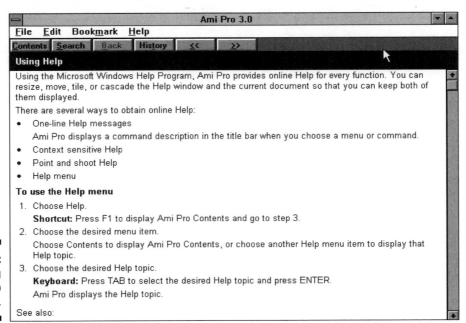

Figure 6-16:
The Using
Help
window.

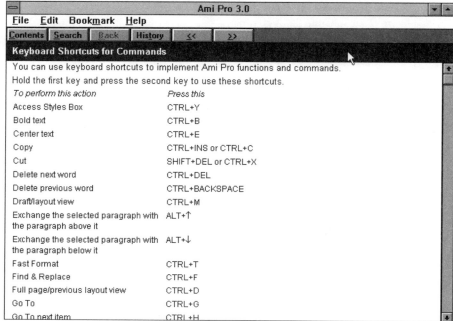

Figure 6-17:
Keyboard
Shortcuts
for
Commands
window.

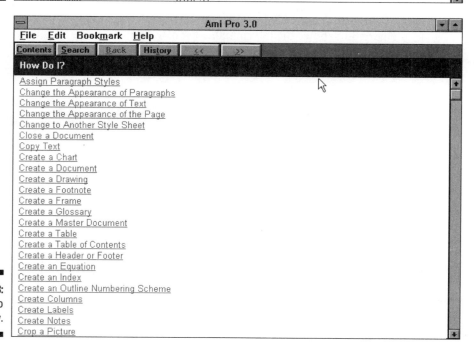

Figure 6-18:
The How Do
I? window.

Checking out the Help menus

The Help window has its own menus, besides the buttons you read about earlier. You can do quite a few mainly useless and distracting things with those menus. For example, you can add a note to a help file. You might actually add something smart to all that dumb information, though I never use this feature.

Instead of using the Always on Top command, I find it helpful to use Windows techniques to place the Help file side-by-side with my document. Figure 6-19 shows an example. That way, you can read and scroll in the Help file and work in the Ami Pro file without having the Help file disappear when you're in the Ami Pro file (and vice versa.)

Help as your constant guardian

The Help menu offers an interesting choice called Always on Top. You might find it useful, especially in your first days of Ami Pro. Try it out this way:

1. **Open a Help window (by clicking one of commands).**

   In this example, choose the How Do I? command to open a Help window.

2. **Size the Help window so it takes up only part of the screen (drag the sides in).**

3. **Click Help in the Help menu.**

The Help Help menu drops down. See the accompanying figure.

4. **Click the Always on Top command.**

Now the Help window should stick on top of your file like a Secret Service person to the President. You won't be able to get it off.

If you click anywhere inside of Ami Pro, the Help file stays on top of your Ami Pro file. To disable this feature, go back to the Help Help window and click Always on Top again. You also can use Windows techniques to move or resize the window.

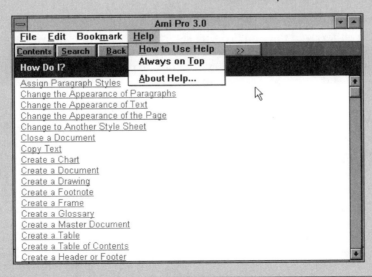

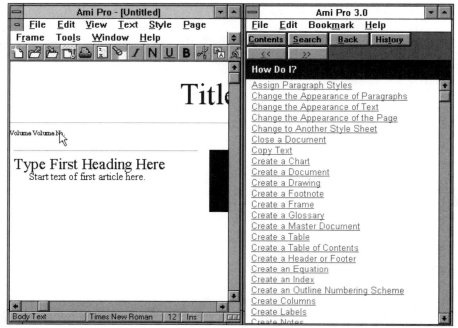

Figure 6-19:
You can put
Help side
by side with
Ami Pro.

Help has a few other menu choices besides the ones I wrote about in this section (although, hypocritically, the Help menus don't provide a line of menu help in the Title bar). You can browse through them at your leisure if you want, though that's a little like asking an accident victim to browse through the emergency room while she waits. When you want help, you usually want it right now.

Begging for a basic tutorial

You either used the Ami Pro QuickStart Tutorial right away when you installed Ami Pro, or you will never use it — not, at least, in the heat of battle. It's too slow a way to find out something like how to move a frame around. If you're on salary and somebody is content that you learn at a leisurely pace, the tutorial might not be useful to you.

When you are first getting to know Ami Pro, though, it's great. Check it out for a second:

 1. From the Help menu, choose QuickStart Tutorial.

   The tutorial starts, as shown in Figure 6-20.

Social scientists who are experts at making things easy to use have designed this, so it should be easy, fast, and effective. To me, it's as boring as daytime TV programming.

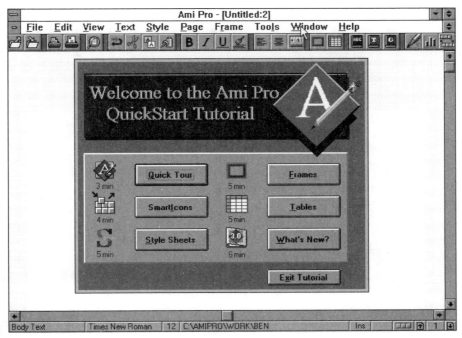

Figure 6-20:
Ami Pro
QuickStart
Tutorial.

Denouncing About Ami Pro

I hate the Help command called About Ami Pro. A person can click it 50 or a hundred times before finally giving up and realizing that it's never going to be any more than it is (other than a pure nerd, who would, of course, do this only once). I mean, you're flummoxed over something and looking for help. You see this category and, before you can stop yourself, think, "Oh, this is About Ami Pro. Well, my question's about Ami Pro. Maybe what I need is in here." But it isn't. There's nothing in there. It's a practical joke perpetrated on the world by Bill Gates and his cronies at Microsoft.

I realize that every Windows program has About Whatever-the-Program-Is in its Help menu. I think that's a lame excuse. This isn't "about" anything. It's one line about how much memory is available, and only technical people use that line anyway. It's dumb. It's like the disclaimers the baseball announcers read during every game. "This broadcast is for the exclusive use blah blah blah." I hate it. It should be named "Two Words About Ami Pro Memory." No, it shouldn't be there at all, and it certainly shouldn't be masquerading as some full-fledged menu choice.

There are some other tools that can bail people out and make them look smart almost as well as Help does. In the next chapter you expose yourself to three of them — the Spell Checker, Thesaurus, and Grammar Checker.

Reverently glimpsing Macro Doc

There is an item on the Help menu called Macro Doc. This one is definitely for nerds only. It's a complete tome hidden on your disk about how to create and perfect your own macros. Macros are programming, pure and simple. Except in the simple form you'll read about in Chapter 18, they aren't something you'll use much. The accompanying figure shows a typical Macro Doc Help file.

Do you get a queasy feeling in the pit of your stomach, as if you're leaning over the railing and looking into the Grand Canyon? If you let go, you'll turn into a nerd and never get back to normal again. Ignore this info and you'll feel much better.

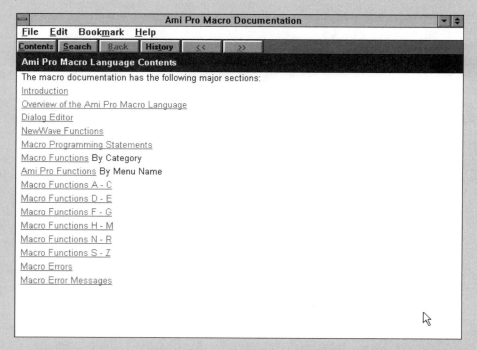

Chapter 7

Spell Check, the Thesaurus, and Its Cronies: Like Having a Chef in a Jar

• •

In This Chapter

▶ How to spell check your document

▶ How to find a better word for *late*

▶ How to put out an All Points Bulletin to find a word

▶ How to find a word and substitute another for it, over and over and over

▶ How to check your grammar and why you might not check it all that often

▶ How to resist sins of the Flesch

▶ How to determine the number of words in your document

• •

*A*s a general rule, most people want to look like they can do things that they can't, such as spell. A generation has grown up with two things that all earlier generations should've had: handheld calculators and spelling checkers. This chapter has nothing to do with calculators, but it *does* deal with Ami Pro's Spell Checker, which is a sort of built-in genie that checks your spelling. With Ami Pro, you also get a genie who helps you think of new words to replace the old ones you've been using. And you get yet another genie who makes sure that you stuck commas where you should have and didn't stick them where you shouldn't have. (Of course, after these genies have been around awhile, you may feel like strangling them.)

To switch to the Proofing set of SmartIcons (which is perfect for this chapter), click the SmartIcon button in the Status bar (bottom-right area of screen with three blue boxes, remember?) and select Proofing.

Fixing All Those Misspellings

F. Scott Fitzgerald was a terrific writer but a notoriously bad speller (too bad he didn't have Ami Pro). Figure 7-1 shows a short letter, full of spelling errors, that he didn't really write to his publisher. You can use it to practice spell checking a document if you follow along with this example.

To follow along with the example, create a new document using the _MEMO1.STY style sheet, save the document as SCOTT.SAM, and type in the contents of Figure 7-1 (be sure to leave in the spelling errors!). Now with some misspellings in front of you, you're ready to transform them miraculously into correct spellings without having to be able to spell yourself.

Fixing a single word

You may often find yourself puzzling over one single word, as in: "Is *apple* spelled with one *p* or two?" Or: "Where does that double *a* appear in *aardvark?*" In the pre-Ami Pro days, when faced with this situation, you just had to take your best guess. Well, OK, there were dictionaries around, but if you tried to keep a bound dictionary by your desk, someone was always stealing it to do a crossword puzzle and then throwing it out with the Sunday papers. But nobody's going to throw out Ami Pro Spell Checker — the thief would have to know about DOS commands and subdirectories and stuff.

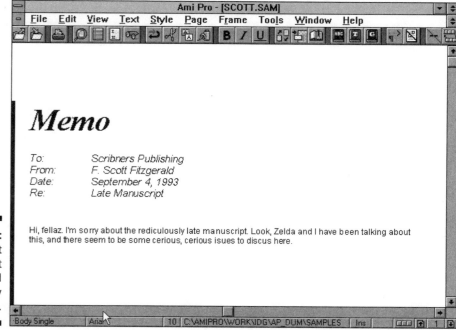

Figure 7-1:
A letter that
F. Scott
Fitzgerald
didn't really
write.

Consider the example in Figure 7-1. Suppose you thought that maybe the word *rediculously* looked a little suspect. Here's what to do if you want to check spelling on one word or a group of words:

1. **Select the word or group of words to spell check by highlighting the selection.**

   In this case, select the word *rediculously.*

2. **Click the Spell Checker SmartIcon (shown in the margin).**

   Some great, invisible spelling bee champion inside Ami Pro scrutinizes the word. If the word is spelled correctly, Ami Pro doesn't do a thing. If the word is spelled incorrectly, however, as in this case, Ami Pro presents a dialog box (see Figure 7-2).

   If the word appears in the Spell Check dialog box, that means Ami Pro finds it suspicious. You then decide whether Ami Pro's suspicion is justified. You look over the list of words in the Alternatives box, all of which are spelled correctly (by smart people whose job it is to do that) to see whether one of them is the word you are looking for. In this example, only one word appears in the Alternatives box anyway, so it's that word or nothing.

Figure 7-2:
The Spell
Check
dialog box.

3. **Click the correct word in the Alternatives box to select it.**

   In this example, click *ridiculously.*

4. **Click Replace.**

   Spell Checker puts the new word that you've selected into your document (see Figure 7-3) and disappears into its genie jar to wait for you to summon it again.

Remember, you don't have to select a single word at a time. When you click the Spell Checker SmartIcon, Ami Pro checks the spelling of whatever text you've selected. You can select and spell check phrases, sentences, paragraphs, the whole document — any text you want. Simply pressing the Spell Check icon without any text highlighted checks the whole document.

Spell repairing a whole document

Once in a while, you may check the spelling of a single word or group of words on the fly, but most people get carried away in the heat of composition and don't check their spelling until the end (by which time they're tired and more than willing to do a mundane task such as spell checking).

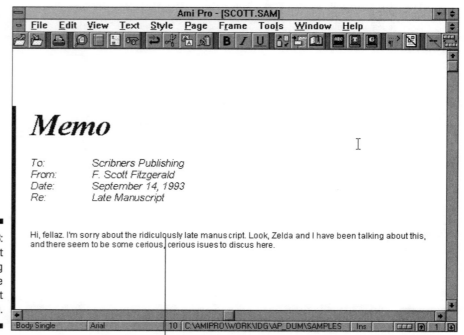

Figure 7-3: The correct spelling replaces the incorrect spelling.

Word spelled correctly now

Spell Checker also makes a great proofreader. If you accidentally type a word wrong or leave out the space between two words or put in some random letter of the alphabet by accident, Spell Checker finds it. It reveals whether you typed a word twice without meaning to and, in general, makes a nuisance of itself at a time when that's precisely what you need.

If your spelling mistake is an actual word but not the one you intended, Ami Pro doesn't catch it. Suppose you wrote "I made some big many last week" but you obviously meant *big money,* not *big many.* Well, as you know, *many* is a word. Therefore, Ami Pro doesn't detect it as an error, which is why such correctly spelled wrong words are the most common mistakes to creep into formal business letters in this age of electronic spell checkers.

To spell check an entire document (in this example, the bogus F. Scott Fitzgerald letter), do the following:

1. From the Tools menu, choose Spell Check.

A Spell Check dialog box appears to glean a bit more information from you before embarking on the actual check. See Figure 7-4.

2. Select the check box labeled Check from beginning of document.

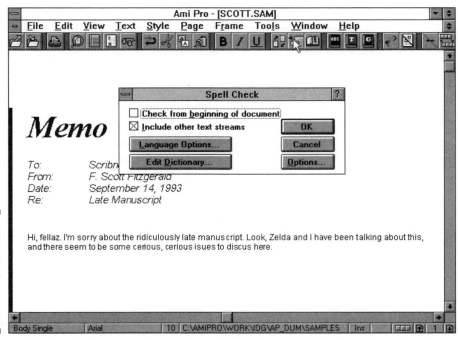

Figure 7-4:
The Spell
Check
dialog box
before you
check a
document.

Sometimes you may decide to stop Spell Checker part way through a long document so that you can do a bit of rewriting or make some other change that you can't make inside Spell Checker. To avoid going over all the words that you've already checked, be certain that you have unselected the Check from beginning of document check box.

3. Click OK to start Spell Checker.

Skipping all instances of a word

Spell Checker often points to a word that you know perfectly well is spelled correctly (such as your own name). You can have it ignore all instances of the term by clicking the Skip All button when the term appears.

For example, Spell Checker flags the term *Scribner's* in the document SCOTT.SAM, the valid name of the publisher. Click Skip All to keep it from pointing out the term again any time during the current checking session.

One disadvantage to stopping in the middle of Spell Checker and then restarting it is that when you restart, you have to remind Ami Pro again of the words it should skip. In other words, you have to click Skip All again for each term you want it to skip.

Replacing a word

You click Replace when checking a whole document the same way you did earlier in the chapter when you spell checked a single word. Click the word that you want in the Alternatives box and then click Replace to replace the misspelled word.

Typing in a correct spelling

Sometimes it *does* help to know how to spell when using a spell checker, as is the case in our example when Spell Checker catches the word *fellaz.* Continue with the Spell Checker until *fellaz* appears in the Replace with text box.

Spell Checker's proposed alternative, *fleas,* is hardly the one you want (see Figure 7-5).

When Spell Checker's alternatives are way off base, you can simply type the alternative yourself:

1. Type your desired word in the Replace with text box.

With *fellaz* selected, type **fellows** into the text box instead. The corrected spelling appears now in the Replace with text box (see Figure 7-6).

2. Click Replace.

If Spell Checker does not recognize the word you type, it will run the spelling check on the new word and offer you other alternatives. This might be helpful if you don't actually know the proper spelling of the word. Otherwise, just click Skip.

Spell Checker puts your version into the document.

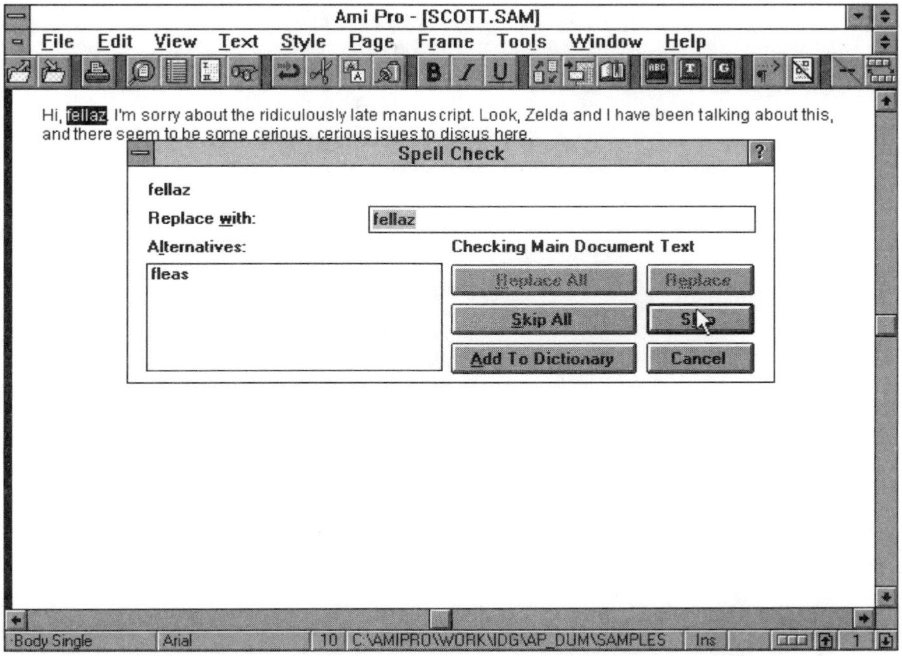

Figure 7-5:
Sometimes
Spell
Checker
offers comic
alternatives.

Figure 7-6:
Type the
correct
replacement
yourself.

Looking over your rights in Spell Checker

You can go gaily along in Spell Checker using only the Replace, Skip, and Skip All buttons. You have a couple of other choices, though:

Button	What It Does
Add To Dictionary	Use this to add the word to the list of words Ami Pro goes to when it decides whether a word is spelled wrong. After you add the word, Ami Pro skips over it in the present checking sessions and all future ones.
Replace All	Replace all, as the name implies, replaces all instances of the current word with the new word you have selected. This is a helpful option if you have habitually spelled a particular word incorrectly.

You can put any word you want into the dictionary. You can put in *ain't* or *recieve* or *rabit*. However, once the word is in its dictionary, Ami Pro (fool that it is) thinks it's spelled correctly. So be very careful with what you put into the dictionary's list of acceptable words. You mite end up looking cilly.

Options

Even though Spell Check is sometimes a professional nuisance, it wants to be as unobtrusive as possible. To help make itself that way, it offers you some choices to control what it looks for and, in so doing, enables you to cut down on the number of times it intercepts words. The following examples show you how to use these options:

1. Click the Spell Check SmartIcon.

The Spell Check dialog box appears.

2. Click Options in the Spell Check dialog box.

The Spell Check Options dialog box comes up (see Figure 7-7).

From here, you can select or unselect the check boxes for any of the four Spell Check options:

- **Check for repeated words:** This option tells the Spell Checker to check for words that appear twice in succession (I'd leave that one checked, because it happens often).

- **Check words with numbers:** This tells Spell Checker to check words that have numbers in them. (This is mainly a nerd thing. I'd leave the check box selected because, as a non-nerd, you don't have many numbers in your words anyway.)

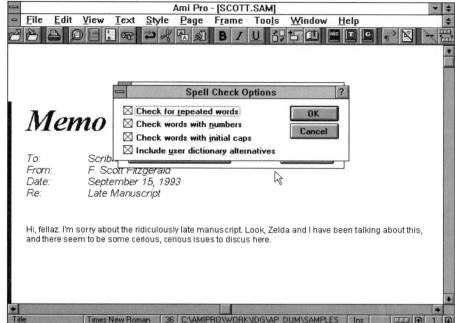

- **Check words with initial caps:** This tells Spell Checker to check words that start with capital letters. (This might be worth unchecking. It avoids flagging words such as *Scribner's* and your own name but means that you had better not have any misspellings in the first word of any sentence.)

- **Include user dictionary alternatives:** Know what this one is? (It's not what you think — you don't have a choice about having alternatives appear in the Alternatives box.) This choice determines whether Spell Checker displays the alternatives that *you* may have added to the user dictionary with the Add To Dictionary option. I'll bet not many people know that. Apparently this choice is to prevent you from offering yourself your own misspellings as alternatives. Weird.

3. **Click Cancel to close the Spell Check Options box without making any changes.**

Language Options

About the only reason to fool with this — unless you're a spy and have to change between American and British identities — is because you're curious about it.

1. **From the Spell Check dialog box, click Language Options.**

    The Spell Check Language Options dialog box opens (see Figure 7-8).

Figure 7-8:
The Spell
Check
Language
Options
dialog box.

If you really wanted to, you can change to a list of British spellings to check your words (with things like "gaol" for "jail" and other spellings that red-blooded Americans don't use).

2. Click Cancel to keep American English as the default language.

Edit Dictionary

Once you add words to the dictionary list that Ami Pro checks, it's not a dead-end street. You *can* take the words out if you change your mind:

1. Click Edit Dictionary in the Spell Check dialog box.

A document, LTSUSER1.DIC, appears on-screen with a list of the words you have added to the dictionary. I'd show you my list, but I think it would just confuse you. Yours may be just about empty right now.

2. To take words out of the list, select and delete words just like you would in any other document.

3. Click File, Save to save LTSUSER1.DIC with the new changes.

This step saves your changes.

4. Click File, Close to close the user dictionary file.

You should return to your original document.

Include other text streams

"What in the heck," you may well wonder, "are text streams, anyway? And why are more than one involved?" Good question. I don't quite know why this choice is here because you usually want to check everywhere if you're checking the whole document. Ami Pro regards your main document text as one stream, kind of the *mainstream,* as it were. It looks at text in tables, frames, and margins as other streams and doesn't check them if you unselect the Include other text streams check box.

In all probability, whatever stream you're in, you want Ami Pro to check your whole document when you use Spell Checker and don't have a word or phrase selected. But if you're in a table, margin, frame (or other text stream if there is one), Ami Pro basically checks only that stream.

You can go crazy trying to figure out why Spell Checker isn't working. The solution is usually to put the cursor into the main body text and be sure that you've selected Include other text streams.

Completing your spell checking

With what you now know about Spell Checker and its buttons and options, you can finish checking a document on your own. Note that in the F. Scott Fitzgerald example, Spell Checker passed right over *discus* because it knows about the round heavy thing that is hurled in the track-and-field event. Correct it manually (and learn another lesson about looking out for correctly spelled, yet *wrong* words). When you finish the check, the dialog box closes. Figure 7-9 shows the corrected document.

I'll have a Danish

You don't have it on your disk, but if you asked the people at Lotus, you can get a primary language dictionary and Thesaurus in French, German, Dutch, Spanish, Italian, Norwegian, Swedish, or Danish.

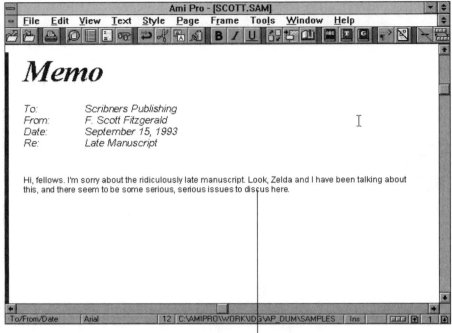

Correctly spelled but incorrectly used

Figure 7-9:
The pretend
Fitzgerald
letter after
spell
checking.

What's Another Word for Late?

Where the Thesaurus is concerned, I've never fully recovered from my freshman English instructor, Ridgely Pearson, who firmly told us all to "stay out of the library." Cowed by him and the institution he represented, I never went near a Thesaurus for years thereafter. Now I do turn to them at times, but often with disappointment. (I don't know — most of the time, the words in the Thesaurus don't seem to be as good as the ones that I can think of on my own.) Nevertheless, the Thesaurus is a good way to overcome a mental block when you're trying to think of a word.

Starting the Ami Pro Thesaurus

Suppose that you want to find a better word for *late*. Here's how to proceed:

1. **Place the cursor anywhere in the word *late* (or, if you prefer, select it).**

2. **From the Tools menu, choose Thesaurus (or click the Thesaurus SmartIcon).**

   The Thesaurus works a great deal like the Spell Checker. A Thesaurus dialog box comes up and asks you to decide whether to make a change. See Figure 7-10.

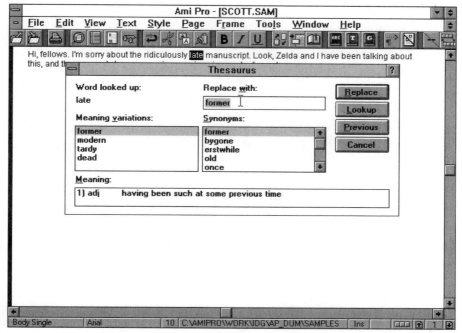

Figure 7-10:
The
Thesaurus
dialog box.

You can use the Thesaurus as a dictionary. In the Meaning box at the bottom is a definition of the word at hand. Actually, the definition is for one variation of the meaning — the variation expressed in the word highlighted in the Meaning variations box and appearing in the Replace with box. This is how you would determine the meaning of *discus,* for example.

Getting to the meaning you really wanted

Chances are that the first guess of the Thesaurus is not really the variation you want. (It almost never is, it seems.) You have only to read through the list of alternatives in the Meaning variations box and click the one you want. In this specific example, I chose *tardy.*

The selected word then appears in the Replace with box (Figure 7-11 shows my example) and its definition appears in the Meaning box.

Picking a synonym

Once you've got the meaning variation you want (because, after all, *late* can mean many things, including *dead*), you can look through the synonyms to find one you want.

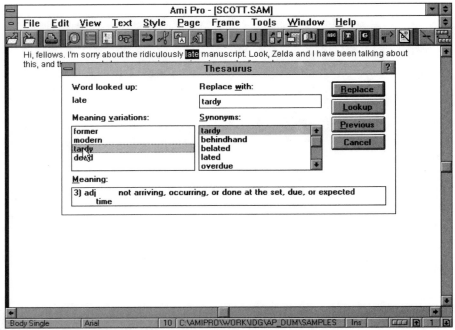

Figure 7-11:
Click a word
you want to
use.

The selected synonym goes into the Replace with box, but in this case, the meaning doesn't change. Figure 7-12 shows what happens when you choose *unpunctual* to replace *late*.

Scoping out the synonym

The biggest hazard of using synonyms is that you may use a word with the wrong connotation. To help meliorate that risk, you use the Lookup button.

1. **With the synonym of choice in the Synonyms box, click Lookup.**

   In this example, *unpunctual* should be in the Synonyms box. The Thesaurus looks up *unpunctual*, but doesn't find it. It gives you a message box to this effect.

2. **Choose OK in the message box to try again.**

   The Thesaurus jumps to the top of the column (in this case, the word *former*).

3. **Click *tardy* again in the left box to look for another synonym for it.**

4. **Select a new word in the right box, then click Lookup.**

   In this example, click *overdue*.

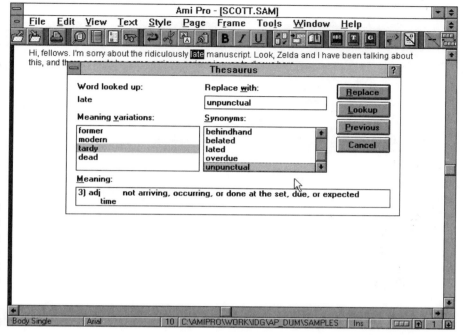

Figure 7-12:
The synonym you select goes into the Replace with box.

The Thesaurus looks up the word, but goes right back to *tardy* in the Replace with box. I mean, that's no help. I hate that. If I wanted to go in a circle, I would have clicked a button that said Go in a Circle or at least clicked on the Previous button. Figure 7-13 shows where Lookup takes you in this case, which is a big bag of nothing as far as I'm concerned, but that can happen in any Thesaurus, electronic or not.

Going back a step

If you want to get back to the word you looked up before, you click the Previous button. (See Figure 7-14.)

It's easy to chase your own tail with the Thesaurus. As you click Lookup, you frequently find yourself back where you started, even though that may not be where you want to go. Thesaurus doesn't take you on a truly Byzantine path of synonyms the way I like. For that, use a bound Thesaurus.

With the electronic Thesaurus, there's no guarantee that because a word's in the Synonyms list, the Thesaurus will have a synonym for it. As for clicking Previous, that's a pretty sure way to take yourself back to where you've already been. But sometimes it doesn't take you anywhere.

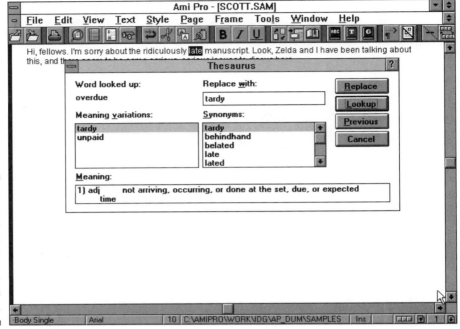

Figure 7-13:
When you
click
L̲ookup,
Thesaurus
looks up the
word in the
S̲ynonyms
box.

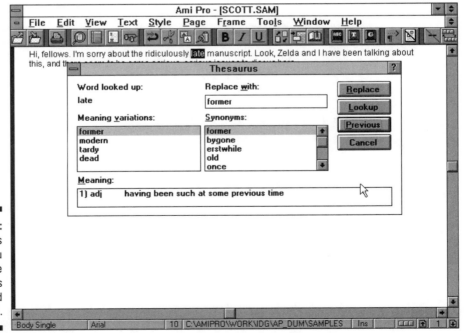

Figure 7-14:
P̲revious
takes you
back to the
previous
word
selected.

Replacing the word

Once you do find a word that you like, be sure it's in the Replace with box.

1. Click your new word so it's in the Replace with box.

In this example, click *tardy.*

2. Click Replace.

Thesaurus replaces the word in the document. Figure 7-15 shows how *tardy* has replaced *late* in the SCOTT.SAM letter.

3. To close the Thesaurus, click Cancel.

Word replaced in document

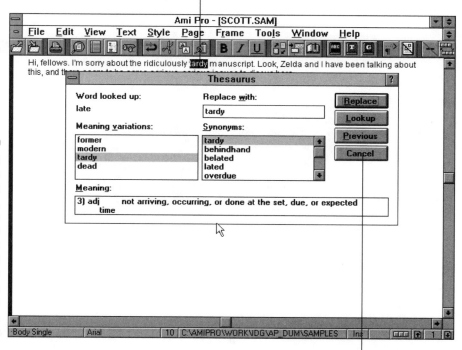

Figure 7-15:
When you
click
Replace,
Ami Pro
replaces the
word in the
document
with the
word in the
Replace
with box.

Cancel to close Thesaurus

In general, it's best to take a quick-and-dirty approach to this electronic Thesaurus. Scan quickly through the synonyms. If you find something you like, take it. If not, cut your losses and get out of the Thesaurus. You're going to waste time if you stay. Guaranteed.

Finding an Evil Word, Replacing It with a Virtuous Word

Spelling words and finding synonyms is one thing. Sometimes, though, you just want to find a specific word in a document — usually, of course, in a document that's longer than one paragraph. Maybe you want to find a word to help you locate the place you left off in a document. Maybe you want to replace this word with another word.

To find a word in your document, follow these steps:

1. From the Edit menu, choose Find & Replace.

The Find & Replace dialog box opens, as shown in Figure 7-16. Suppose, for this example, that you want to replace the word *hello* with *goodbye*.

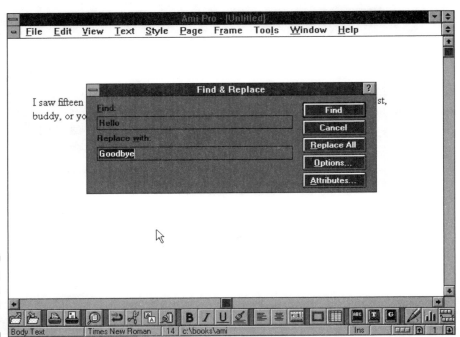

Figure 7-16:
The Find & Replace dialog box.

 "But I just want to find a word and that's it. I don't want to replace it," you may think. In Ami Pro, you still use the Find & Replace command. You simply ignore the replace part. I don't like having it there and having to ignore it, but it's just one of those things you have to learn to live with. Sigh...

2. Type your word of choice and click Find.

In this example, type **hello**. Ami Pro finds the next instance of the word and highlights it. Figure 7-17 shows the found word.

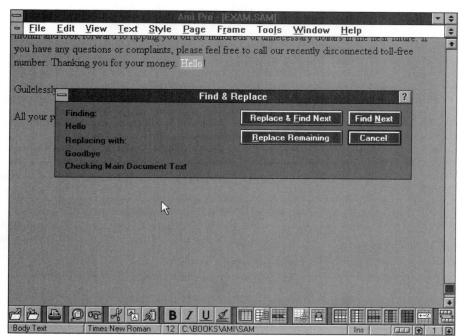

Figure 7-17:
If the word
is there,
Find &
Replace
finds it.

3. In the Find & Replace dialog box, click Cancel.

The box closes, and you are back in the document, having found the word.

Finding a wayward word and replacing it

You may want to change a word a number of times throughout a document. This exasperating state of affairs is often not your choice. Someone higher in the chain of command, having sat in on several weeks of meetings (usually at posh resort areas in warm climates) may come back and tell you, "We never say *joke* any more. Go back and change every instance of it to *witticism*."

Suppose, in this example, that you wanted to change every instance of *serious* in the Fitzgerald letter to *mortifying:*

1. **From the Edit menu, choose Find & Replace.**

   To make sure that your search is complete, you should be at the top of your document when starting this find and replace.

2. **In the Find & Replace dialog box, type the word you want to find in the Find box.**

   In this example, type **serious**.

3. **Type the new word in the Replace with box.**

   In this example, type **mortifying** in the Replace with box. Figure 7-18 shows the completed box.

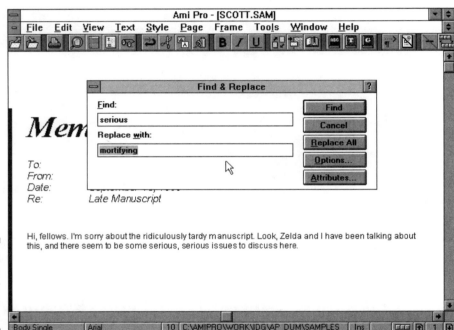

Figure 7-18: The dialog box, ready for search and replace.

4. **Click Replace All.**

   A different Find & Replace box shows the progress of your snoop and supplant activity. Figure 7-19 shows this sneaky business.

5. **Click Replace & Find Next.**

   In this example, Ami Pro changes the first instance of *serious* to *mortifying* and moves to the next. Figure 7-20 shows the progress.

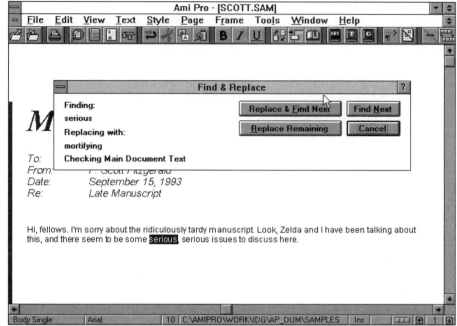

Figure 7-19:
A box
shows the
progress of
the search
and replace
command.

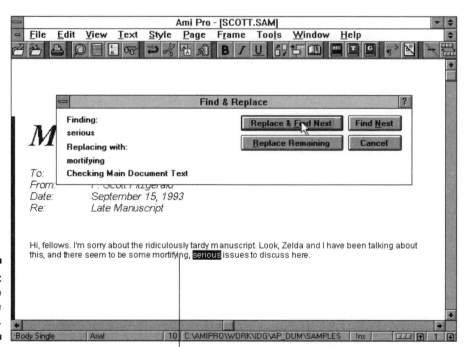

Figure 7-20:
Ami Pro
replaces the
word.

Replaced word

6. **When you are satisfied, click Cancel to close the dialog box.**

   If you want to skip an instance of a word, click Find Next. To replace all instances of a word without having the option to skip each one, choose Replace Remaining.

Using options to narrow the search

Whether you're doing a Find or a Find & Replace, you can implement a few nerdy, confusing tactics to narrow your search by using the Options menu in Find & Replace:

1. **Click Find & Replace in the Edit menu.**

2. **Click Options.**

   The Find & Replace Options dialog box appears, where you can make a bunch of fine distinctions that don't really matter most of the time. Figure 7-21 shows this dialog box. The next section tells you a little bit about these options.

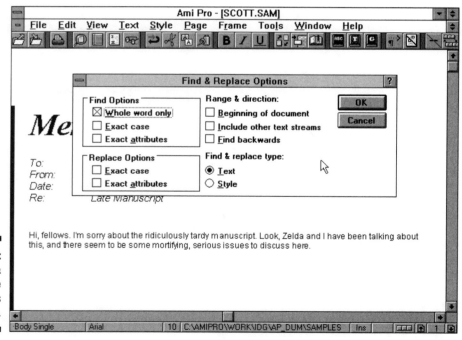

Figure 7-21:
The Find & Replace Options dialog box.

Here are some of the options for Find & Replace that you can implement:

- ✔ **Whole word only:** This option, at times, is indispensable. It tells Ami Pro to find the whole word only, not if it's part of another word. Suppose that you wanted to look up the word *I*. The searching process would last days without this option. Think of other examples on your own. *Not* can come up frequently as a part of other words (*note, nothing*) or, for a truly maddening example, how about the word *able*.

- ✔ **Exact case:** Sometimes you may want to be sure to find and replace a word with a specific capitalization, such as all instances of *Jimmy* used as a name but none with a small *j* when it's used as a verb.

- ✔ **Exact attributes:** This option enables you to search for words with a specific text attribute applied to them. For example, you might want to find the word *to* only when it's italicized. By selecting this option, you can search for words that are bold, italic, underlined, small caps, and the like.

- ✔ **Find & replace type:** If you click <u>S</u>tyle, you can find a particular paragraph style. Perhaps you've created a fresh style, called Main Text and want to find all instances of Body Single and change them to the new text. You can search and replace for a style.

- ✔ **Range & direction:** These options do just what their names suggest. If you're far along in a document and want to find the most recent time you used a term, it may be helpful to use <u>F</u>ind backwards.

It's easy to forget that you've clicked <u>F</u>ind backwards. If you notice your Find activities behaving bizarrely and not locating words you know are there, you may want to be sure you're searching in the correct direction.

Checking for Passive Resistance, Hung up Modifiers, and Stultifyingly Unedifying Prose

A true grammar checker is one of those "too good to be true" things that in fact turns out to be too good to be true. Grammar is one of those ugly, unpopular, unfathomable, utterly despised concepts that most people don't like and no one ever masters. It's a nice thought that you might be able to do your original writing (which many people enjoy) and then turn to some canned grammarian to correct a grammatical faux pas without having to think about it. But I don't know, after an initial infatuation with it, I stopped using my grammar checker. You probably will, too. (See Chapter 20, "Ten Great Ami Pro Capabilities I Almost Never Use.")

Making a few mistakes to learn from

First, so that you can see the grammar checker in action, look at a couple of grammatically bad sentences. In this example, we'll look at some grammar problems in the SCOTT.SAM document.

You can select a particular sentence to check it, just as you can select a single word for Spell Checker to scrutinize. To use your Grammar Checker for a specific section:

1. Select the sentence(s) you want to check by highlighting them.

In this example, I select *I'm sorry about the ridiculously tardy manuscript.*

2. Click the Grammar Check SmartIcon, shown in the margin.

The Grammar Check dialog box appears. Figure 7-22 shows it.

3. Click OK.

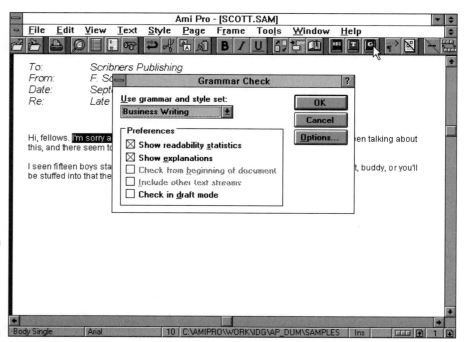

Figure 7-22:
The
Grammar
Check
dialog box.

In the example of the sentence *I'm sorry about the ridiculously tardy manuscript,* Grammar Checker makes no recommendations because it finds nothing wrong. It instead shows a screen telling you everything you never wanted to know about the Fog Index and stuff like that. I'll take some cheap shots at that screen in a moment.

Although you can check the grammar of a word or phrase, I doubt if many people ever do that. Mostly, you check the grammar of your entire piece of writing.

Scrutinizing a complete work

Usually you use the proofing tools all at the same time, after you've written whatever it is. I mean, proofing is strictly for nerds to begin with. You can spend years, create the Old Testament or something, and some grammarian in glasses and buck teeth will act all superior because you left off a quotation mark some place. But at least you can now proof your own document and not have to deal with some human grammarian. (Well, somebody will still check your grammar, unless you're just writing a letter to yourself.)

To check a whole document with Grammar Checker:

1. **Be sure no text is selected, then click the *G* icon (or select Grammar Check from the Tools menu).**

2. **In the Grammar Check dialog box, click Check from beginning of document.**

3. **Choose OK.**

   Grammar Checker selects the first candidate for a grammatical error and makes suggestions about it. Figure 7-23 shows Grammar Checker finding an "error" in the SCOTT.SAM document.

Skipping a suggestion

Often, you'll want to just flat ignore the advice from the oh-so-smart grammarian. If Grammar Checker suggests a change you want to ignore, simply click Skip. If you want to ignore a particular rule altogether (perhaps you're compiling a list in which each thought is only a partial sentence), click Skip Rule rather than Skip when Grammar Checker questions the broken rule.

Barely discouraged, Grammar Checker goes sniffing for other possible errors. Figure 7-24 shows another instance of the SCOTT.SAM document.

Making a change

To correct a sentence, simply edit it in the text the way you normally do. If you want to accept Ami Pro's suggestion, you can click Replace. Ami Pro replaces your error with its grammatically correct suggestion. In the example in Figure 7-24, you would change *seen* to *saw*.

If you get tired of working on a sentence, even though it may still have errors in it, you can click Next Sentence to force Grammar Checker to stop gnawing on that sentence and move on to the next.

Offending sentence

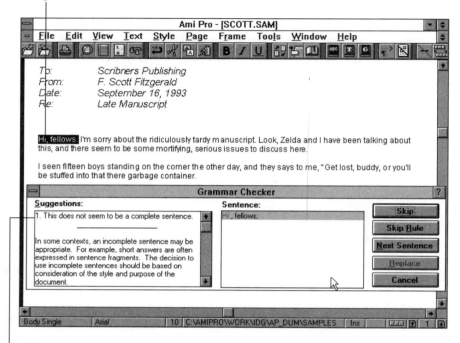

Figure 7-23:
Grammar
Checker
makes
suggestions.

Suggestions

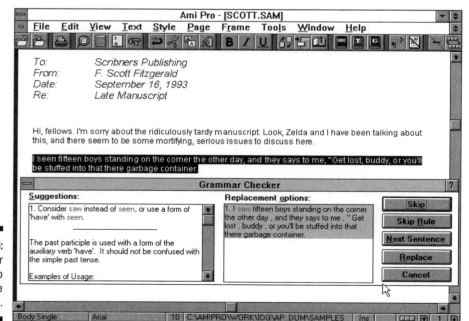

Figure 7-24:
Grammar
Checker to
the rescue
again.

Weighing your preferences

When you begin the Grammar Checker, you can unselect Show readability statistics so you don't get that pseudo scientific analysis of your writing at the end — see the accompanying figure. The categories in the Readability Statistics section are all different ways of saying the same thing — namely, how many big words have you used. Usually, a seventh-grade level for the Flesch Reading Ease Grade Level is a good target.

Readability Statistics			?
Document Statistics			Close
Totals:		Averages:	
Words	70	Words per sentence	17.5
Sentences	4	Sentences per Paragraph	.6
Paragraphs	7		
Syllables	87	Percentages:	
3-syllable words	5	Passive sentences	0%
Readability Statistics			
Gunning's Fog Index:	9.2	Flesch Reading Ease Score:	65.2
Flesch-Kincaid Score:	7.8	Flesch Reading Ease Grade Level:	8.5

You can disable the analysis of your writing style if you want. In the Grammar Check dialog box (Figure 7-22), unselect Show explanations. You may want to get analyzed a few times, but once the novelty wears off, you'll no doubt want to disable this baby.

Overwhelming yourself with rules (for a second)

Want to have a horrifying moment, to see what Kurtz was referring to in *Heart of Darkness* (by Joseph Conrad) when he summed up life by saying, "The horror. The horror"? Look over the collection of rules applied to your document:

1. **Start the Grammar Checker with the icon or menu commands.**

2. **From the Grammar Check dialog box (Figure 7-22), click Options.**

    The Grammar and Style Options dialog box opens, as shown in Figure 7-25.

I suggest you not mess much with these options, except the Grammar and style set option, which is discussed in the next section. You'll probably never have much use for any of the other options.

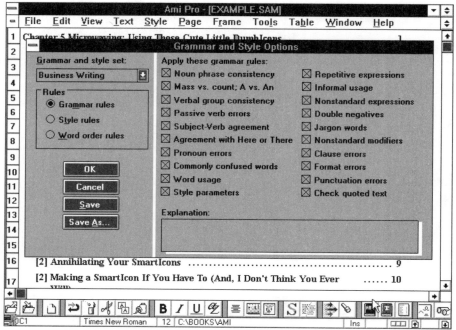

Figure 7-25:
Grammar
and Style
Options
dialog box.

Choosing a set of rules

If you use Ami Pro at work, you should probably stick with the set Ami Pro recommends, namely Business Writing; but you can choose the set of rules Ami Pro uses to evaluate your document. Figure 7-26 shows the drop-down list of the different types of grammar sets you can use when analyzing your work. Different sets include different grammar rules, depending on the formality of your writing. To change the set of rules, follow these steps:

1. **Start the Grammar Checker with the icon or menu command.**

2. **In the Grammar Check dialog box, pull down the options in the Use grammar and style set box by clicking the arrow.**

   A drop-down list shows all the possible styles you can use, as shown in Figure 7-26.

   Each set uses some or all of the rules in the Grammar and Style Options dialog box.

3. **Click the set of your choice.**

   In this example, click Fiction Writing.

4. **Click Options.**

   Clicking Options while selecting a set brings up the Grammar and Style Options dialog box, which shows you the rules applied to this particular set. Figure 7-27 shows the rules used in the Fiction Writing set.

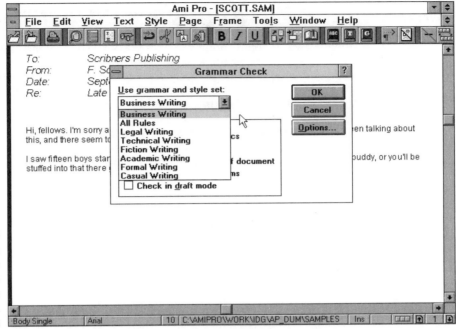

Figure 7-26:
All the possible style sets you can use.

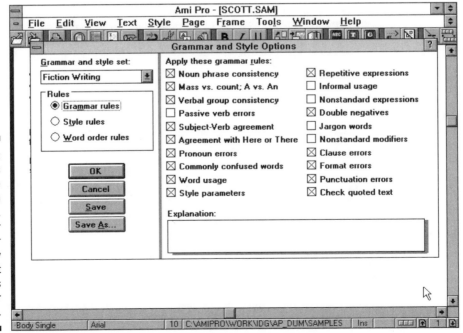

Figure 7-27:
The rules used in the Fiction writing set. Grammar Checker applies only the rules it thinks suitable for fiction.

Counting the Words in Your Document

Unfortunately, word counts don't end after you leave behind the high school teachers who ask for "500-word essays, typewritten, on one side only, and be sure that your name is at the top." All sorts of people want documents of a certain length — for reports, articles, speeches, and so on — and words are a pretty good way to judge length.

One way to find out how many words you have in a document is to run the Grammar Checker. (Perhaps you'd like some splints shoved under your fingernails, too.) No, you have a more direct route to word count: the Doc Info dialog box.

To count the words in your current document, follow these steps:

1. **From the File menu, choose Doc Info.**

   The Doc Info dialog box comes up. The Statistics box at the bottom may lead you to believe that the document has no words, no characters, and no size, because it is almost completely blank, as in Figure 7-28. But the blank screen is easy to correct.

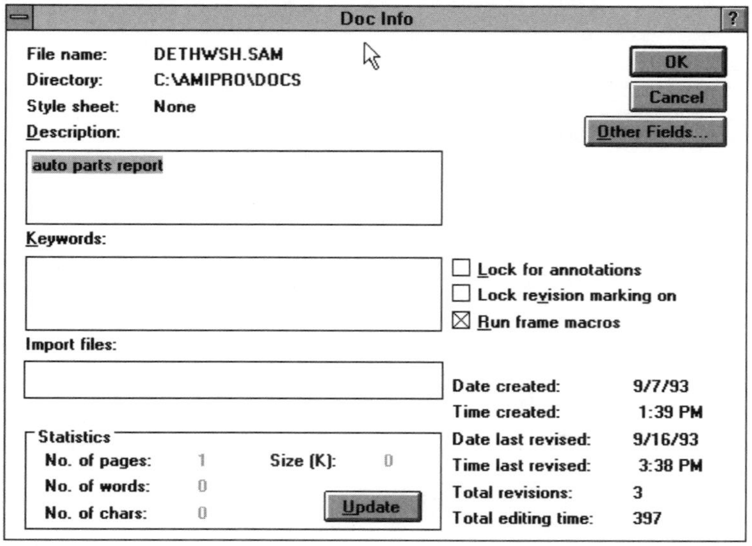

Figure 7-28:
The Doc Info dialog box before you click the Update button.

Doc Info		?
File name: DETHWSH.SAM		OK
Directory: C:\AMIPRO\DOCS		Cancel
Style sheet: None		Other Fields...
Description:		
auto parts report		
Keywords:		
	☐ Lock for annotations	
	☐ Lock revision marking on	
	☒ Run frame macros	
Import files:		
	Date created:	9/7/93
	Time created:	1:39 PM
Statistics	Date last revised:	9/16/93
No. of pages: 1 Size (K): 0	Time last revised:	3:38 PM
No. of words: 0	Total revisions:	3
No. of chars: 0 [Update]	Total editing time:	397

2. **Click the Update button.**

   The Statistics box now shows you the number of words in the document and such related information as the number of pages and the number of characters (see Figure 7-29).

```
┌─────────────────────────────────────────────────────────────────────┐
│ ⊟                              Doc Info                           ? │
├─────────────────────────────────────────────────────────────────────┤
│  File name:    DETHWSH.SAM                        ┌──────────────┐    │
│  Directory:    C:\AMIPRO\DOCS             ⌖       │      OK      │    │
│  Style sheet:  None                               ├──────────────┤    │
│  Description:                                     │    Cancel    │    │
│  ┌──────────────────────────────────────┐        ├──────────────┤    │
│  │ auto parts report                    │        │ Other Fields...│  │
│  │                                      │        └──────────────┘    │
│  └──────────────────────────────────────┘                           │
│  Keywords:                                                           │
│  ┌──────────────────────────────────────┐  ☐ Lock for annotations   │
│  │                                      │  ☐ Lock revision marking on│
│  │                                      │  ☒ Run frame macros        │
│  └──────────────────────────────────────┘                           │
│  Import files:                                                       │
│  ┌──────────────────────────────────────┐  Date created:    9/7/93  │
│  │                                      │  Time created:     1:39 PM │
│  └──────────────────────────────────────┘  Date last revised: 9/16/93│
│  ┌─ Statistics ──────────────────────┐     Time last revised: 3:38 PM│
│  │ No. of pages:   1    Size (K):  5 │     Total revisions:   3      │
│  │ No. of words: 136                 │     Total editing time: 421   │
│  │ No. of chars: 755    [ Update ]   │                              │
│  └────────────────────────────────────┘                             │
└─────────────────────────────────────────────────────────────────────┘
```

Figure 7-29:
The Doc Info dialog box after you click the Update button.

You can play around in the Doc Info dialog box on your own to see the other information in it, or you can press F1 (with the dialog box open) to read Help on the dialog box. Some fields, such as the Date created field, are self-explanatory. Other options, such as the Lock for annotations option, smack of nerdiness. For my part, I'm done writing about Doc Info.

Close the window in the usual way, by either clicking Cancel to toss the changes or by clicking OK to accept your changes.

Checking your grammar and even your spelling are optional (though it is a good idea to do it). Printing, though, is something you usually have to face whether you want to or not. The next chapter pokes into that topic a bit.

Part III

Some Stuff You'll Hate, and Tools That Help

The 5th Wave   **By Rich Tennant**

"WHY A 4GL TOASTER? I DON'T THINK YOU'D ASK THAT QUESTION IF YOU THOUGHT A MINUTE ABOUT HOW TO BALANCE THE MAXIMIZATION OF TOAST DEVELOPMENT PRODUCTIVITY AGAINST TOASTER RESOURCE UTILIZATION IN A MULTI-DINER ENVIRONMENT."

In this part...

Printing your document? It's right up there with taking castor oil and vodka. The printer jams. The computer jams. The band next door jams and drives you crazy. This part does its best to help you face the task of printing, changing elements in your work environment (like the DOS directory where Ami Pro automatically stores your stuff), and generally cleaning up after yourself. Nobody likes these chores, but they're part of life, and these chapters bravely face that fact.

Chapter 8
Printing: Getting the Oven to Work

· ·

In This Chapter
▶ Installing your printer
▶ Printing your document
▶ Changing printing options
▶ Inserting page numbers in your document
▶ Previewing your document before printing
▶ Printing on an envelope (solving the age-old conundrum)

· ·

Are You Ready for the Printing Commitment?

It seems to me that we would all be better off (from the non-nerd's point of view, of course) if a person never had to take what's on-screen and put it on paper. The screen is, oh, kind of slippery and slooshy. It's like being in Disney World: Parades go by; you take rides; you talk to Goofy and Mickey. It's kind of a dream state, where you can put anything and change anything, and nobody ever gets a permanent fix on you and says, "That's wrong."

But the printed page is cruel, hard, and permanent. It represents a kind of commitment that — in an ideal world, at least — a person just ought not to have to make on an everyday basis. When something's not permanent, some-one can accuse you of having made a mistake, and you can say in all honesty, "I don't remember" or, in the more famous phrase of the Watergate defendants, "I don't recall." When your statement is printed, however, it's harder to repudiate.

Except for a real brief look at printing in Chapter 1 (where you needed it, you may remember, to help you steal a speedboat), I haven't said much about printing until now. I don't see how I can put it off any longer, however (although you may well choose to exercise your constitutional right to skip this chapter).

You Are a Samurai Warrior

You can type the following example for practice, if you want. It is the example I use throughout the chapter when showing you the various printing options. You don't have to make you own version of the document in order to follow along, however.

Suppose, for this chapter, that you were a Samurai warrior and wanted to order a new sword from a mail order company. You can write this letter and then throughout the chapter I'll show you show how to print it and do other things with it. To create the file, follow these steps:

1. **Create a new document using the style sheet named _LETTER1.STY.**

   Review Chapter 3 if you can't remember how to use the style sheets.

2. **In the Default Information dialog box, press Cancel.**

3. **Save the document with an appropriate name.**

   I called my file SAMURAI.SAM.

4. **Select the Your Company Name option and type the name of the company.**

   For this example, I typed **Super Samurai Swords**.

5. **Type the rest of the letter.**

   You can type the text as you see it in Figure 8-1.

6. **Save the document again.**

Setting Up the Printer

Well, you have finished your masterpiece, and you are ready to share it with all your 10 or 20 coworkers (who are, no doubt, waiting for it with bated breath). Step one is making sure your printer is installed.

If you are lucky, your printer is already installed and ready to go. Skip to the section entitled "Printing Your Document."

If you're not the lucky sort, however — and how many of us really are? — you easily can run into special considerations in printing (translation: PROBLEMS). One major prob. . . er. . . consideration is installing the printer.

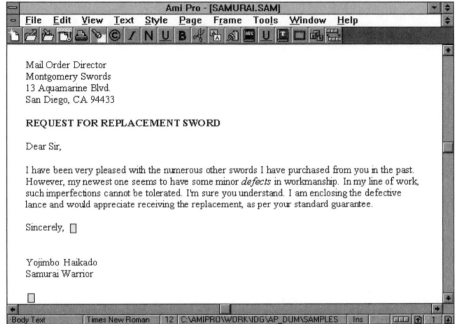

Mail Order Director
Montgomery Swords
13 Aquamarine Blvd.
San Diego, CA 94433

REQUEST FOR REPLACEMENT SWORD

Dear Sir,

I have been very pleased with the numerous other swords I have purchased from you in the past. However, my newest one seems to have some minor *defects* in workmanship. In my line of work, such imperfections cannot be tolerated. I'm sure you understand. I am enclosing the defective lance and would appreciate receiving the replacement, as per your standard guarantee.

Sincerely, ☐

Yojimbo Haikado
Samurai Warrior

☐

Figure 8-1:
On-screen, the letter looks just as it will look when it is printed.

Installing the printer

When you install Ami Pro (or, if you're lucky, when someone else installs it for you), you tell the nice program what printer or printers you have attached to your computer. If you haven't done this step, Ami Pro can't help you.

Your Windows programs can work only with the printers you have installed to work with it. There are hundreds of different printers, and they all have their own special codes, called *printer drivers,* that turn them on and tell them how to work. Your hard disk would be entirely filled up if you installed the drivers for all the possible printers, so you don't have them all on your computer.

If you aren't sure which printer Windows is using, choose Printer Setup from the File menu and see what printer is highlighted in the Select Printer dialog box. Press Esc or Cancel to get out without disturbing anything.

If you want to use a particular printer that isn't installed already, you have to install the driver by doing the following steps:

1. **Click the Control button at the very top left of the Ami Pro screen.**

   The Control menu appears. (Don't double-click or everything shuts down.)

2. Click the Control Panel option.

The Windows Control Panel appears, as shown in Figure 8-2. (This screen is part of the Microsoft Windows program, not part of the Ami Pro program.)

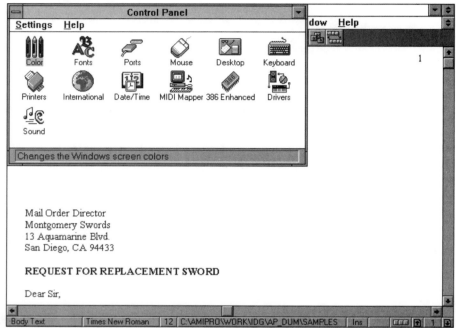

Figure 8-2:
The
Windows
Control
Panel.

3. Double-click the Printers icon.

4. In the Printers dialog box, click the Add button.

A list of printers appears, as you can see in Figure 8-3.

5. From the list of printers, you highlight the printer you want to install, click the Install button, and follow the instructions from Windows about putting in a disk.

6. Click Cancel to close the Printers dialog box and then double-click the Control button in the top left corner of the Control Panel window to close that window.

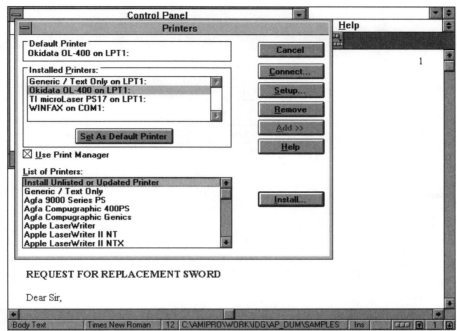

Figure 8-3:
The Printers
dialog box,
with a list of
printers you
can install
in your
computer.

Choosing the printer you want

After you've installed the printer drivers that you may be using, you can choose
any of the installed printers to be the one you use at any given moment. This
feature is especially helpful for those of you who may work in offices that have
several printers available to you. To choose a printer for your document, do the
following:

1. **Choose Printer Setup from the File menu.**

2. **In the Select Printer dialog box, click the printer you want to use and
   then choose OK.**

   Figure 8-4 shows the Select Printer dialog box for my computer, which
   almost certainly doesn't contain the same printers as yours.

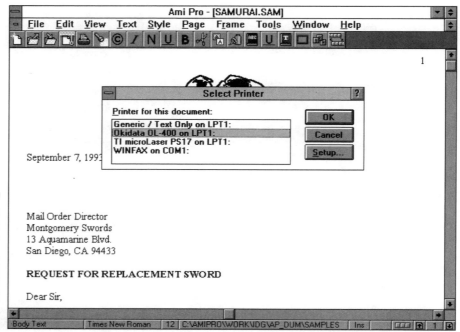

Figure 8-4:
The Select
Printer
dialog box,
where you
find a list of
all installed
printers.

Printing Your Document

If you're lucky, you don't have to do anything special when you decide to print
your document. Just click the Printer icon (as I discussed in Chapter 1) and
happily take your printed work off the printer and shove it into somebody's
waiting hand. Well, unfortunately, you often have to make changes to your
options (sigh). The following sections discuss some of the options you are most
likely to use when printing.

Printing more than one copy

Most of the time, you'll probably be content to print one copy of a document
and leave it at that. However, what do you do if you want to print more than
one copy at a time? You easily can make this printing adjustment by doing the
following steps:

1. **Click the Printer SmartIcon.**

   The Print dialog box appears, as in Figure 8-5. You now can decide how
   many copies to print.

2. **Click the up arrow next to the Number of copies box to select the number of copies you want (or type in the number).**

3. **Choose OK to close the dialog box.**

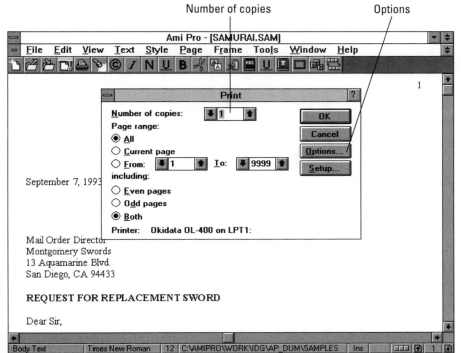

Figure 8-5:
The Print dialog box.

Changing your Setup options

A nice feature about Ami Pro is that it makes decisions for you, such as how dark to print your documents or whether to print them the long way (*Portrait style*) or the wide way (*Landscape style*) on your printer. If your boss wants that overhead in Landscape mode rather than Portrait mode, however, you easily can use the Setup button in the Print dialog box to make some basic changes to your printing. The choices that are available to you vary according to the kind of printer you have — so don't panic when your screen doesn't look like Figure 8-6. My printer is an Okidata OL-400, which performs like an HP LaserJet II.

Exercising your printing options

There are many options for printing that you'll find in the Print Options dialog box (see accompanying figure). I describe a few you might find useful:

➤ *Reverse order:* Prints the last page of the document first, then the next to the last page, and so on.

➤ *Collate:* Prints an entire copy of the document before printing the next copy. If you want more than one copy printed but don't specify this option, Ami Pro prints all copies of page one, then all copies of page 2, and so on.

➤ *Crop marks:* Ami Pro prints thin lines indicating the corners of the page. If you wonder why you need this, you don't.

➤ *Without pictures:* Prints only the text in the document. Frames with pictures in them print as blank frames. Printing with the artwork slows down the printing and eats up printer ink. Save time and printer ink by not printing the artwork until the final draft.

Feel free to experiment with all the options in this box, although I haven't found a use for most of the other options yet.

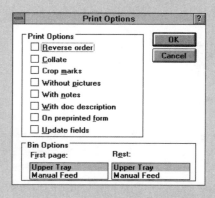

To make changes to your Setup options, do the following:

1. In the Print dialog box, click the Setup button.

In the Setup dialog box, you can choose your paper orientation. Ami Pro makes it easy to remember the difference between Portrait and Landscape orientations by giving you a graphics representation of the option you choose in the Orientation box. Click the options and watch the graphics image change right before your eyes.

2. In the Setup dialog box, click the Options button.

The Options dialog box in Figure 8-7 appears. Now you can change the Dithering from Coarse to Fine. (*Dithering* is the substitution of black and white dots with shades of gray, which makes your characters look less jagged. Nobody ever makes this change. Ami Pro just has the option here

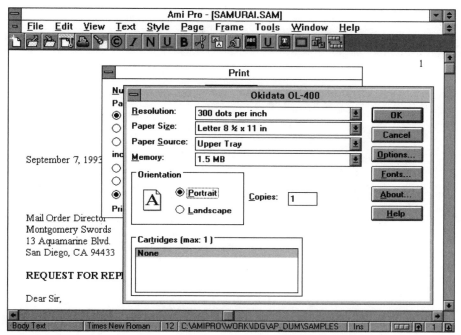

Figure 8-6:
The Setup
dialog box
for the
Okidata OL-
400 printer.

to show off.) You can modify the Intensity Control (the darkness of print).
And you can select the Print TrueType as Graphics option (which deals
with Windows TrueType fonts). You probably won't select this option very
often unless you have many graphics and not very many TrueType fonts.

3. After you have made your changes, choose OK.

If you don't make any changes, choose Cancel.

After you have all your printing options in place and you have indicated to
Windows and Ami Pro which printer to use, the printing is a one-step process:
Just choose OK in the Print dialog box (refer to Figure 8-5) and the document
prints.

Be aware that the options you specify in the Windows Control menu apply to all
files printed under Windows, not just the current document and not just your
Ami Pro files. If these options are not standard to your Ami Pro printing needs, I
suggest returning to File, Printer Setup and resetting the options to your
default.

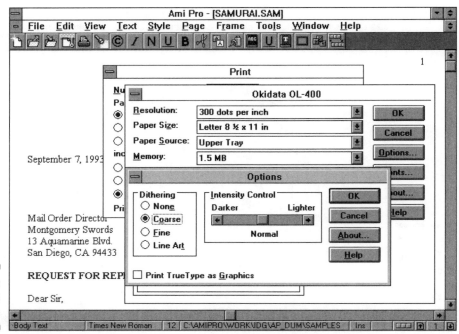

Figure 8-7:
The Options
dialog box.

Adding page numbers

Page numbers may not seem like much when you read a book or a newspaper, because you probably take them for granted as convenient references. Adding page numbers to a document correctly is no small undertaking, however. After you spend days getting a big proposal ready — using the Spell Checker and Grammar Checker and dressing up the fonts — you print the document and realize that you forgot the page numbers. (This always happens to me!) Nobody is going to be impressed with a document that doesn't have any page numbers, no matter how great it looks.

Unfortunately, Ami Pro doesn't put page numbers in a document automatically. However, with a little practice and these easy steps, you easily can add page numbers to all your Ami Pro documents:

1. Be sure that you are in Layout mode in your document.

To switch to Layout mode, choose the View menu and then click Layout mode. You also can press Ctrl+M to switch among modes.

Putting in page numbers is one of those things you just can't do unless you're in Layout mode. I suppose that it makes sense to be in Layout mode, if you think about it, because you actually can see where you're placing the page numbers on-screen.

2. **Click the mouse pointer in the top margin, within the shaded part of the document.**

   These margins aren't sacrosanct. You select them and type in them.

3. **From the Page menu (Figure 8-8), choose Page Numbering.**

Cursor placed here

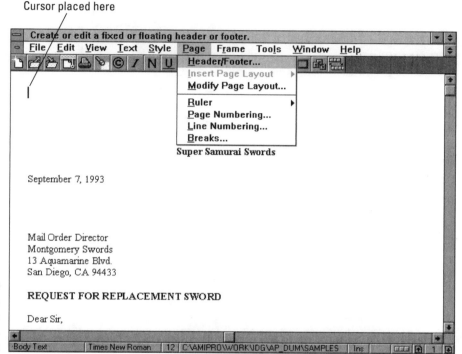

Figure 8-8:
The Page
menu.

4. **In the Page Numbering dialog box, choose OK if you like the style that appears in the Style box (see Figure 8-9).**

   If you don't like the numbering style, click the down arrow to show the choices in the drop-down listbox and make your selection here before you choose OK.

5. **A page number appears on the first page and on all successive pages.**

   Page number 1 appears at the top left of the page, where you probably don't want it, of course. You can select and edit the page number, just as you do with other text (refer to Chapter 2).

6. **Highlight the page number and, from the Text menu, choose Alignment and then Right to move the number to the right side of the page, as in Figure 8-10, or Center to move the number to the middle of the page.**

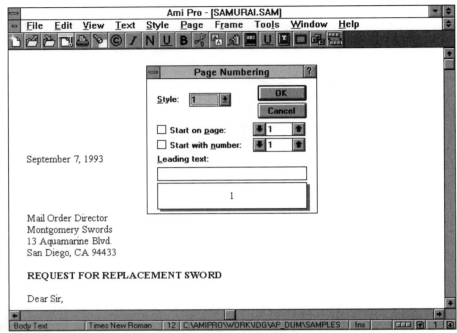

Figure 8-9:
The Page
Numbering
dialog box.

Page number

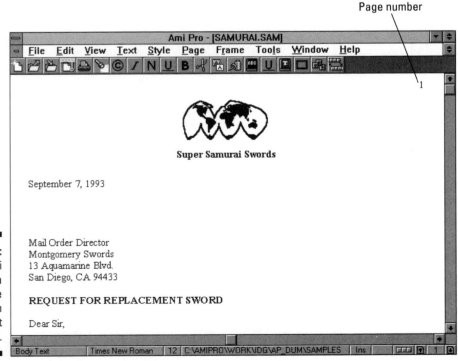

Figure 8-10:
The Samurai
letter with a
page
number in
the top right
corner.

Instead of clicking in the margin, which I think is the easiest way, you also can use headers or footers to insert page numbers into your document as well. To do this, choose <u>H</u>eader/Footer from the <u>P</u>age menu and follow along.

You may not think that it could ever happen, but you *can* forget that you're working in the margin instead of in the document when you start playing around with page numbers. The other night my son spent an hour or two typing an essay in the top margin, thinking he was in the document. Then he came whining to me, saying, "Daddy, I did all this work, and I can't find it. Ami Pro lost it." This situation happens more often than you think (especially to me — which is why I was able to figure out what happened to him).

Be aware that Ami Pro separates the margin material from the document material. If, for example, the cursor is in the margin when you try to do a Search and Replace function, Ami Pro searches only the margin and not the document (which is probably what you really intended to search). Until I figured out this little shortcoming, I had many frustrations in trying to find material that I *knew* was in the document. Why doesn't Ami Pro stop and think for a minute? Why would I want to do a major search in the margin, which has only a page number in it? Talk about dummies! Computer programs take the cake.

Previewing Your Printed Page

Raise your hand if you've heard the term *Print Preview* before. See, many of you have. If you haven't, then, fine, keep your innocence and forget I mentioned it, because you don't have to worry about this term in Ami Pro. If you've used WordPerfect or Microsoft Word or some character-based word processor, though, you've had the experience of typing your essay on the page, putting codes in it, and then wondering what it will look like when it becomes a *real* document (a printed one). With those other word processors, instead of printing your creation to check it out, you can preview it on-screen.

I confess that when I first got Ami Pro, I started looking around for Print Preview. I asked one of the program's designers about it, and he looked at me with amusement. "You don't need it," he said. What you see on the page is already what you get when you print it. For a print preview, just look at the page — it's as simple as that.

On-screen, the document from Figure 8-1 that you've been using already looks like a letter. You can tell what the margins look like, how the bold and italic texts look when printed, and so on. When printed, the letter looks just the way it looks on-screen. However, as you are preparing the letter for printing, you can look at it in several different ways — or *views*. I briefly discuss the different ways you can view a document on-screen next.

Layout mode

Unless you've experimented with different views, you're probably in Layout mode already, because it is the default mode when you begin a new document. But in case you don't know what mode you're in, it's easy to find out. Just drag the scroll box to the top of the vertical scroll bar. (You don't have to go to the top of a document to change views. I just want you to get the view from the top of the document.) In the View menu, you probably see a check mark by the Layout Mode option, which indicates that you are, indeed, in Layout mode. To change the viewing mode, just click any of the viewing options.

In Layout mode, what you see is altogether what you get when you print. You just don't need Print Preview in Ami Pro. (That concept still boggles some part of my text-based word-processor mind. A fully loaded word processor without Print Preview? How can that be?)

Figure 8-11 shows the Samurai letter in Layout mode — with the fancy logo that the style sheet maker put there, the margins in a slightly darker color than the text, and everything looking the way it will when printed.

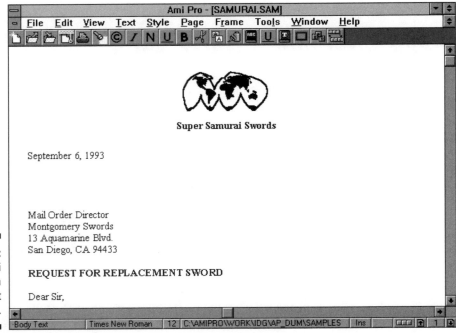

Figure 8-11:
The Samurai
letter in
Layout
mode.

You may run into a problem when you're working in Layout mode. As you're typing at the bottom of one page, Ami Pro suddenly spins you across the margin and onto the top of the next page. You can't even see any of what you were just typing on the preceding page. Some people may not mind not seeing all the text on-screen, but I don't like it and, therefore, rarely work in Layout mode until the end of a document, when I'm trying to get something to look right.

Draft mode

Often as you're working, you don't need to worry about seeing the page exactly as it will be when printed, with its fancy margins and logos. All you are really interested in seeing is the text of the document, so that you can write and edit the text and get it ready for its final form. If you put something into italics, for example, you want to see italics and not some off-beat color. To work in an uncluttered environment on-screen, Draft mode is for you. To get into Draft mode, click the Draft Mode option in the View menu.

Figure 8-12 shows the same Samurai letter in Draft mode. You no longer have the fancy margins on-screen, nor does the logo appear. Notice how much more room you have to work in on-screen without the margin restrictions. Unless you happen to get hooked on Outline mode (as I am), you should get in the habit of using Draft mode when you put your thoughts down with Ami Pro.

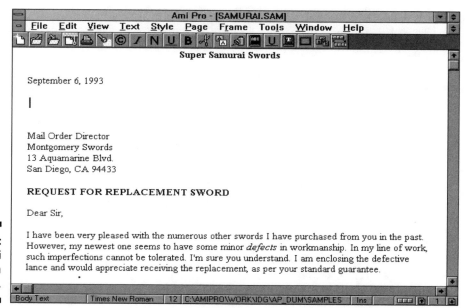

Figure 8-12:
The Samurai
letter in
Draft mode.

Outline mode

The View menu offers one other choice of viewing modes — the Outline mode. To view a document in Outline mode, as in Figure 8-13, click the Outline Mode option in the View menu.

Outline buttons

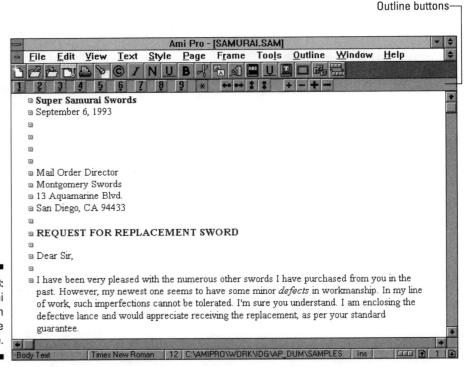

Figure 8-13:
The Samurai
letter in
Outline
mode.

Notice that the program inserts a new line of tools across the top — the Outline buttons. Notice, also, that each time you press Enter after typing text or inserting lines of spacing, the program inserts a box in the left margin. These boxes are codes indicating what type of outline paragraph you have.

For now all you have to worry about is how the different views appear on-screen. If you want to find out more about Outline mode now, however (because you just can't wait), refer to Chapter 11, where I have dedicated the entire chapter to the topic. (I'll still be here when you get back.)

Full Page view

If you want to know the *entire* truth about looking at a page in Layout mode, it really isn't like looking at a printed page, because you can't see the *whole* page.

Ami Pro has anticipated this criticism, however, by providing a solution called Full Page view.

When you are in Full Page view, you can look at an entire page of your document, just as in Figure 8-14. Admittedly, the page is so small that you need a microscope to read it (unless you have a movie screen for a monitor), but you can still see how the text and graphics look on the page. Full Page view is great for seeing the margins, seeing whether the text is laid out proportionately, and seeing whether you have your graphics in the right places.

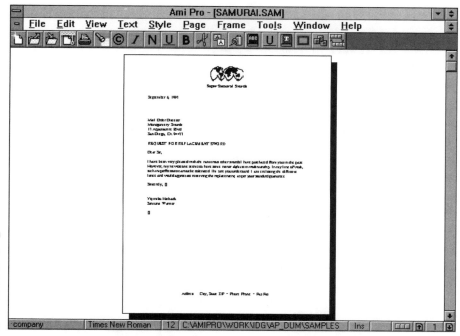

Figure 8-14:
The Samurai letter in Full Page view.

If you've worked with a Print Preview page from WordPerfect or some other word processor, this point may amaze you (the way it amazed me when I first learned about it). In most Print Preview modes, you only can view the document — you can't edit it, too. However, in Ami Pro, you *can* edit when you are in Full Page view in just the same way as you edit in any other view. If you think that you should have more line spacing between your body text and the salutation in a letter, for example, you can insert the extra spacing right in Full Page view and see how it will look on the entire printed page. Don't take this revolutionary change for granted — it is a daring break with the past and an efficient time-saver, too.

To get into Full Page view, first make sure that you are in Layout mode, because you can't get into Full Page view if you are currently in either Draft mode or Outline mode. This little inconvenience is one of those hyper-correct menu gray-outs that I've complained about before. Ami Pro could switch to Layout mode and give you a Full Page view; however, it chooses to embarrass and frustrate you and as much as say, "How could you have a Full Page view, dummy? You don't have pages in Outline mode." When I get around to building a Windows program someday, there won't be anything grayed out in the menus! After you get into Layout mode, you simply choose the Full Page option from the View menu.

Facing Pages view

When you have material on more than one page, you may want to see how the pages look next to one another (usually to make sure that you have them reasonably balanced and don't have all the text except a line or two on just one page). Using Facing Pages view is particularly helpful when you want to check how your pages look with newsletter style sheets, but it is also useful when you write letters, memos, and any other document in which it is important to have a balanced appearance. Again, you must be in Layout mode to use the Facing Pages view. Simply choose the Facing Pages option from the View menu, and your screen should look like Figure 8-15.

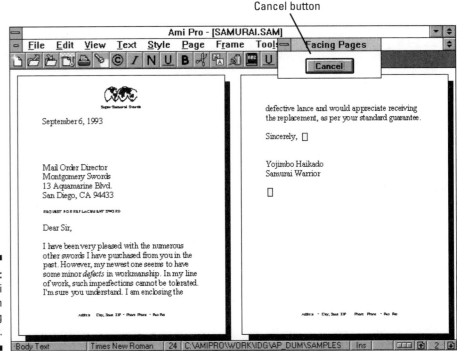

Figure 8-15:
The Samurai letter in Facing Pages view.

As of right now, the Samurai letter takes up only one page. You may have only one-page documents, too. How can you get SAMURAI.SAM, or any one-page document that you may want to work with, to expand to two pages, so that you can view it in Facing Pages? I changed the letter to 24 point and the letter spilled over onto another page.

Now that your document has two pages, you can see what the two pages look like in Facing Pages view:

1. **Choose F̲acing Pages from the V̲iew menu.**

2. **When you're finished looking, click Cancel.**

    The document goes back to Layout mode.

Unlike in Full Page view, you can't type or make editing changes while you're in Facing Pages view. I guess Ami Pro went to its limit in giving us a revolutionary Full Page view and kind of lost steam when it got to Facing Pages view. However, the Facing Pages view is still helpful for you to use in checking out your documents before printing, even though you can only look and not touch.

Other views

You probably won't be using the other views on the V̲iew menu as often as the ones I have already discussed (with the exception of the C̲ustom 91% view, which is the default view); however, I do want to briefly explain these views to you.

The E̲nlarged view option, as shown in Figure 8-16, is good if you're very nearsighted. But seriously, the Enlarged view does come in handy for viewing some applications in graphics work, such as examining a font in detail, or when drawing.

The S̲tandard view option, as shown in Figure 8-17, shows the page in the same size as other Microsoft Windows applications (which, of course, Ami Pro is one). This view is also a bit tricky to use, because the document that fit so perfectly on-screen in Custom view doesn't quite fit there any more. You have to use that pesky horizontal scroll bar again to be able to see both ends of your lines — kind of like reading a badly bound book, where the words get lost in the binding and you have to flatten out the book to read them.

The view you use when you start, C̲ustom 91%, is a percentage of the Standard view. In Chapter 9 you find out how to use View Preferences to change the percentage. I assume that some Ami Pro engineers faced a big problem when the Standard Microsoft screen size didn't fit on the Ami Pro page. They then came up with this Custom view as a solution and (like any good marketer) decided to pass off the finagled solution as a great asset.

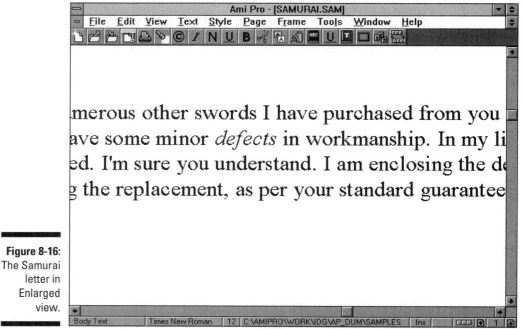

Figure 8-16:
The Samurai
letter in
Enlarged
view.

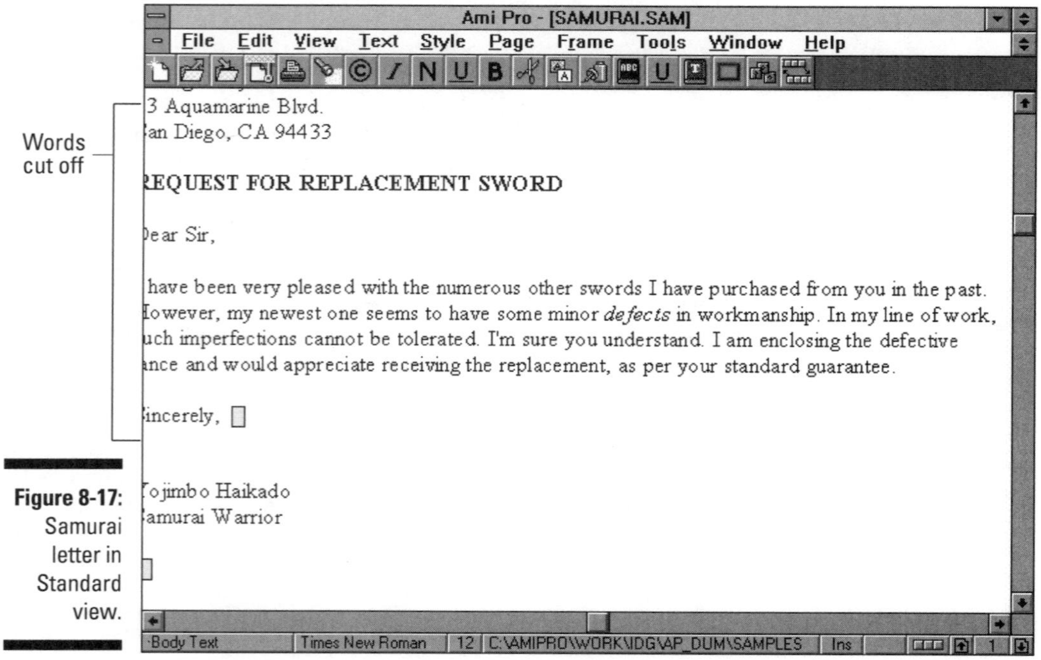

Figure 8-17:
Samurai
letter in
Standard
view.

Printing Envelopes

For years, I aspired to be able to print envelopes on my printer. I was tired of keeping a typewriter by my desk so that I could address envelopes on it. (For heaven's sake, even *nerds* keep typewriters by their desks for this purpose!) Recognizing the problem, Ami Pro has decided to help by giving you the capability to print envelopes on your printer. Just follow these steps:

1. **In the document, select the address for which you want to print an envelope.**

   In the Samurai letter example, I highlighted the mail order address as shown in Figure 8-18.

2. **From the File menu, choose Print Envelope.**

   The Print Envelope dialog box appears, also shown in Figure 8-18.

3. **Choose your envelope size.**

   The standard legal size envelope is the default size, but you can change this size by clicking the size envelope you want.

   Before you choose OK, be sure that your printer is ready.

4. **Put the envelope, facing the right way, in the top feeder of the paper tray.**

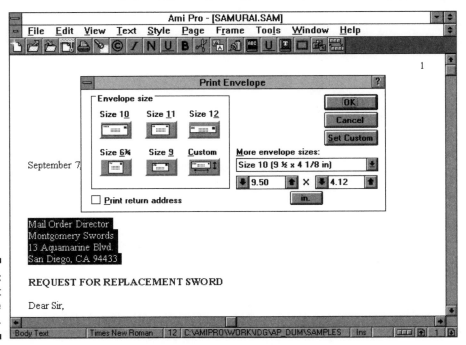

Figure 8-18:
The Print
Envelope
dialog box.

To find out the right way to put an envelope in the paper tray, I first had to experiment a few times. When I finally discovered the right way, I took a sample envelope and wrote the instructions on it: "This way down, this side right." Because I print an envelope only once every week or two, I don't want to rely on my memory for putting the envelope in the paper tray correctly. Having my trusty envelope in the desk helps me to remember each time. If you don't know how to feed an envelope, check with your printer manual.

With the printer ready to receive the envelope, you can take the final step with Ami Pro.

5. **Click OK in the Print Envelope dialog box.**

If your printer is like my printer, you may have to press Form Feed to get the envelope to print. (So what if the envelope comes out crinkled — at least the address is in the right place!)

You probably will have to fiddle around with your envelope's position several times before you find the right way to get your specific printer to print the address correctly.

Printing can be about as big a deal as you want it to be, but almost everybody has to confront it sometime. Great-looking documents aren't going to impress anybody if they're just great-looking documents on-screen. You have to try to turn them into great-looking documents on paper.

Chapter 9
Setting Up the Kitchen

• •

In This Chapter

▶ How to start each new document with your favorite style sheet

▶ How to save your documents to a specified directory

▶ How to choose other setup options

▶ How to lose sight of your SmartIcons (and how to get them back)

▶ How to put a mighty ruler on the page (and how to get it back off)

▶ How to get a clean screen (and how it can leave you helpless)

▶ How to choose options with View Preference

• •

*T*his chapter is about setting things up. If you're like me, it's not your favorite topic, because you like to do things rather than take the time to set them up: You like to go to a party, not decorate the hall; you like to drive your car, not tune it up. (Nerds tune carburetors and change filters and belts and set buttons on the dashboard. Dummies, like me, just push pedals, steer, and drive places — usually having to stop and ask directions a few times and still getting lost.)

All word processors give you choices about how you can set up your screens, your documents, your printing, and so on. I feel that Ami Pro really empowers you to put your own personal touches in your computer work. In Chapter 5, you learned how to take advantage of the SmartIcons to personalize your screen. In Chapter 8, you learned how to choose which view of your document to work in. Now that you have a little more experience using Ami Pro, it's time to examine even more ways you can personalize the way you set up the program. (And I'm talking about many, many ways — a mind-wrenching surfeit of them!)

You're the Wacko Waco

If you want to, you can follow along by creating the document shown in Figure 9-1. Keep in mind that you don't have to create the document to understand the example — the figures in the chapter clearly illustrate the example and the concepts.

Suppose, for the example, that you're a struggling, disillusioned auto parts sales manager in Waco, Texas, who is about to quit, and you've been asked to file a report on sales trends that you've witnessed. Figure 9-1 shows the report (named DETHWSH.SAM) you create using the _REPORT1.STY style sheet.

Changing Your Workplace with User Setup

You probably are content with most of Ami Pro's default settings, but you may have run across a few options that you may like to change. In this section, I'll discuss the most common changes that people make to their settings.

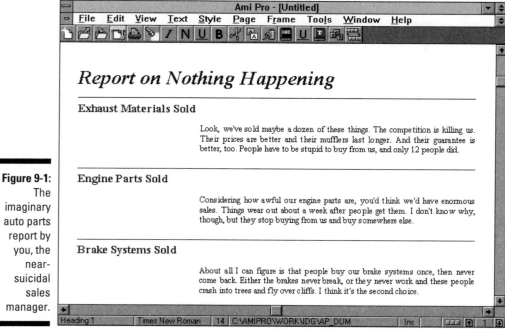

Figure 9-1: The imaginary auto parts report by you, the near-suicidal sales manager.

Viewing the possibilities

The User Setup area has many features you may want to change or try. Choose User Setup from the Tools menu. Figure 9-2 shows the dialog box you receive. Following is a brief discussion of some of the more helpful options.

✔ The **File saving** option activates Ami Pro to save your open files every few minutes. By choosing the Auto timed save box, you can have Ami Pro save all open files every five or ten minutes. Just click the minutes box to choose the time. By clicking Auto backup, you tell Ami Pro to keep a backup copy of every file you save (that is, creating two versions of the file).

✔ The **Undo levels** option has to do with how far back you can go in undoing what you just did. The maximum is four levels — which I always use, because I figure I'm going to mess up big time, and I'll want to get my old stuff back.

✔ The **Recent files** option pertains to how many recently used files display at the bottom of the File menu after you open it. Remember that you can open a recently opened file by clicking its name at the bottom of the File menu. This is where you indicate how many of those filenames you want to appear in the File menu.

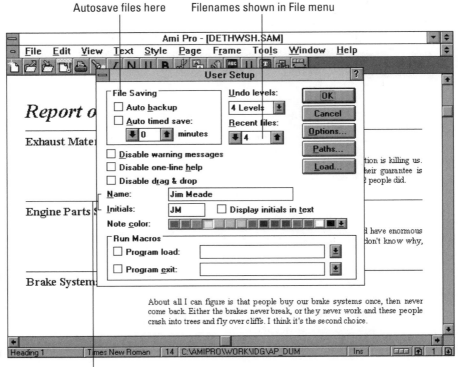

Figure 9-2:
The User Setup dialog box.

You probably won't be using the other options in the User Setup dialog box very often. In fact, these options are designed for nerds just looking for ways to make their lives more difficult, but I'll go over some of these options anyway.

- ✔ Warning messages are designed to protect you from inadvertently removing material from your documents or your program that you may regret later. After you engage the **Disable warning messages** option, you prevent the program from prompting you with a warning. I once met a nerd who hated being asked whether he really wanted to delete something. "Of course I want to delete it," he said. He hated those warning messages — but this guy is really unpopular, forgets to lace his shoes, can't carry on a normal conversation, and thinks that watching C-SPAN is having a really great time. The rest of us take comfort in those messages and do not select this option.

- ✔ The on-line help messages are friendly little messages that give helpful information. They appear in the Title bar after you select a menu item. Now who would want to atomize such helpful things? (Although I usually forget to look at them, it's comforting to know they're there.) If you select the **Disable one-line help** option, however, you nuke those little guys right off the face of your screen.

- ✔ For those of you who edit by using the drag and drop feature (see Chapter 2), you know how handy it can be; however, you also may have experienced how easy it is to skewer some pretty good prose when you really don't mean to. If you find the drag and drop feature to be a nuisance, disable it by selecting the **Disable drag & drop** option. Personally, I find this feature too fancy and advanced to part with, so I never disable it. You never know when it might come in handy.

- ✔ When you install Ami Pro, you enter your name. Unless you join a rock band, get married, get divorced, or decide to take on a pseudonym, you will probably never have cause to change the **Name** option.

- ✔ Ami Pro is showing off with the **Note color** option by giving you the option to put text notes in another color. You should probably use this option some time, just to make Ami Pro happy. Notes are little asides (that don't print) that you stick in the document, such as *Don't forget to get dog food on the way home.* I discuss these notes in Chapter 16.

Changing your default style sheet

Suppose that you know you'll be using the same report style sheet for many reports — one for the head honchos at headquarters in New York, one for the state regulatory agencies, and several for your own personal purposes. You easily can set up Ami Pro to start with that report style sheet (and set up a few other options at the same time).

To establish a new default style sheet, do the following:

1. **From the Tools menu, choose User Setup.**

   The User Setup dialog box opens, as shown in Figure 9-2, where you can have a field day changing the way things happen.

2. **Click the Load button.**

   The Load Defaults dialog box opens (refer to Figure 9-3), where you can change your defaults for the view you want to start with (Chapter 8), the mode you want to work in (Chapter 8), or the style sheet you want to use (Chapter 3).

3. **Scroll down the Style sheet list and click the style you want to be the default.**

4. **Click OK to close the Load Defaults dialog box.**

Now when you start Ami Pro the next time, this style sheet is automatically the default. If you want to pick a different style sheet, you can do that, as normally, in the File, New dialog box.

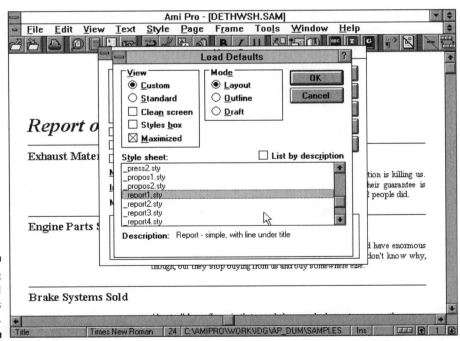

Figure 9-3:
The Load
Defaults
dialog box.

Changing the path to your Ami Pro documents

If you know DOS paths, you may want to set up Ami Pro to open by a path that you design. If you don't know DOS paths, to quote Yeats, "Horseman, pass by." In other words, skip this section!

Although you are not limited by DOS in this way, I usually change only one path when I'm working in Ami Pro — the document path. The *document path* is the directory and/or subdirectories that contain your document files. You can set up directories for categories of your work. Go back to the disgruntled salesperson example. You can set up a directory for hate letters, one for sabotage planning, and so on. Then when you save your documents, you automatically save them to the default directory unless you specify another one when you save. You even can specify a new default directory.

To change the document path, follow these steps:

1. **Choose Under Setup from the Tools menu.**

   The dialog box you receive is shown in Figure 9-2.

2. **Click the Paths button.**

   The Default Paths dialog box emerges, as shown in Figure 9-4. As you can see from the DOS codes in my own document path, I've changed my document path.

Ami Pro - [DETHWSH.SAM]

File   Edit   View   Text   Style   Page   Frame   Tools   Window   Help

User Setup

File Saving   Undo levels: OK

Default Paths   ?

Document: c:\amipro\work\idg\ap_dum   OK

Report   Style sheet: c:\amipro\styles   Cancel

Backup:

Exhaust Mat   Macro: c:\amipro\macros

SmartIcons: c:\amipro\icons

☒ Use working directory

Note color:

Run Macros

Engine Parts   ☐ Program load:

☐ Program exit:

Figure 9-4:
The Default
Paths dialog
box.

Brake Systems Sold

Title   Times New Roman   24   C:\AMIPRO\WORK\IDG\AP_DUM\SAMPLES   Ins   1

Most of these paths are for Ami Pro's own uses. The Macro option indicates where Ami Pro saves the macros (refer to Chapter 18). The Style sheet option indicates where Ami Pro saves its style sheets.

To create the subdirectory you want to use, refer to Chapter 2. Ami Pro refuses to enable you to close the Default Paths window if you put in a path that doesn't exist yet. Ami Pro should be polite and offer to create the path for you, but it doesn't do that. It just adamantly refuses to budge.

3. **In the Document box, type the drive, path, and subdirectory of your new file location.**

   For example, if you created a directory called REPORTS and a subdirectory called SALES (and assuming your main drive is C), you would type the following line into the Document box:

   ```
   C:\REPORTS\SALES
   ```

   Remember that you have to create the directory (in Windows or DOS) before you can set it up as the default. Chapter 2 explains how to create a directory in Windows.

4. **Click OK to make your new document path the default.**

   The next time you start Ami Pro, this new path will be the default.

Exploring other setup options

For lack of a clearer name, Ami Pro lists some additional setup choices under the Options button in the User Setup dialog box. Choose User Setup from the Tools menu, as usual, then click the Options button. The User Setup Options dialog box, shown in Figure 9-5, appears.

You can choose from several options in the Typographic Options box.

✔ The **Widow/Orphan control** is for dilettantes — I know that I like this option. The Widow/Orphan control prevents single lines at the beginning or end of paragraphs from showing up at the top or bottom of the page. You still may get single lines at the top or bottom of your pages, however, even after you select the Widow/Orphan control. To prevent these stray single lines from occurring in your text, modify the style of the paragraph and change the Breaks option so that you don't allow breaks within the paragraph (see Chapter 4).

✔ The **Pair kerning** option is pure showing off, as in, "We have pair kerning, and WordPerfect doesn't." Pair kerning is for printers (by which I mean people who run professional print shops) and has to do with the spacing between characters.

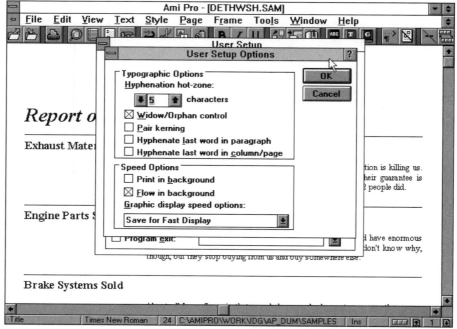

✔ The **Hyphenation hot-zone** option, aside from being quite a tongue twister, is not for ordinary mortals, either. This hyphenation option has to do with how many spaces you want at the end of the line before Ami Pro decides whether to put a hyphen in a word.

The most useful option in the Speed Options box is Print in background.

✔ The **Print in background** option can be a good Setup option for normal people, because this option means that you can work in Ami Pro even if the program is taking its time about printing some 200-page tome at the same time.

When the Print in background option is checked, sometimes Ami Pro has a bit of a struggle doing more than one thing at a time. You may find that Ami Pro is unable to do some tasks while printing. (I had trouble when printing certain large graphics images, for example.) You may have to disable the Print in background option when you run into difficulty; however, it is a great feature to use when everything works as it should.

Choose OK to close the User Setup dialog box to implement any changes you may have made. Except for a few useful options, such as changing the default path, selecting your favorite style sheet, and choosing a note color (NOT), you probably will not be using the User Setup dialog box very often.

Changing Your Workplace with the View Menu

User Setup is one place to fiddle with your environmental controls, but you also can use the V̲iew menu, which I discussed in the preceding chapter. The possibilities for changing Setup options in the V̲iew menu also should be taken with a grain of salt — or approached with a ten-foot pole. To access all the possible changes you can make with the V̲iew menu, as shown in Figure 9-6, choose V̲iew.

Concealing your SmartIcons

SmartIcons are a great visual tool for most users of Ami Pro. If the SmartIcons aren't visible, you can't use them. What good is a visual tool if you can't see it on-screen? Apparently, some nerds have such important things to do on-screen that they can't afford the space for the SmartIcons, however, so they select the Hide Smart̲Icons option.

Gulp. Those helpful, friendly little babies disappear. I mean, what kind of person would want to do that? The screen takes on a very lonely look, as you can see in Figure 9-7. For the life of me, I just can't relate to removing the SmartIcons from the screen. Would you want a car dashboard without instruments? A TV without a remote control?

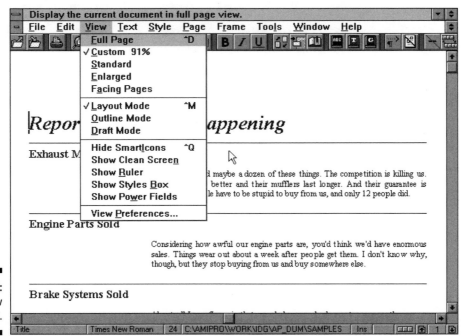

Figure 9-6:
The V̲iew
menu.

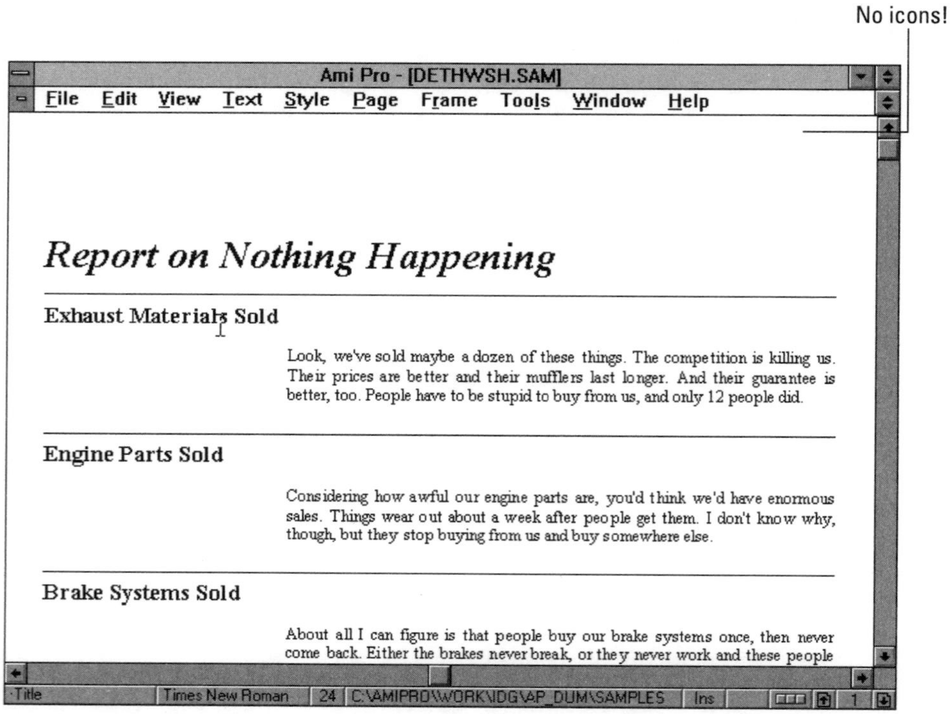

No icons!

```
┌──────────────────────────────────────────────────────────────┐
│ ─                Ami Pro - [DETHWSH.SAM]              ▼ ♦      │
│ ▭  File  Edit  View  Text  Style  Page  Frame  Tools  Window  Help   ♦ │
│                                                                │
│                                                                │
│                                                                │
│     Report on Nothing Happening                               │
│                                                                │
│     Exhaust Materials Sold                                    │
│                        Look, we've sold maybe a dozen of these things. The competition is killing us. │
│                        Their prices are better and their mufflers last longer. And their guarantee is │
│                        better, too. People have to be stupid to buy from us, and only 12 people did.  │
│                                                                │
│     Engine Parts Sold                                         │
│                        Considering how awful our engine parts are, you'd think we'd have enormous │
│                        sales. Things wear out about a week after people get them. I don't know why, │
│                        though, but they stop buying from us and buy somewhere else.              │
│                                                                │
│     Brake Systems Sold                                        │
│                        About all I can figure is that people buy our brake systems once, then never │
│                        come back. Either the brakes never break, or they never work and these people │
│ ◄                                                           ►  │
│ ·Title        Times New Roman   24  C:\AMIPRO\WORK\IDG\AP_DUM\SAMPLES  Ins      1 ◄│
└──────────────────────────────────────────────────────────────┘
```

Figure 9-7:
A screen without SmartIcons is like a day without sunshine.

To get the SmartIcons back, open the View menu again and choose the command, which has now changed to Show SmartIcons. (You also can press Ctrl+Q to toggle between showing and hiding them.) After you click Show SmartIcons, those precious little pictures come back home where they belong.

Bowing to the mighty ruler

For the most part, I find the ruler as unessential as I find the SmartIcons essential. You can use the ruler to position items exactly as you want them on the page, to add tabs, and it's most likely to be valuable when laying out the page for final printing or for placing graphics just so. I use the ruler only when I really need it. At other times, I just keep it hidden.

To display the ruler, as in Figure 9-8, choose Show Ruler from the View menu. To get the ruler out of the way, choose the Hide Ruler option from the View menu. (Notice the change in the command name again.)

Ruler

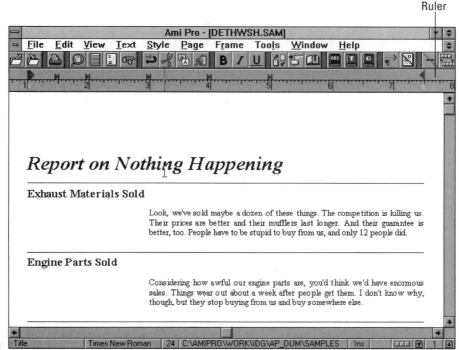

Figure 9-8:
A screen
with the
ruler.

Wiping the screen clean

If hiding the SmartIcons makes you nervous, wait till you choose the Show Clean Screen option. *Everything* (well, almost everything) disappears from your screen but your editing area. Ami Pro is quite proud of this feature, new in Version 3, because it enables you to maximize your editing workspace. Hey, no thanks. I've got plenty of editing workspace as it is. This choice is scary because, if all the controls are gone, how do you get anything done?

Well, take the plunge and try this option, but don't lose this book in the middle of your attempt, because there will be no menus or controls left on-screen to get you out of this mess. If, from the View menu, you chose Show Clean Screen, your screen would look something like Figure 9-9.

Everything disappears except for one friendly little icon at the bottom of the screen, which allows you to reestablish all your screen controls. (You find out later in the chapter how you can make this icon disappear, too.) Well, there it is — you've maximized your workspace. If this editing screen appeals to you, fine. For my part, it makes me nervous.

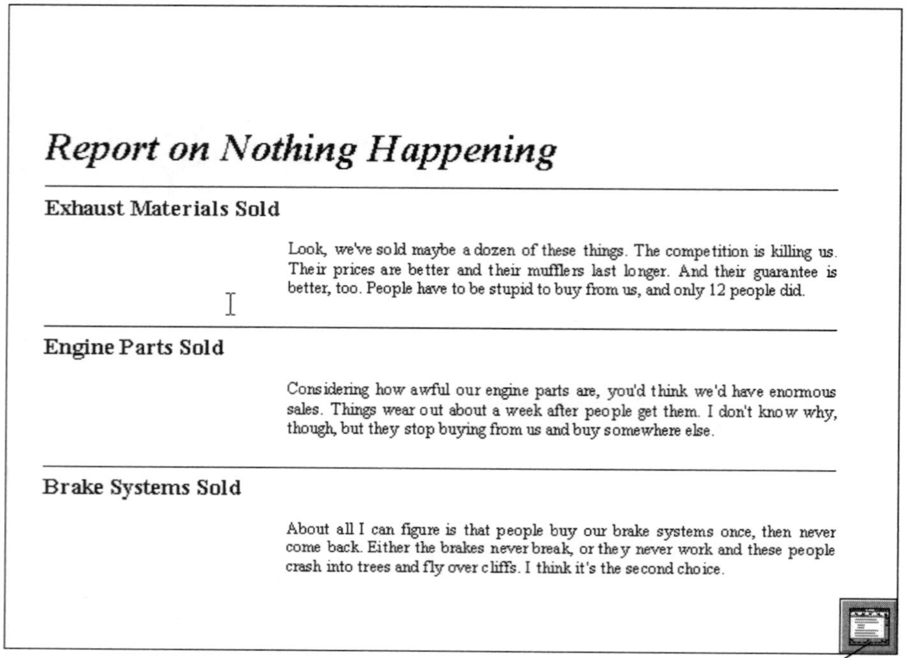

Report on Nothing Happening

Exhaust Materials Sold

Look, we've sold maybe a dozen of these things. The competition is killing us. Their prices are better and their mufflers last longer. And their guarantee is better, too. People have to be stupid to buy from us, and only 12 people did.

Engine Parts Sold

Considering how awful our engine parts are, you'd think we'd have enormous sales. Things wear out about a week after people get them. I don't know why, though, but they stop buying from us and buy somewhere else.

Brake Systems Sold

About all I can figure is that people buy our brake systems once, then never come back. Either the brakes never break, or they never work and these people crash into trees and fly over cliffs. I think it's the second choice.

Reassuring icon

Figure 9-9:
The screen with the clean-cut look (yikes).

How do you do anything after the menus and SmartIcons are all gone, not to mention the Title bar and the lovely, responsive Status bar? Well, you have to use that bane of all dummies: your memory. By now, you should know that the hot key for the View menu is a *V*. Just press Alt+V to get to the View menu so that you quickly can reestablish your helpful screen controls. (Or — and this approach is so much easier — click the friendly little icon at the bottom of the page to reestablish all your screen controls.)

To get some work done when you have a clean screen, you don't have to remember how to open every menu. You just have to get one menu on-screen (for example, press Alt+F for the File menu), and then you can use the horizontal arrow keys on the keyboard to move back and forth from menu to menu.

Changing Your Workplace with View Preferences

The View Preferences option in the View menu provides even more setup options for your screen. After you click View Preferences, the View Preferences dialog box appears, as you can see in Figure 9-10.

Examining the View Preferences options

Most of the options are self-explanatory (except for Outline buttons, which I haven't discussed yet, or Marks, which can be about anything), but I'll go over these options with you briefly, anyway. Remember that you can choose as many or as few of these options as you want.

✔ The **Tabs & returns** option is helpful during proofreading, because you can actually see the paragraph and tab marks on-screen that you have inserted in your text. If you have extra tabs or returns, you easily can find and remove them with this option activated.

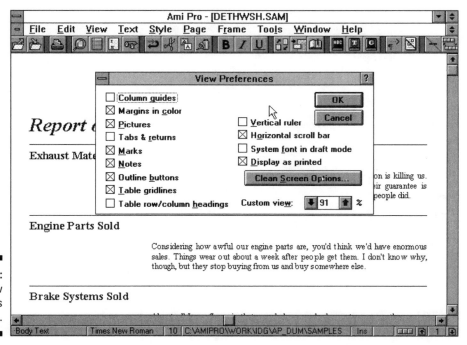

Figure 9-10:
The View
Preferences
dialog box.

✔ The **Vertical ruler** option is even less useful than the horizontal ruler, except when you need to place graphics specifically in a certain place to line them up properly.

✔ Figure 9-11 shows how your screen looks after you select both the Tabs & returns option and the Vertical ruler option.

✔ Clicking the **Notes** option just means that you can see any notes you add to your file. (Notes are discussed in detail in Chapter 16.) You may find a time when hiding these notes (a love letter, perhaps) is a better option.

✔ The **Marks** option is for nerds only. Clicking this means that if you have any embedded codes (for example, a page break or a footer), Ami Pro shows you a code where these would appear.

✔ The **System font in draft mode** option is another for-nerds-only option. Ami Pro runs faster while you're in draft mode, so after you select this option, the program displays whatever font Windows 3.1 feels comfortable with. You do not see the font that you'll get when you print. Nerds can give up their WYSIWYG (what you see is what you get) if they want. The rest of us should not give up what it took us so long to get!

Return mark

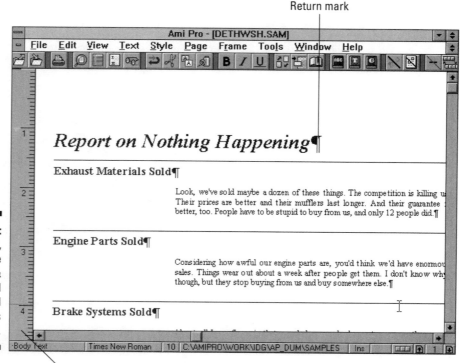

Figure 9-11:
Your screen, with the Tabs & returns and the Vertical ruler options checked.

Vertical ruler

Scoping out the clean screen options

In a previous section, I told you that there is a way to remove the friendly little icon at the bottom of the clean screen. You can add or remove this icon, along with other options, after you choose the Clean Screen Options in the View Preferences dialog box. Choosing this option produces the Clean Screen Options dialog box, shown in Figure 9-12.

The options in the Clean Screen Options dialog box enable you to decide which screen controls you want to display after you choose the Show Clean Screen option from the View menu. Be sure that you always have the Return icon option selected so that you quickly can go back to your original screen after you have edited in Clean Screen. You can choose also to display any or all the other options, too. But if you do decide to display the other options on your Clean Screen, it wouldn't be clean for very long, would it?

After you have made your selections, click OK to close the Clean Screen Options dialog box and then click OK once more to close the View Preferences dialog box.

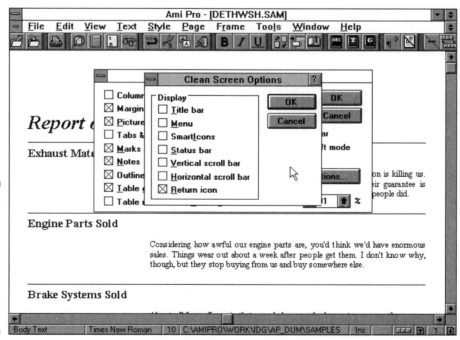

Figure 9-12:
The Clean
Screen
Options
dialog box,
with the
Return icon
option
selected.

Be extra careful about unselecting the Return icon option in the Clean Screen Options box. If you unselect it, the icon doesn't appear in the bottom right of the screen as it does in Figure 9-9. Without this friendly little icon, you have to rely on your memory to use a keyboard command to open a menu (such as Alt+V to open the View menu). Without this icon, you find yourself with no controls on-screen and no way to get them back if you have a bad memory. Take it from me, don't unselect the Return icon.

When you use Ami Pro, you don't have to submit helplessly to your environment the way you find it. (But as you can see from this chapter, the more you submit to your environment the way it is, the better off you are!) Just keep in mind, however, that changing controls can mess up your friendly computer workplace, so remember that "if it ain't broke, don't fix it." At times, though, you may want to straighten up your environment by moving and deleting files. You find out how to do these things in the next chapter.

Chapter 10

File Management:
Reorganizing the Kitchen

. . . .

In This Chapter

▶ Why file management pertains to you

▶ Why you may prefer the Windows File Manager

▶ How to stoke up the Ami Pro File Manager

▶ How to copy a file

▶ How to rename a file, move it, and send it off to meet its maker

▶ How to alchemize a WordPerfect file into an Ami Pro file

. . . .

*E*verybody — even a nerd (in most cases) — would rather have somebody else do the cleanup work on a project. Everyone enjoys participating in a project, but no one enjoys straightening up afterwards. Still, as you work in Ami Pro, you're going to pile up more and more documents. If you don't put your files in some kind of order, you'll soon find it very hard to find them. And when your files get too messy, you'll find it hard to think straight.

Why File Management?

Organizing your files in different directories is a good idea. Normally, people separate files by type or subject matter; for example, you might want to put all your tax information files in a directory called C:\YUCK, whereas your files of poems you wrote would be in the C:\POEMS directory. There are concrete benefits in organizing your files in different directories, including the following:

🗸 Your files are organized in such a way that they are intuitively easy to find.

🗸 The fewer files you have in one directory, the less hunting and scrolling you have to do.

🗸 Other people can find information without knowing exactly where you put it.

🗸 You can control the number of versions you have in one directory.

Once you become accustomed to managing your files in this way, you'll never want to go back!

Looking Longingly at the Windows File Manager

When you're using a Windows program, you don't really have to use any file manager other than the one that comes with Windows. Chapter 2 discusses switching to the Windows File Manager and using it to create directories.

I leave my Windows File Manager open most of the time when I'm in Windows, so I can readily copy files to my floppy disk, move files around, and other clean-up actions.

Just as a review, this is how you switch to the Windows File Manager:

1. **Click the Ami Pro Control button (top left of the Ami Pro window).**

2. **From the Control menu, choose Switch To.**

   The Task List dialog box appears.

3. **Highlight Program Manager and choose Switch To.**

4. **Open the Main window in Program Manager by choosing Window, then Main.**

5. **Double-click the File Manager icon, as shown in Figure 10-1.**

   The Windows File Manager opens.

The Windows File Manager has a great file Search capability, which the Ami Pro File Manager doesn't have. With the Search capability, you can search your entire disk to find an errant file.

Refer to Chapter 2 to create directories and move files in the Windows File Manager. Chapter 10 covers these actions in Ami Pro.

Coming Home to the Ami Pro File Manager

You can do all your file management in the Windows File Manager (which I prefer) when you're in Ami Pro; however, you also can use the Ami Pro File Manager.

To use the File Manager to get your files in order, first choose File Management from the File menu. The Ami Pro File Manager starts up (a program within the Ami Pro program), as shown in Figure 10-2.

File Manager icon

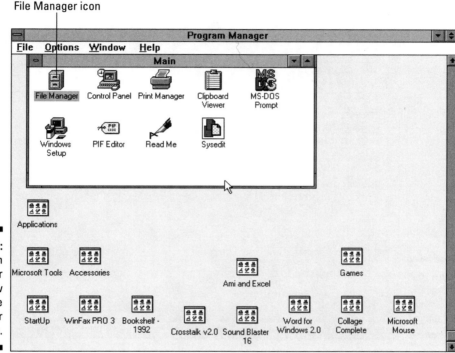

Figure 10-1:
The Program
Manager
window
showing the
File Manager
icon.

I know that the name *File Management* sounds stilted. My guess, unsubstanti-ated by any hard information, is that Ami Pro didn't want to look like it was infringing on the Windows File Manager name, so it came up with a different one that is understandable, if somewhat formal.

Moving around in the File Manager

The File Manager that you see in Figure 10-2 shows the contents of the C:\AMIPRO\DOCS directory, which contains a number of the sample docu-ments I've created in earlier chapters in the book. Suppose that you want to move to the C:\AMIPRO directory (one level up). To move one level up in a directory path, simply double-click the two dots in the brackets at the bottom of the list of files. The File Manager now displays the directory above the current one in the path (see Figure 10-3). You also can click the letters in brackets to change drives.

To move down a level in the directory path, double-click the name of the directory you want. In my example, you can double-click the DOCS directory (in brackets) to move back to where you started.

Directory name   Files

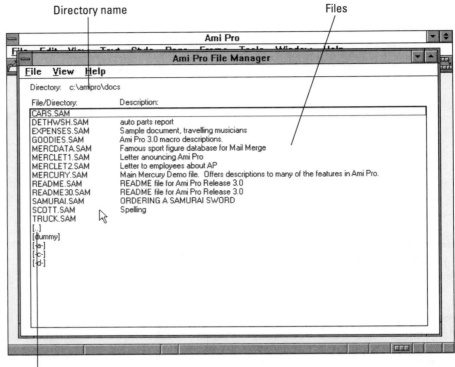

Figure 10-2:
The Ami Pro
File
Manager.

Two dots

Moving around in the File Manager is nothing more than clicking the two dots to move up in the directory path and clicking the names of directories to move down the path.

Copying a file

Suppose that you want to copy a file from one directory to another. Just take the following easy steps to do so:

1. **In the Ami Pro File Manager window, click the name of the file you want to copy in order to select it.**

   Suppose, again, that you want to copy the file TRUCK.SAM from C:\AMIPRO\DOCS to C:\AMIPRO\DOCS\DUMMY. Click TRUCK.SAM to select it, as in Figure 10-4.

   You don't have to work with (i.e. move, delete, copy) just one file at a time. You can choose multiple files. After you click the first file to select it, hold down the Ctrl key while you click additional names to select them, as well.

2. **From the Ami Pro File Manager File menu, as shown in Figure 10-5, choose the Copy command.**

   The Copy dialog box opens, as shown in Figure 10-6.

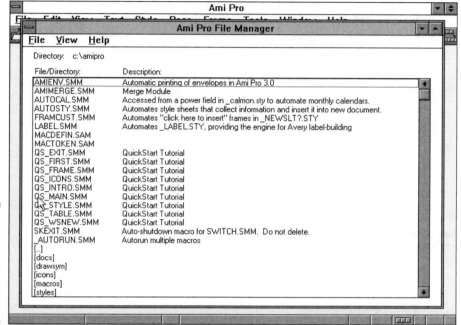

Figure 10-3:
The new
directory,
one level up
from the
preceding
directory.

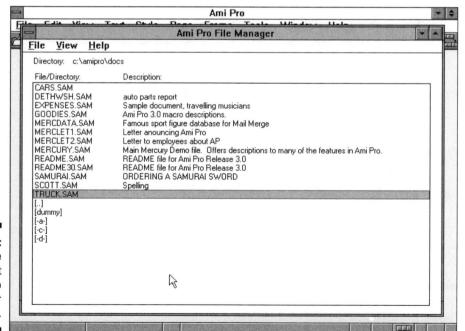

Figure 10-4:
Select the
file you want
to copy to
another
directory.

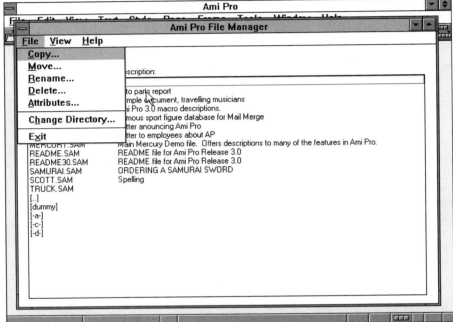

Figure 10-5:
The Ami Pro
File
Manager
File menu.

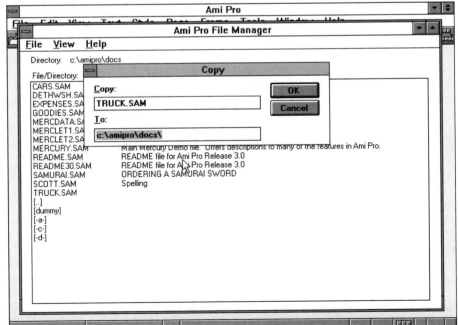

Figure 10-6:
The Copy
dialog box.

Because you selected a file before choosing the Copy command, the dialog box appears with stuff already in the Copy box (the name of the selected file) and the To box (the name of your default directory). If you chose the Copy command before selecting a file first, the boxes are blank. (This little idiosyncrasy dawned on me one day when I was working with blank boxes and finding it annoying to type in all those DOS backslashes.)

3. Type in the name of the directory path to which you want to copy the selected file.

For my example, click at the end of the line in the To box (to avoid deleting the text already in the box) and type **DUMMY**. The complete entry in the To box now reads C:\AMIPRO\DOCS\DUMMY.

If you type a directory that doesn't exist, Ami Pro doesn't warn you — it makes a copy of the file with the bad directory name. Double-check that what you type is correct before pressing OK.

4. Choose OK.

The File Copy Options dialog box appears, as in Figure 10-7. This box represents the real advantage of using the Ami Pro File Manager instead of the Windows offering, because the Ami Pro File Manager is sensitive to style sheets. (On the other hand, it's a bit aggravating to have to think about style sheets when all you're thinking about is copying a dumb file.) In the present example, I had already saved the style sheet with the document (refer to Chapter 1), so the Style Sheet option is grayed out on the figure.

Figure 10-7:
The File
Copy
Options
dialog box.

5. Choose OK.

The File Manager copies the file.

If you want to make sure the file was copied:

6. Double-click the new directory to switch to that directory.

In the example, double-click [dummy] to switch to that directory. A copy of the file TRUCK.SAM is now in the directory, as you can see in Figure 10-8.

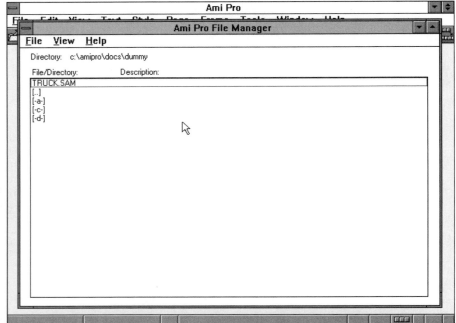

Figure 10-8:
The
TRUCK.SAM
file has
found a new
home in the
DUMMY
directory.

Crazy things can happen to the files you're working on, causing you to lose them for one reason or another. Get in the habit of using the Copy command frequently as you work to copy your stuff to a separate disk in the A: drive.

Renaming a file

The other File commands work in the same way as the Copy command does. You first select the file(s) to work on, and then you choose the command. Try some of the other commands with one of your files or follow along with the TRUCK.SAM file.

To change the name of a file, follow these steps:

1. In the File Manager, click the file to select it.

Click TRUCK.SAM.

2. From the File menu, choose Rename.

3. In the Rename dialog box, shown in Figure 10-9, type the new name for the selected file in the To text box and choose OK.

In this case, type **MACK.SAM** and click OK. The File Manager renames the file.

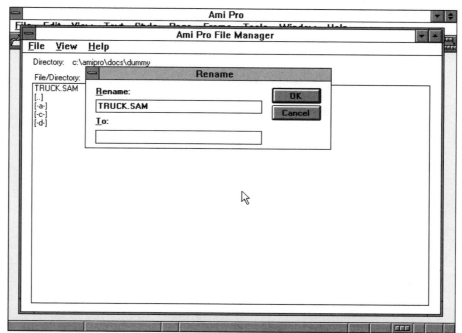

Figure 10-9:
The Rename
dialog box.

Moving a file

When you copy a file, you leave the original in place and make a second one — an activity that most dummies (like me) much prefer to moving or deleting a file. You can't do too much damage when you copy a file, because you can always use the one you started with, if you want. When you move a file, however, you change its position in a directory, but you don't delete anything.

Be careful not to copy too frequently to another drive because you might end up with 24 versions of 12 different files — not a great allocation of hard disk space.

To move a file to another directory, do the following:

1. In the File Manager, click the file you want to move.

For this example, click MACK.SAM.

2. From the File menu, choose Move.

3. **In the Move dialog box, as shown in Figure 10-10, type the new path where you want to move the file and click OK.**

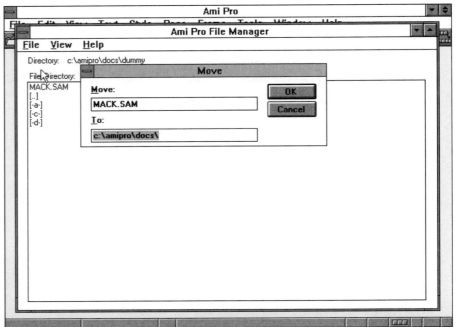

Figure 10-10:
The Move
dialog box.

The File Move Options dialog box appears, as shown in Figure 10-11.

4. **After you make your $\underline{S}$tyle Sheet decisions, choose OK.**

   File Manager moves the file to the directory you indicated. In this case, the file moves to the default directory, C:\AMIPRO\DOCS.

5. **To see the document listed in its new directory home, click the two dots below the filenames to bring up the new directory file list.**

   MACK.SAM is now in its new location in Figure 10-12.

Nuking a file

Nothing you can do to straighten up your disk is quite as satisfying and down-right effective as deleting stuff. Nothing matches the trash can as a house cleaning tool.

Everyone who has used computers for any length of time can attest to using care when deleting files. If you don't know what it is and don't know what's in it, *don't delete it!* You might end up deleting some important Windows or DOS files and having a major system crash on your hands.

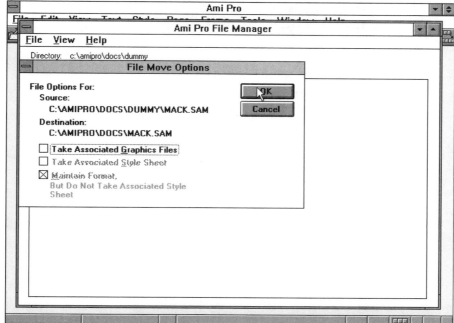

Figure 10-11:
The File
Move
Options
dialog box.

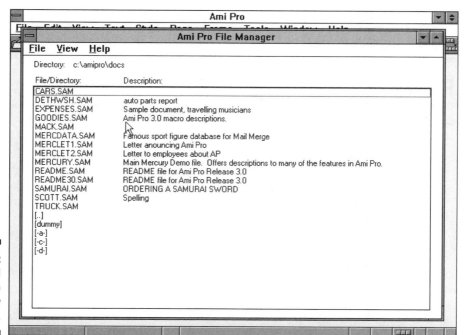

Figure 10-12:
MACK.SAM
moves to
its new
location.

To delete a file, follow these steps:

1. **In the File Manager, click the file you want to delete.**

   In this case, click MACK.SAM.

2. **From the File menu, choose Delete.**

3. **In the Delete dialog box, shown in Figure 10-13, choose OK.**

   The file kicks the bucket.

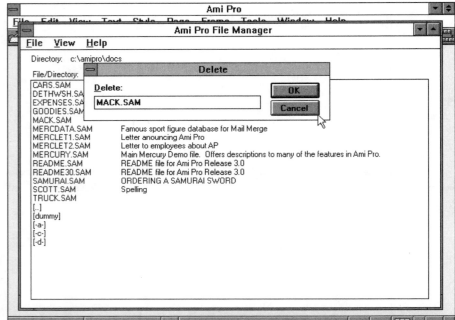

Figure 10-13:
The Delete
dialog box.

Bidding File Manager a fond adieu

The Ami Pro File Manager, in my opinion, is pretty good at what it does: It helps you deal with the perplexing DOS directory structures as you move things around. Still, reorganizing files gets old pretty fast; therefore, to close the File Manager, choose Exit from the File menu, and the File Manager beats a hasty retreat.

Opening a file in a different program

All along, you've been working strictly with Ami Pro documents, the ones with the offbeat .SAM extension. In the real world, however, you're going to encounter files from all kinds of other programs. You open them in almost the same way you do your Ami Pro files (and pray that when you do open the file, you get something there).

To open a file from another program, do the following:

1. **From the Ami Pro File menu, choose the Open command.**

2. **In the Open dialog box, click the arrow to the right of the List files of type listbox.**

   A list of file types drops down, as you can see in the accompanying figure.

3. **Click the appropriate file type in the listbox.**

   The List files of type listbox now shows the file type that you chose.

   For this example, I chose a WordPerfect 5.0 & 5.1 file.

4. **Scroll through the Files box and double-click the old file.**

   And if you're religious at all, pray! Depending on the file and its program, you may have to make some choices in a couple

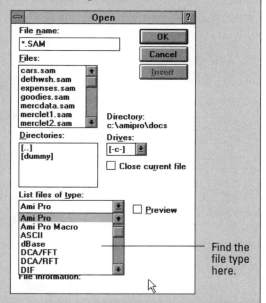

Find the file type here.

more dialog boxes. If you receive any dialog box, click OK to accept the default settings.

Then, the document should come in with all the formatting for an Ami Pro document.

5. **Name the file with the Save command.**

   Ami Pro automatically adds its own extension, .SAM.

Reverting to a Preceding File

In the twisted world of personal computing, you can spend time making things happen and then wish they never had happened. In life, you usually don't get a second chance. Ami Pro, however, tries to go life one better by giving you a second chance to correct your mistakes with the Revert to Saved command (when you bollix things up but good).

If you are working on a file that you have previously saved, for example, and you have added material to that document, you can remove all the new material from the document (without searching it out individually) with just a few clicks of the mouse. I find this feature to be handy, especially when I come back to a file after leaving it for awhile. I may go off the track and then remember what I really had in mind. If I haven't saved my file (or if my computer hasn't automatically saved it for me on a timed save), I can invoke this capability to get me back to where I started. This feature is also good when you accidentally delete a whole bunch of stuff, which, as I say, can happen.

To get back to your original saved document after you have made changes to it, simply click the Revert to Saved command in the File menu. A friendly reminder comes up (see Figure 10-14) telling you that you'll blow away everything you've done since you last saved the document. You probably know that this will happen, but the question is worth considering again. About half the time, I change my mind here and choose Cancel. But if you truly want to get rid of the new material, choose OK and watch your document revert back to its original saved form (minus the changes).

Figure 10-14:
The Revert to Saved warning box.

Ami Pro

This will undo all the changes you have made since you last saved. Are you sure?

OK   Cancel

After you save a document, you can't use the Revert to Saved command to get back to an earlier version, so be sure that you are completely happy with the material that you enter into your document before you save it.

You can fight the battle of keeping order among your documents by using the Windows File Manager or the Ami Pro File Manager. Either one helps you move files from place to place and to remove what you don't want any more.

One of the best ways to organize your thinking, though, is by following a logical structure. Ami Pro helps you get organized when you use its Outliner, described in the next chapter.

Part IV
Do You Have To Be So Graphic about It?

"I SAAIID WHAT COMPANY DO YOU REPRESENT?"

In this part...

In this part, you'll master Ami Pro art and frames. You also find out about the Outliner, which isn't exactly about graphics, but does enable you to see your document in many different ways.

Chapter 11

Keeping Things Straight as You Cook with the Outliner

· ·

In This Chapter

▶ How to get going *a la* Outline mode

▶ How to snap heads up into main headings and down into subheadings

▶ How to see only one level, nothing below it

▶ How to squash things into the heading and blast them out of it

▶ How to take an axe to parts of your outline

▶ How to add features to an outline

· ·

The Benefits of an Outliner

Outlines take a bum rap. Nobody likes outlines or the thought of outlining because outlines seem rigid and unimaginative. What was the worst homework assignment you ever had? Outlining an American history chapter in eighth grade? (This was the worst I ever had. Mr. Daly. Roosevelt Jr. High School. It was pure, rote grunt work. It wasn't learning. It was punishment, day after day, week after week.)

Nevertheless, I confess to a fondness for Ami Pro outlining. For people who think that logic is not one of their greatest strengths, the Ami Pro Outliner helps you build in a logical structure without much effort. Illogical people who use an outliner write in a more organized fashion and more coherently than logical people who don't. It's just too hard to do the stuff that an outliner does for you in your own head.

Outlining a Money-Laundering Scheme

Suppose you wanted to write a business plan for a money-laundering company. When your company is into illegal actions, it's important to have everything organized so you can stay a step ahead of the law. (You can follow along with this example or outline your own file; instructions are included to do both.)

To follow the example:

1. **Create a new document using _DEFAULT.STY as the style sheet and save it as LAUNDER.SAM.**

2. **Type the title and the main subheads as Body Text, as follows**

   Business Plan — The Money Laundry, Inc.

   Executive Summary
   Marketing Plan
   Business Plan
   Management Team
   Projected Revenues

Figure 11-1 shows what your file looks like so far.

Scrambling into Outline mode

Some people work in Outline mode most of the time. It's a great way to organize and reorganize your thinking as you go. From the View menu, choose Outline Mode.

A new row of buttons appears on-screen, and a menu choice for Outline appears in the Menu bar. Figure 11-2 shows the new mode with its different icons.

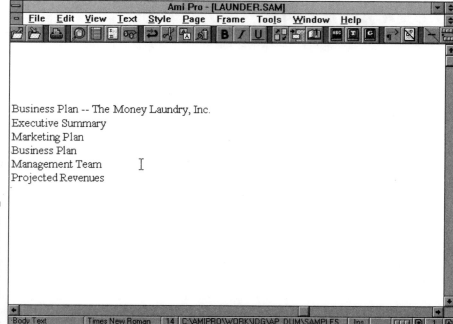

Figure 11-1:
Title and
main
subheads
for your
outline
document.

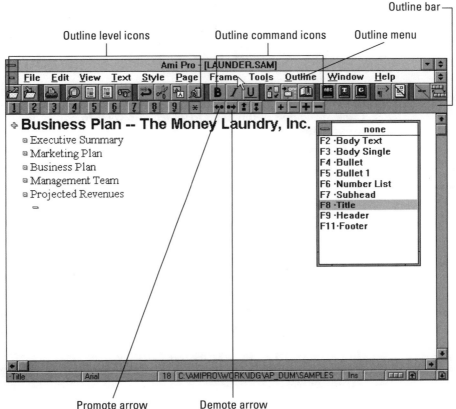

Outline bar

Outline level icons   Outline command icons   Outline menu

Promote arrow   Demote arrow

Figure 11-2:
Placing your
file in
Outline
mode.

Sprouting some main heads

You can readily use the outline gadgets at the top of the screen to transform the bland-looking text in Figure 11-1 into an outline.

1. **Display the Styles box by clicking <u>V</u>iew, Show Styles <u>B</u>ox.**

2. **Put the cursor anywhere on the first level of text and click the left arrow (called the *promote arrow*) in the group of outline command icons shown in the margin.**

   You also can use Alt+left arrow to do this.

   In this example, put the cursor on the first line, *Business Plan,* and click the promote arrow. The line changes to Title style, and a plus sign appears next to it. It is now an outline level — level 1.

3. **Select the second level text and click the *demote* arrow, shown in the margin.**

   You also can use Alt+right arrow to do this.

In this example, select the remaining five lines of text and click the demote arrow. Figure 11-3 shows the outline with two levels of headings.

Sprouting some subheads

You can type new paragraphs into the outline as well.

1. **Click at the end of the head to which you want to add subheads and press Enter.**

   In this example, click at the end of *Marketing Plan* and press Enter.

2. **Click the demote arrow.**

3. **Type the subheads you desire.**

   In this example you can type the subheads shown in Figure 11-4 (pressing Enter at the end of each line).

4. **Repeat Steps 1-3 to add subheads to any other headings.**

   Figure 11-4 shows the outline in this example.

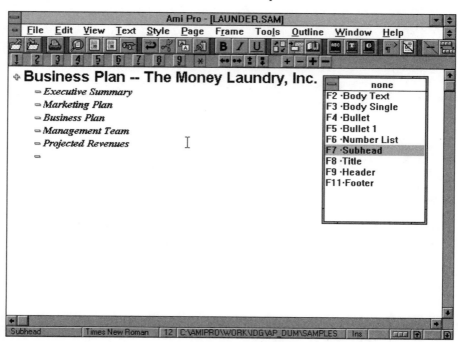

Figure 11-3:
The outline with two levels of headings.

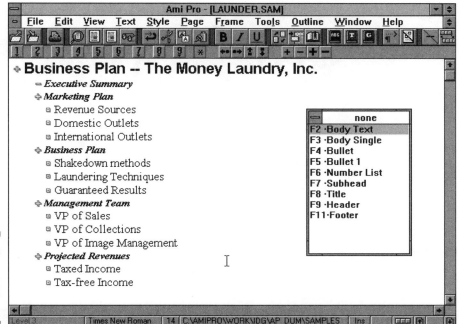

Figure 11-4:
A completed outline with additional subheads.

Making Some Levels Appear, Others Disappear

After completing your outline, you'll probably need to change it several times. Of course, no major undertaking is going to go straight from the blueprint to final production. There's likely to be many suggestions and changes in the plan.

Seeing only certain levels

You can use the outline level icons to see certain levels of the outline and no more. To implode the outline so you see only certain levels of text, you simply click the corresponding number in the Outline menu bar. The outline implodes into itself (known in the trade as *collapsing*, much like the universe falling into a black hole in space).

For example, if you were to click the number 1 button, you would see only the top level heads. Figure 11-5 shows what you'd see in this example.

Outline level 1 button

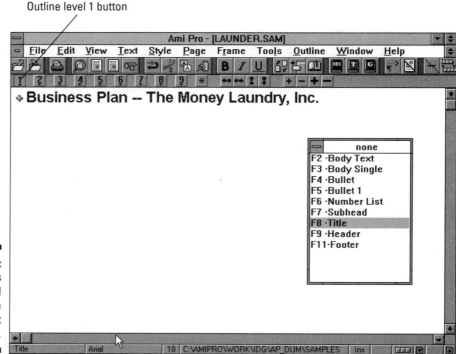

Figure 11-5:
All levels
burrow and
hide inside
the first
level.

If you were to click the number 2 button, as another example, you would see second and first level heads (see Figure 11-6). Note that the higher levels always appear as well.

Click the star button to display all the outline levels.

Deciphering the outline hieroglyphics

You may notice that there are little plus and minus signs and boxes next to various levels. The plus and minus signs indicate headings. Some text has only a *box button* next to it, which means that it does not have any outline level; it's just plain text.

If a head has a plus sign, it has other levels inside itself. You can think of it as being pregnant, I suppose. If it has a minus sign, it's got nothing more to share. What you see is all there is.

If the plus button is filled, the head has subheads and more text under the subheads. If the plus button is not filled, the subheads have no additional text.

You can even double-click these terse graphics to see what's in them. If you double-click a plus sign that's showing its subheads, the subheads will collapse into the heading and the heading will turn green. If you double-click a filled plus, it displays all headings and text.

Star button

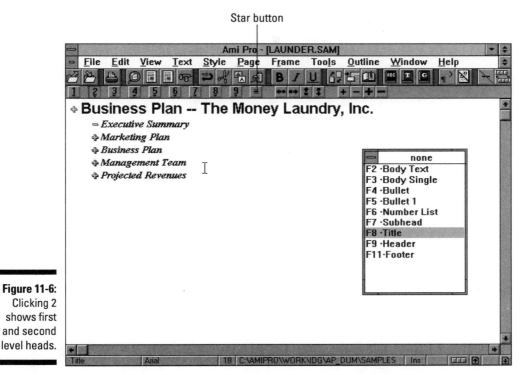

Figure 11-6:
Clicking 2
shows first
and second
level heads.

Scrunching and Unscrunching the Topics

You can use the plus and minus signs on the outline bar to expand and contract parts of the outline. Notice that there are two types of plus and minus signs in the outline bar at the top of the screen — a fat plus and minus and a skinny plus and minus. When you click the fatter of the two plus signs, it explodes all the text under the selected head for you to view, whereas the skinny plus sign explodes only one heading at a time. The fat minus sign, consequentially, implodes all text under the selected head when clicked; the skinny minus sign implodes only the next heading. Figure 11-7 shows these buttons.

To absorb all subheads and text using the fat minus sign, for example, you put the cursor on the highest level head and click the fat minus sign. The subhead sucks all other subheads into itself. Figure 11-7 shows what happens to the chapter example when you do this.

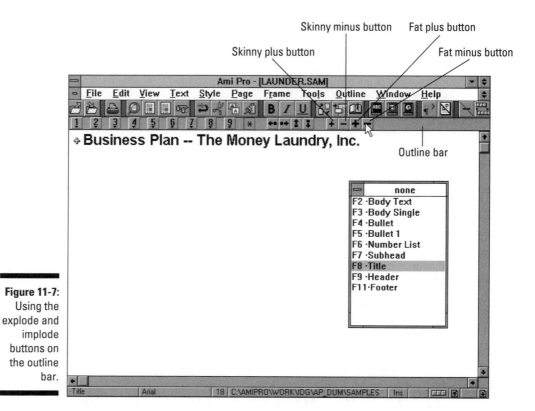

Figure 11-7:
Using the explode and implode buttons on the outline bar.

With everything contracted into the top head, you can display additional heads one level at a time. For example, if you were to click the skinny plus sign, the next level heads would emerge. Figure 11-8 shows this phenomenon with the chapter example.

Sliding Topics Up and Down

One of the purposes of an outline is so that you can move pieces of your document around with ease.

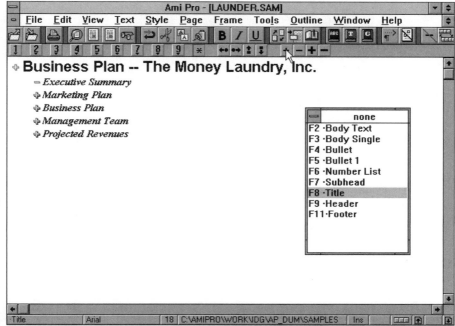

Figure 11-8:
Click the skinny plus sign to bring out one level at a time.

Using the buttons

Suppose, in the chapter example, that one of the higher-ups in your organization insisted that the business plan was more important to investors than the marketing plan. You can move a level head down (in the example, the *Marketing Plan*) by following these instructions:

1. **Double-click the plus sign next to the heads involved in the move to tuck all their heads inside them.**

    In this example, double-click the *Marketing Plan* plus sign and the *Business Plan* plus sign.

2. **With the cursor anywhere in the head you want to move, click the up arrow to move the section up a slot or click the down arrow to move it down a slot.**

    In this example, clicking the up arrow on *Business Plan* moves that section up a slot, as shown in Figure 11-9.

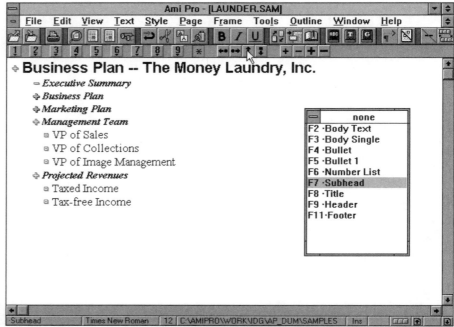

Figure 11-9:
By clicking
the up
arrow, you
can move
sections up
a slot.

3. Click the * command button to display all the levels.

Figure 11-10 shows the rearranged outline for this example.

I'm not sure why the Outliner was designed this way, but if you move a heading up or down when its content is displayed, *just the heading moves.* The content stays where it was. There may be some esoteric advantage to this flaw, but I haven't found it yet. So heed my warning and implode all text under the heading before moving it.

Using the menu commands

I've forgotten to mention, up to now, that you can use the menus to do most of the things you can do with the command buttons (with the exception that you can't designate a certain level of heading to display).

Although I don't use it much, the Outline menu may be your best bet if you are keyboard-oriented. Figure 11-11 shows the Outline menu and its commands.

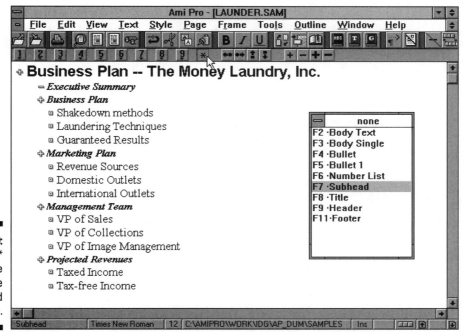

Figure 11-10: Clicking * shows the complete rearranged outline.

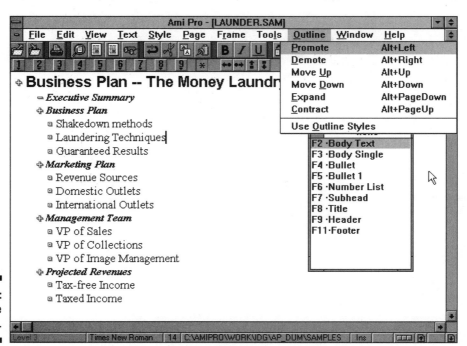

Figure 11-11: The Outline menu.

The only command that should look foreign to you in the <u>O</u>utline menu is the Use <u>O</u>utline Styles command. Clicking this command enables you to use the formatting information in the _OUTLINE.STY style sheet, including the typeface, point, size, and color of the heads. Because Ami Pro does not actually apply these styles to your paragraphs, when you return to another mode, your document uses its original paragraph styles. This command is just a convenient way to change the look of your heading levels until you return to another mode.

Notice that there are keyboard combinations for all the commands on the menu. Use the method you find is easiest for you.

Chopping Off Parts

Deleting sections in the outline isn't much different than deleting text anywhere else. You simply select text and delete it. To delete a section, follow these simple steps:

1. **Click and drag the symbol next to the section to highlight the whole section.**

    Figure 11-12 shows how I highlighted the *Management Team* section.

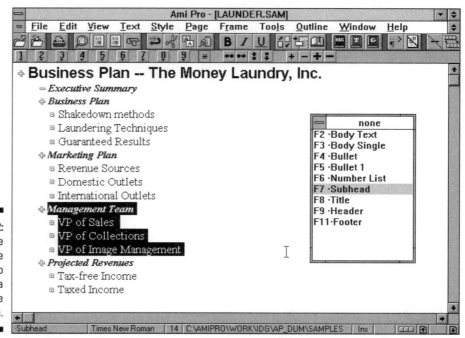

Figure 11-12: Click the outline symbol to select a whole section.

2. Press Delete.

The offending text disappears into the spiritual world. (You can Undo it, though.)

If you implode all the headings into a higher heading before pressing Delete, you can delete all the headings at once.

Be careful when deleting single words at the end of a line in a collapsed heading. You may accidentally delete the headings that follow. If you double-click the words to select them and then press Delete, you might just delete all the subheads as well. I've never seen this little foible documented anywhere, but it has caused me many a nervous start (and occasional rewriting). To avoid it, don't double-click to select the word at the end of a line. Select the word by clicking and dragging over the word. Or, even better, place the cursor after the word and press Ctrl+Backspace to delete the word from right to left.

Creating the Final Outline

When you print your outline, it doesn't look the way it does in Outline mode.

Switching to Layout mode

To see what your outline really looks like, switch to Layout mode by choosing Layout mode from the View menu. Figure 11-13 shows the laundering outline in Layout mode using the __OUTLIN1.STY style sheet. The appearance of the plan depends entirely on the style sheet that you're using.

Any style sheet will look about like any other in Outline mode, but the appearance varies after you get back to Layout mode (the mode that shows what the document will look like when printed).

Adding style to the outline

You can change the look of the numbering, the levels of the headings, and a few other things for your outline styles with the Style menu. You simply click the Outline Styles command from the Style menu. The Outline Styles dialog box, shown in Figure 11-14, opens.

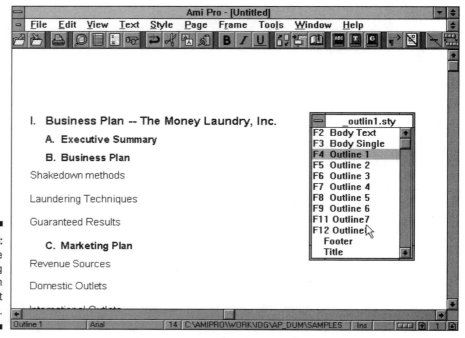

Figure 11-13:
The
Laundering
outline in
Layout
mode.

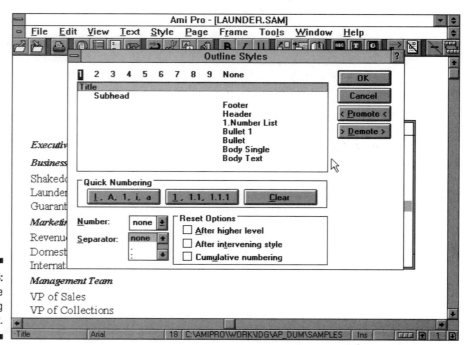

Figure 11-14:
The Outline
Styles dialog
box.

You can use this dialog box to modify the appearance of your outline in a way quite similar to the way you use the Modify Styles dialog box to change the appearance of paragraphs. If you find yourself outlining often, you may want to press F1 and do some serious cohabitating with this box and its possibilities. The Quick Numbering buttons are the ones I use the most. Figure 11-15 shows the sample document when you click a Quick Numbering button and then click OK.

There are no spaces after the numbers in most of the cases (such as *A.Executive Summary*), which I think looks like heck. Nevertheless, the numbering in itself is a good thing.

Outlining, in my usually jaded view, is a sweetheart capability. It helps a dumb person look smart and makes a smart person too stubborn to use it look dumb. It's enough to help you get over outline phobia. Nah. I guess it's not that good. But give it a try anyway — you might end up depending on it.

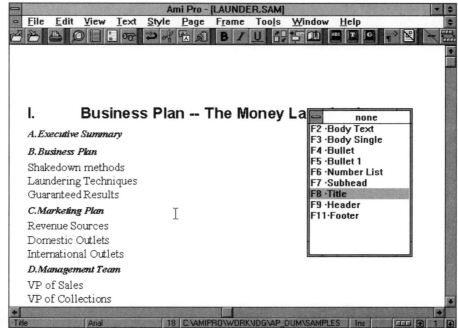

Figure 11-15:
The
document
with
numbering.

Chapter 12

Frames: Cooking on Extra Burners

• •

In This Chapter

▶ What it takes to make a frame (not much)

▶ Why you might want to make one (usually, you don't)

▶ How to suck a picture into a frame

▶ How to order the frame around, all over the page

▶ How to stretch and shrink the frame

▶ How to stretch and shrink the picture inside the frame

• •

What Is a Frame?

Although style sheets and SmartIcons were the first two great inspirations of Ami Pro, *frames* are right up there with them. Frames make actions that were close to impossible before so easy now that even a computer-illiterate monkey has a shot at doing them. A *frame,* in essence, is a rectangular-shaped area on-screen that you'll create and use to arrange text or graphics.

You probably won't need frames every day or every year. Nevertheless, I think they are a nice thing. They're easy to use, and they open the world of graphics and page layout to you and your word processor. With frames, you can:

✔ Place text in a box in the middle of the main text

✔ Place a picture in the box and have text wrap around the box

✔ Edit the picture or text within the box

✔ Move the box around to different places, object intact

Framing Your Frame

The mouse is the easiest way to create a frame and I hesitate to mention that you also can create the frame with the menus and specify the exact size and position of the frame. If you're doing government work and have really exact specifications, maybe you need the menus. The only way I make one, though, is with the mouse.

Before you create the frame, get a document to work with and choose a set of SmartIcons.

Preparing your screen for frames

Follow these steps to prepare your document for a frame:

1. **Open the document to which you want to add a frame.**

   In this example, I use TRUCK.SAM from Chapter 5.

2. **Switch to the Graphics SmartIcons (click the *change SmartIcon set* button in the Status bar and choose Graphics).**

   You'll need this different set of icons for all the cool actions you take to create your frame.

Being a frame maker

Your file of choice is open and, you have switched to the Graphics SmartIcon set— you are ready to create your first frame:

1. **Be sure you're in Layout mode by clicking View, Layout Mode.**

 2. **Click the Add a frame SmartIcon (shown in the margin).**

   When you move the pointer into the document, the pointer turns into the shape of a frame with a little arrow at one corner. (This arrow indicates which corner of the frame is anchored to the document when you click and drag it to create your box.) Figure 12-1 shows the pointer as a frame.

 Didn't your pointer turn into a frame? You *have* to be in Layout mode to work with frames. Click the View menu and make sure Layout Mode is checked. You would hope that Ami Pro would tell you that when you clicked the frame icon from one of the other modes, but noooo, it just sadistically lets you spin slowly in the wind.

3. **Move the icon to where you want the picture to start.**

   In this case, place the icon to the left of the page (but not into the margin).

4. **Hold down the left mouse button to anchor the frame and, without releasing the mouse button, drag the frame down and to the right until it's the size and shape you want. Then release.**

   Any shape is OK because you can always size it. Don't worry, the text will move out of the way of the frame.

Frame pointer

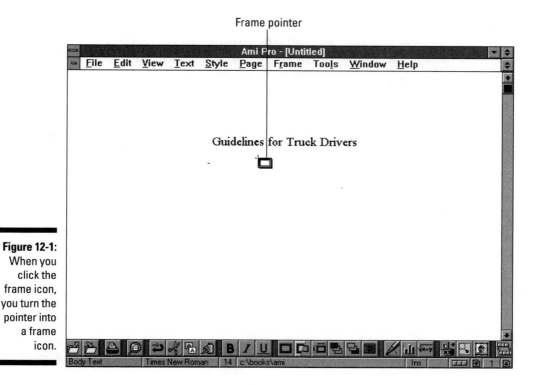

Figure 12-1:
When you
click the
frame icon,
you turn the
pointer into
a frame
icon.

Figure 12-2 shows what you should get when you click and drag the frame pointer. The tiny black squares you see around the box are called *handles,* and you click and drag these to change the size of the box.

That's it. *Creating a frame* sounds like something a novice would never do, but nerds who go around bragging about their frames all the time are just perpetrating a big ruse.

Unselecting the frame

When you first create the frame, it's *selected,* which means, as I wrote about in Chapter 2, that Ami Pro knows that you want to work with it and not with something else. The handles you see in Figure 12-2 appear only when the frame is selected. Click anywhere outside the frame to unselect it. The handles on the frame disappear, as shown in Figure 12-3.

Handles

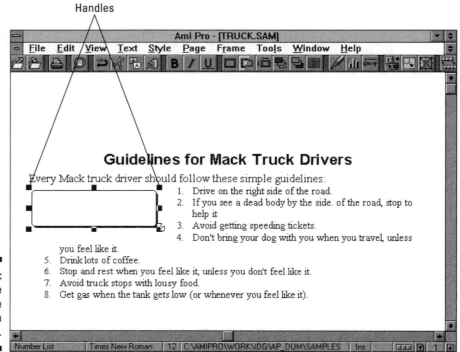

Figure 12-2:
Drag the
frame to the
shape you
want.

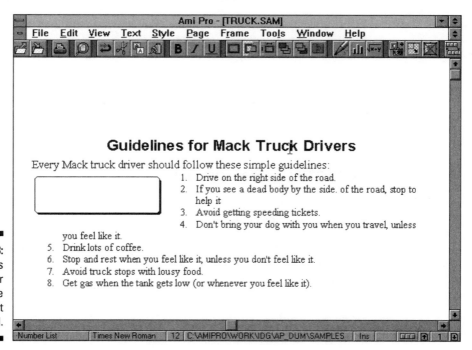

Figure 12-3:
The handles
disappear
when the
frame is not
selected.

Adding a Picture to the Frame

You can put drawings, tables, equations, words, even your little brother in a frame. To learn how to add text to a frame, see Chapter 13, which discusses drawing and charting. Adding a picture to a document brightens it up considerably and it's not as hard as you might think. The next sections teach you how to do it.

Selecting a frame

Selecting a frame, as you might suppose, is pretty much like selecting a person whom you want to borrow a tissue from; you tap him or her on the shoulder and ask:

1. Move the pointer over the frame until the pointer takes the shape of an arrow (Figure 12-4).

2. Click the frame once.

The frame again becomes selected, as it was in Figure 12-2.

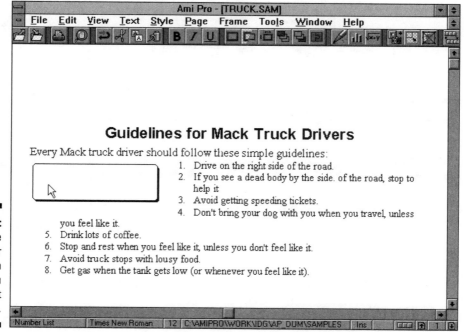

Figure 12-4:
When the pointer becomes an arrow, you can select the frame.

Sucking in the picture

Ami Pro comes with a neat collection of pictures (called *clip art*). The clip art that comes with Ami Pro is sufficient for various overheads, school papers for the kids, birthday invitations, and whatever. To add one of these pictures to your frame:

1. **Select the frame.**

2. **Click Import Picture in the File menu.**

   The Import Picture dialog box opens, as shown in Figure 12-5.

Figure 12-5:
The Import
Picture
dialog box.

3. **In the Files box, click one of the files ending with the extension .SDW.**

   In this example, scroll down and click BIGTRUCK.SDW. (The File type box should have Ami Draw selected.)

4. **Choose OK.**

   The picture of the truck appears inside the frame. Figure 12-6 shows BIGTRUCK.SDW inside the frame.

5. **Click outside the frame to unselect it.**

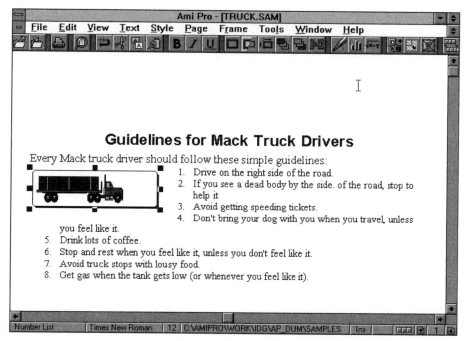

Figure 12-6:
Ami Pro
sucks the
picture into
the frame.

The clip art files are named about as descriptively as DOS filenames can be (Can you guess what's in 35FLOPPY.SDW? How about 3BOXES.SDW?), but you almost always have to see a picture to decide whether it's the one you want. The *Ami Pro User's Guide* has little miniatures of all its symbols, starting on page 559. These little pictures, buried in the back of the giant tome, are the only things that bring me back to the documentation from time to time. It's easier to use the book than open all these files.

Dragging the Frame Around

Once you get the frame on the page, it's yours. It'll follow you anywhere. That's real useful, because many times you'll want to try your picture in about 50 different places before you decide where you really want it.

You can move your frame anywhere in the document by clicking anywhere on it and dragging it (keep mouse button clicked) to its new location. The text in your document automatically *wraps* (folds itself) around the frame! Now this is hot stuff in word processing circles. It's not that easy for the computer to do. Figure 12-7 shows how I moved the truck to the middle of my document.

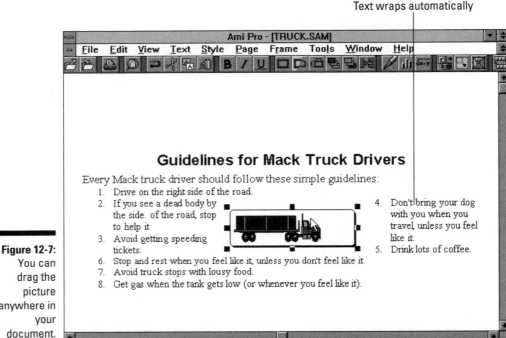

Figure 12-7:
You can
drag the
picture
anywhere in
your
document.

Distorting and Contorting the Frame

The nice people who make the programs that run with Windows (in this case, Lotus) try to set commands and actions to be compatible with Microsoft Windows. That way, you have to learn only one way to do something. Ami Pro frames follow this rule pretty well. You stretch them the same way you stretch any Window window — drag a side handle in and out to move that side; drag a corner handle in and out to move two sides at once.

Figure 12-8 shows what happens when I click the middle bottom handle and drag the frame down. When I release the mouse button, the frame will be the size of the dotted area. I have enlarged it.

Weird, wrapped, warped words

Ami Pro is smart about wrapping text, but not as smart as you are. After moving your picture, Ami Pro will sometimes split words in weird places, as shown in the following figure. So, when you move a frame around, eyeball your text closely to ensure that the words are splitting in an understandable manner.

Bad text breaks

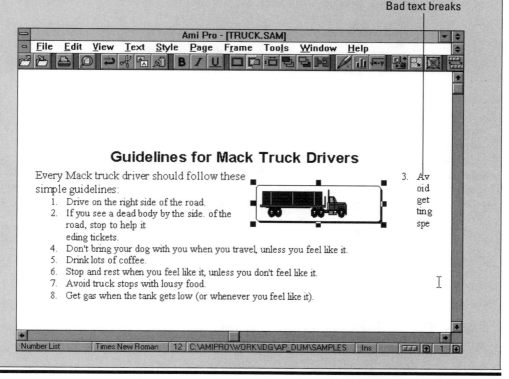

When the pointer becomes a two-headed arrow, it's ready for you to click and resize the frame.

Figure 12-9 shows what happens when I click and drag the lower right corner handle of the frame towards the middle of the frame. Because I'm dragging the corner handle, two sides of the frame move at once. Because I'm dragging the handle back toward the frame, the frame becomes smaller.

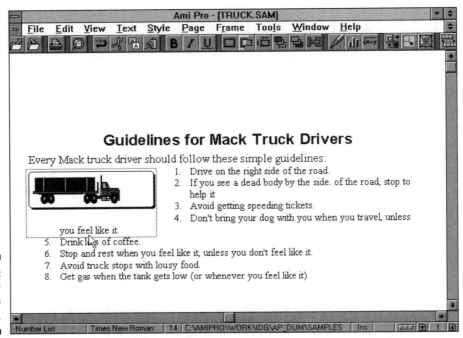

Figure 12-8:
Drag a side
in or out to
move it.

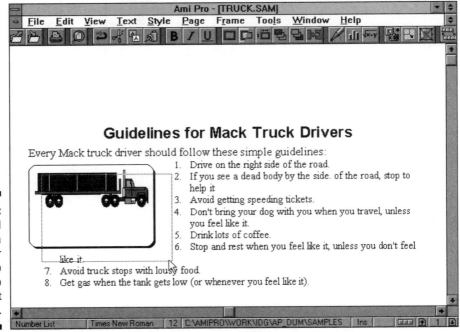

Figure 12-9:
Click and
drag a
corner
handle to
change two
sides at
once.

Doing Stuff to the Picture inside the Frame

The stuff inside the frame enjoys a universe of its own. You can change the size of the picture itself, rotate it, and stuff like that.

Dragging around the picture inside the frame

An admittedly crude way to *crop* a picture (a fancy design term for cutting part of it off) is to move the picture so that only part of it shows in the frame. To do fancy things to the object within the frame, click twice inside the frame. Your pointer is now active inside the frame.

The handles turn gray, but they don't disappear (see Figure 12-10). A new row of icons appears at the top of the screen — drawing icons. I'll discuss them in detail in Chapter 13. For now, just realize that they are used specifically to edit the picture in some way.

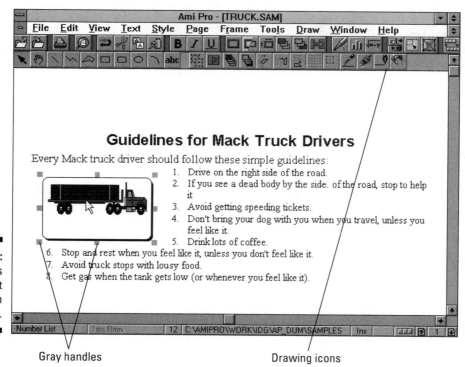

Figure 12-10: Gray handles mean that you are in Draw mode.

Gray handles

Drawing icons

You can click and drag the object to move it anywhere within the frame. Figure 12-11 shows what happens when I drag the truck so the back half disappears behind the side of the frame.

Back half
of truck is hiding.

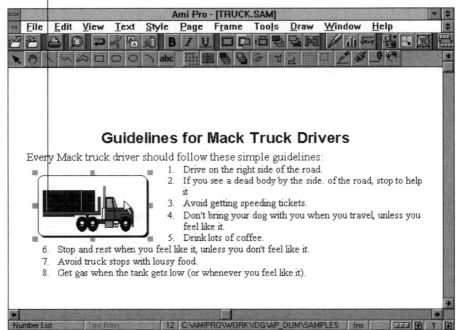

Figure 12-11:
You can
move a
picture
around
inside the
frame.

Selecting and demolishing the picture

You can move the picture without selecting it, because Ami Pro knows you want to work with it when you point to it. To delete it, though, you have to first select it, so Ami Pro knows what to delete. With the gray handles still showing on the frame, click once on the truck to select it. Figure 12-12 shows that additional black handles appear around the object, within the frame.

Once you've selected the picture, you delete it the way you delete anything else, by pressing Delete.

Once you delete a picture from inside a frame, you can't import another picture into it. This is a very maddening problem. I mean, anybody's likely to change his or her mind about a picture and want to use a different one. When you go to add a new picture to your frame, wham, Import Picture is grayed on the File menu. You actually have to delete the frame and make a new one to import another picture. It's an *Ami Pro foible,* a dumb Ami Pro foible. I apologize for it, even though, hey, they never asked me, and I have nothing to do with its being that way.

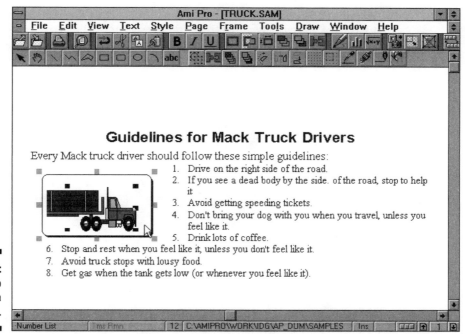

Figure 12-12:
Click once to
select a
picture.

You can always click the Undo icon (or choose Edit, Undo) to get the picture back. This is one of those actions that works with the Undo command.

Ami Pro offers what it calls *image processing,* where you "adjust the gray scales" of an image. But the only images you can use this feature on are .TIFF images, which you scan into Ami Pro using a scanner. Because you, dear reader, and I have no such images in common, I don't run through any examples of image processing in this book.

Remodeling the Frame

"What," you might wonder, "can I do with my frame once I've created it? A frame is a frame is a frame. It's a square box."

Well, apparently somebody put some thought into this question and realized that if frames were really going to be useful to people, they have to be capable of change and modification. Follow these steps to see how to modify your frame:

1. **Click the frame to select it.**

   The handles should appear, as always.

2. **With the frame selected, right-click the mouse to open the Modify Frame Layout dialog box (shown in Figure 12-13).**

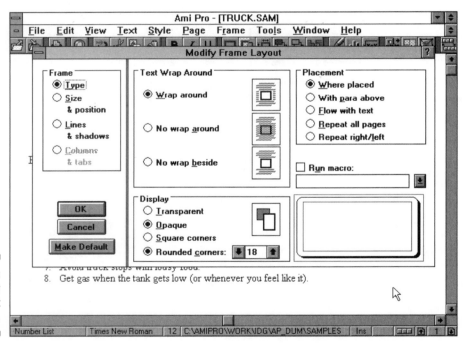

Figure 12-13: The Modify Frame Layout dialog box.

You use this box the same way you use the Modify Style dialog box (from Chapter 4). Clicking a choice in the Frame area changes the options in the rest of the dialog box.

You have many different options in the Modify Frame Layout dialog box. From it, you can create some professional-looking frames. This box includes controls to adjust:

- ✔ The thickness of lines
- ✔ The placement of lines
- ✔ The exact size and positioning of the frame
- ✔ Whether the frame has rounded or square corners
- ✔ Whether the frame has shading
- ✔ Whether the text wraps

And many more options! If you were to click Lines & Shadows in the Frame box, for example, you get the options shown in Figure 12-14. (Notice that in the lower right corner of this dialog box is another *idiot box* that shows you what your change would do.)

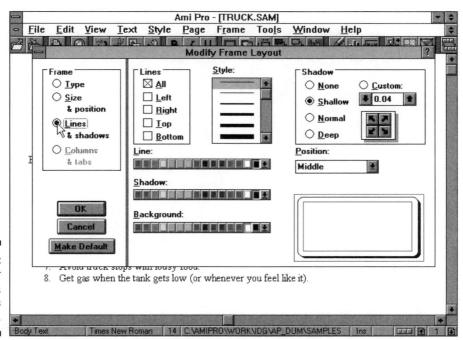

Figure 12-14: Choices for the Lines & shadows option.

The things you do easily with frames are hard to do otherwise. It is hard to put text in a box in the middle of the text you already have. It is hard to move the box around if you can get it there in the first place. Frames, though, are a good thing for beginners. You just point, click, drag, and look like you know something when you think you don't.

Two things you can do inside frames are draw and create charts. You probably won't have much need to draw inside frames, unless you are an artist, but charts are useful and easy to make. Chapter 13 shows you how to draw and create charts in your frames.

The 5th Wave

By Rich Tennant

"WELL, HECK — I CAN'T STEP AWAY FROM THE COMPUTER FOR A SECOND WITHOUT YOU BIRDS GETTIN' ALL RUFFLED ABOUT IT."

Chapter 13
Ami Pro Art:
Decorating the Cake

- -

In This Chapter
▶ Why you might want to chart but wouldn't want to draw
▶ How to start a chart
▶ How to line up your data in a bar chart
▶ How to put a gun on the page
▶ How to dress up what you drew

- -

The Reality of Drawing and Charting

Drawing is hard, painstaking, and dangerous. Even the pros take a long time at it. I once asked a woman who drew symbols for a living how long it took her to draw one of her symbols. I don't remember what she said, but I'll tell you what, it took her at least a few days to draw a single picture.

If it's your job to, oh, run a screw-sorting department or manage a baseball team or sell orange juice or program computers, chances are neither you nor your boss wants to spend a few days sketching a little drawing to embellish some report or other. No way. (If your boss would like to do so, I've got a few investments that might be of interest.)

Hitting the Charts

Of the two capabilities — charting and drawing — charting is the one that might possibly win a place in your heart. Charts now have a solid place in business. A business plan just doesn't warrant a second look unless it has at least one bar chart in it, preferably four or five, as well as a few pie charts.

Take, for example, the money-laundering company described in Chapter 11. The business plan for that company should have some charts in it so that the investors will reach for their wallets.

Fabricating a sample document

To teach you how to create a chart, I create a document to put the chart into. I created the doucment shown in Figure 13-1 with the _OVERHD4.STY style sheet and named the file CHART1.SAM. If you are following along, type the text in Figure 13-1 into your document.

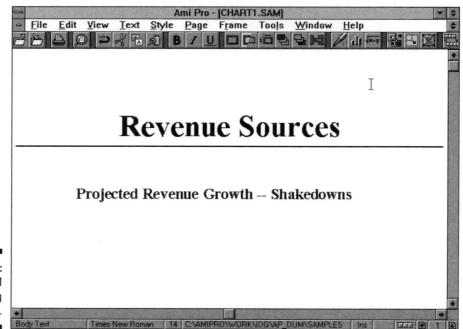

Figure 13-1:
CHART1.SAM
is begging
for a chart.

Pulling the start cord on charting

Before creating a chart, you can switch to the Graphics SmartIcon set by clicking the change SmartIcons set button in the Status bar and choosing *Graphics*.

If you create the frame manually before you start charting, you have greater freedom in moving and resizing the frame.

To create a chart, use the Tools menu and follow these steps:

1. From the Tools menu, choose Charting.

You receive the rather bizarre and discomfiting message (Figure 13-2) that the Clipboard contains no data. I mean, so what? And whoever said the Clipboard should contain some data? I know this chart is about shake-downs in business, but this sounds like a shakedown of its own — "Put some data in the Clipboard, or I'll put a horse's head in your bed." Ami Pro gets all righteous and makes you feel like you made some big mistake when you didn't. You just choose from a menu.

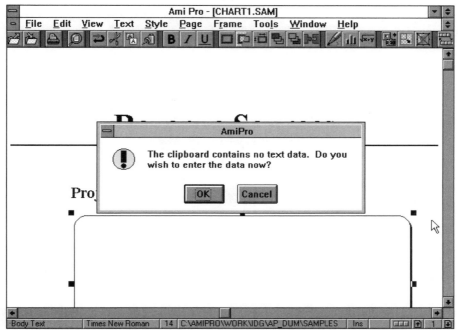

Figure 13-2:
The scary
message
that you
should
ignore.

2. Choose OK.

The Charting Data dialog box opens, as shown in Figure 13-3.

You can put the data for your chart into the Clipboard before you click Charting. The best place to store the data is in a table, though, and you don't find out about tables until Chapter 14. You also can place the data into the Clipboard from another program, such as a spreadsheet like Excel. (I like saying Excel here to tweak the nose of Lotus, which no doubt has the notion that anyone using Lotus Ami Pro uses Lotus 1-2-3.)

3. In the Charting Data dialog box, type the words (or letters) that you want to appear in the x-axis.

For example, assume you were creating a simple chart that showed how much candy you ate during the months of July through September. Here, you would type **Jul Aug Sep.** In this example, I typed **Q1 Q2 Q3 Q4.** Be careful to press the Spacebar between each letter or word, and don't press Enter at the end of the line.

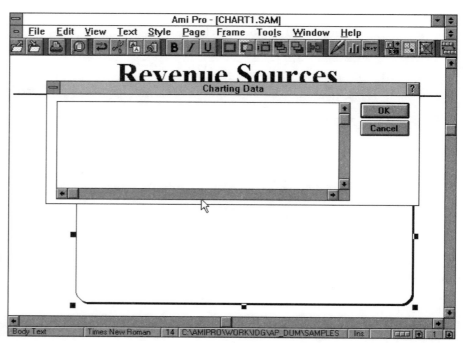

Figure 13-3:
The Charting
Data dialog
box.

4. Click at the start of the second line, type the numerical amount that the y-axis will display.

For the candy example, you would type **5 6 8** if you ate 5, 6, and 8 pounds of candy, respectively. In this example, I typed **5 13 22 39**.

Figure 13-4 shows the Charting Data dialog box with the data I typed in it. It's ugly, I know, and the data doesn't even line up right. It'll work, though.

5. Click OK to accept your data.

When you click OK, a Charting dialog box that's worthy of Ami Pro opens, as shown in Figure 13-5. The Chart Type box on the left visualizes the types of charts you can use. The idiot box shows what the chart will look like for each type.

6. Click the icon of the chart type you want to use.

In this example, I clicked the vertical bar chart icon in the top left.

7. Click OK.

Ami Pro creates the chart, and a handsome devil it is, too, worthy of any boardroom presentation. Figure 13-6 shows the chart I created.

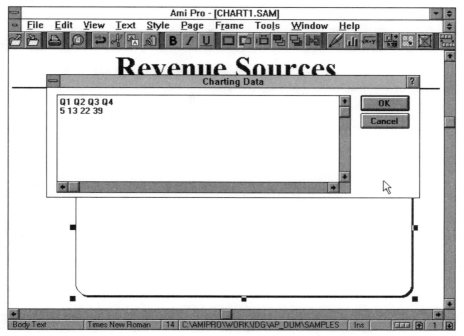

Figure 13-4:
The completed Charting Data dialog box.

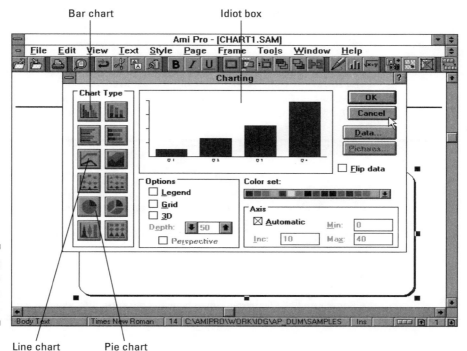

Figure 13-5:
The Charting dialog box.

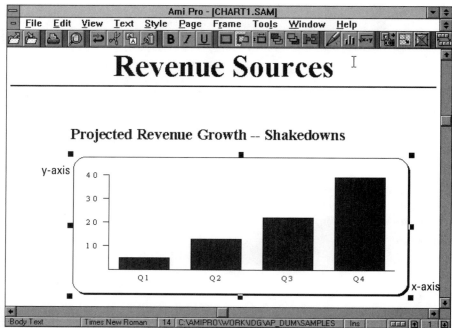

Figure 13-6:
A bar chart
for
projected
shakedowns.

Of course, you can save each chart in a separate document. In fact, you'd want to do that if you were doing a presentation in the boardroom. Simply create a separate overhead for each chart, then choose Charting from the Tools menu.

Use any of the chart types to create a chart that fits your data simply by clicking the chart type icon of your choice. Figure 13-7 shows what my data looks like in a line chart and Figure 13-8 shows the pie chart version, after making a few changes.

Charts defined...

You may be wondering what real differences there are between these different types of charts. Although you may simply take a liking to one chart over another, each chart really does have its own benefits, as listed here:

Chart Type	*Benefit(s)*
Pie charts	Compare proportions to the whole
Line charts	Show trends over time
Bar charts	Show trends over time and relationships between each element

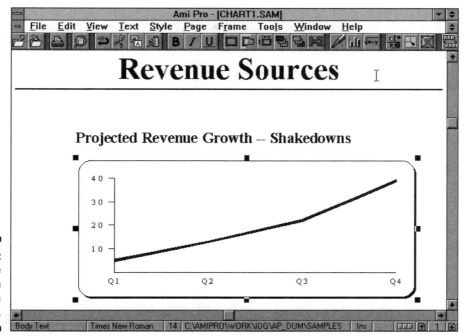

Figure 13-7:
The
shakedown
data in a
line chart.

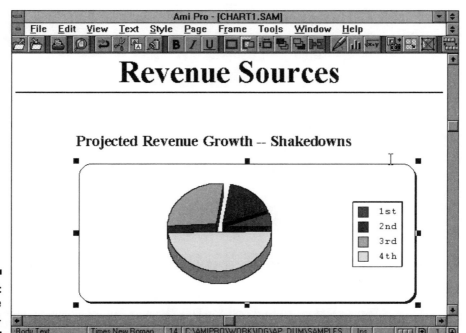

Figure 13-8:
The pie
chart.

TIP

To delete a chart frame, simply select it and press Delete.

Putting a Picture on the Page

It's so much fun to fool around with illustrating tools that I can't usually bear to leave the chart just looking good. I like to try to make it better. One way to enhance your chart is to import a picture into the file:

1. **In the View menu, choose Full Page.**

2. **Put a frame below the chart, where you can put in your picture.**

   Chapter 12 tells you all about putting in frames.

3. **From the File menu, choose Import Picture.**

4. **In the Import Picture dialog box (Figure 13-9), double-click the file of your choice.**

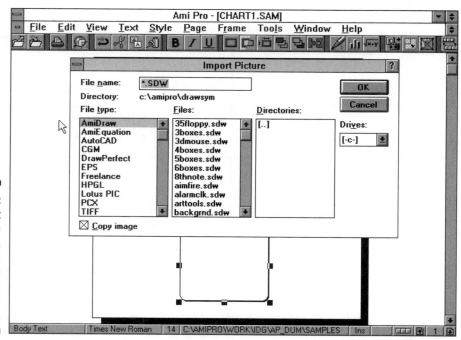

Figure 13-9:
The Import Picture dialog box, where you choose the picture you want to import.

In this example, I choose AIMFIRE.SDW. A sniper appears in a box on the page. Figure 13-10 shows the Full Page view after clicking outside the sniper box.

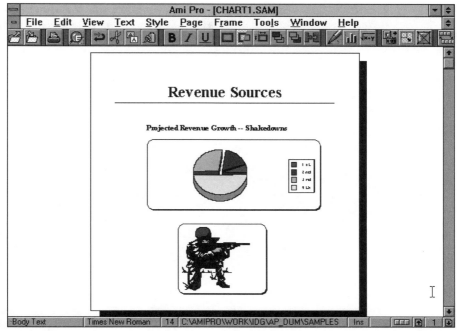

Figure 13-10:
Full Page
view with
the sniper
picture.

Trying Out the Luck of the Draw

Charting, as I mentioned, is a pretty standard business activity. I mean, you can get drenched under a deluge of pie charts, bar charts, pert charts, and heaven only knows what other lines, bars, and squiggles displayed across the page. Even if just out of self defense, every novice should know something about charting.

Drawing, though, isn't in the same category. You really don't have to know much about it in the average business environment. You can use one or two elements to enhance the charts you make, but that's about it. Serious drawing isn't even for nerds. It's for artsy types, I suppose. The rest of us might use drawing to add a little text here and there, maybe a few arrows, and that's it.

Drawing out of the void

You kick in drawing in the same way you kick in about anything else — choose it from the menu. Suppose you wanted to add text to your chart.

Although it's not essential to using the drawing capabilities, I switched back to Custom view because it made the figures in this chapter look a little better.

In order to use the drawing capabilities, you must select a frame. You don't have to use a frame with a chart in it. You can create an empty frame. If you don't select a frame before you start, Ami creates one for you (which is much better than those times that it just sits there or prances out some obnoxious warning box or something).

Once your frame is selected, choose Drawing from the Tools menu. A bar of drawing icons appears at the top of the screen, as shown in Figure 13-11.

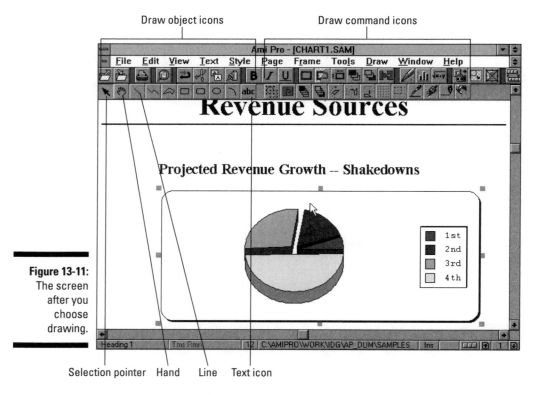

Draw object icons   Draw command icons

Figure 13-11:
The screen
after you
choose
drawing.

Selection pointer   Hand   Line   Text icon

Using the drawing icons

The icons on the left side of the toolbar are called the *drawing object* icons. With these new icons, you can add an infinite amount of features to your chart. The icons on the right side of the toolbar are called *drawing command* icons. They help you fiddle around, waste time, and get really frustrated trying to make the drawing look decent. In the following example, I use both sets of these icons to add and modify lines and text to my pie chart.

Be careful about clicking outside the frame that you're working in as you draw. If you click outside the frame, the drawing toolbar disappears. You have to select the frame again to invoke the toolbar. This accidental click can really slow you down if you are working on a slow machine.

To add a line to your chart:

1. **Click the line icon (shown in the margin).**

2. **Click (in the chart) where you want the line to begin, and, keeping the button pressed down, drag the cursor to where you want the line to end. When the line is exactly where you want it, release the button.**

   Figure 13-12 shows my line added to the pie chart.

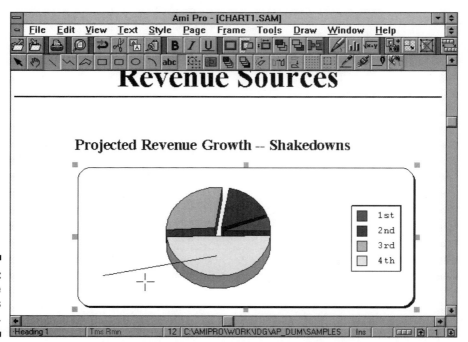

Figure 13-12:
Adding a line
to a chart is
simple.

Suppose you wanted to have the line look a little better than the skinny little nothing in the figure. You can modify the rule to look many different ways. To do so:

1. **Click the selection pointer icon (shown in the margin).**

2. **Click the line to select it.**

   Handles appear at the ends of the lines to show that you've successfully picked it out of the crowd.

In other parts of Ami Pro, the pointer is usually smart enough to change shapes depending on your actions. That fact sets you up to look stupid in drawing, where instead of changing shapes, the pointer remains stuck in a given shape until you tell it to change. You can slide the cursor on top of the line you want to select, but the pointer just won't turn into a pointer until you click the *selection pointer icon* in the toolbar. No doubt the marketing folks say that's a feature, that you'd be messing up the drawing otherwise. Right.

3. From the Draw menu (Figure 13-13), choose the Line Style command.

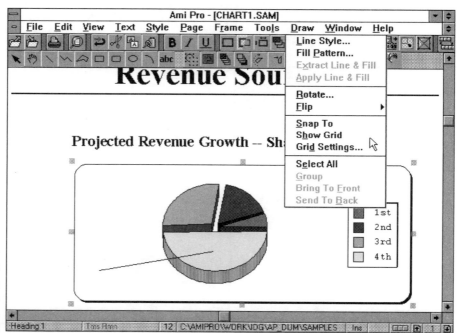

Figure 13-13:
The surprise
Draw menu.

The Line Styles dialog box appears (shown in Figure 13-14).

4. In the Line Styles dialog box, click the line of your choice and choose an ending from the radio buttons, if you want. Notice there is an idiot box that shows you what your line will look like.

5. Choose OK.

The line should take on the characteristics you requested. Figure 13-15 shows my preferences for the pie chart.

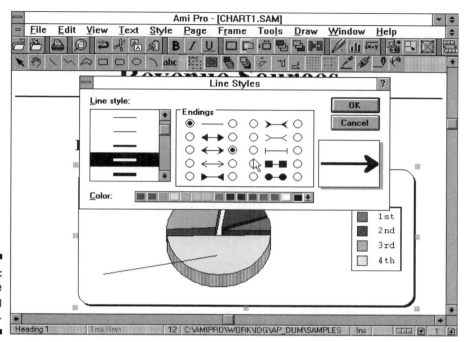

Figure 13-14:
The Line
Styles dialog
box.

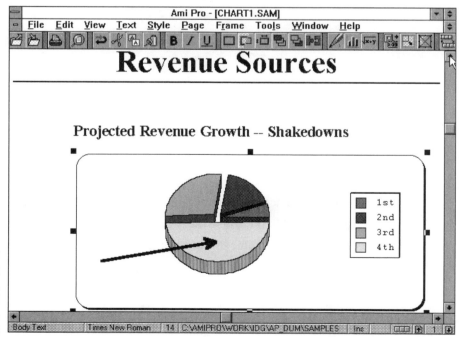

Figure 13-15:
My fat,
remodeled
arrow.

Now you probably want to add text to that arrow. How else will people know what the arrow signifies? To add text to your chart:

1. **Click the text icon (shown in the margin).**

2. **Click once where you want the text to begin.**

3. **Type the text exactly as you want it to appear, including all hard returns.**

Figure 13-16 shows my drawing with the line and the text.

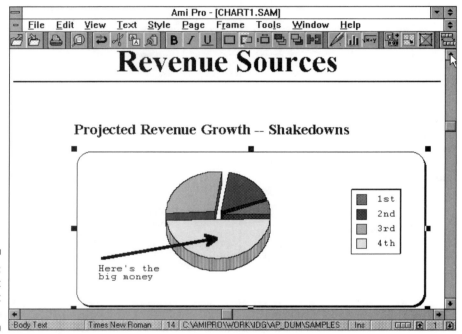

Figure 13-16:
Adding text
with the text
icon.

You can change the text to appear in any font or point size you desire, just as you can in a document. Follow these simple steps:

1. **Choose the selection pointer icon (shown in the margin).**

2. **Click the text in the frame that you want to modify to select it.**

3. **Click the font or point size area on the Status bar to change the text as you desire.**

You can make these changes also from the menus. Figure 13-17 shows how I changed the text in my chart with the Status bar options.

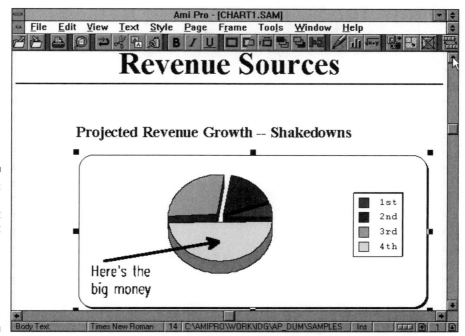

Figure 13-17:
You can
select
drawing text
and change
it with the
regular Ami
Pro menus
and Status
bar.

You can spend hours with little niggling changes and adjustments in the drawing program. The darn stuff never quite comes out right the first time, and you can keep going at it from more and more directions, like sticking your tongue into a sore tooth. But for the most part, it's just not worth it. Make a little enhancement now and then with drawing, if you dare, but then put it behind you as fast as you can. It's the best way. Trust me.

Tables, on the other hand, may well prove to be a special capability that you turn to frequently. I talk about them in the next chapter.

Part V

Avoid This Part: Stuff You Don't Want to Know

"OH YEAH, AND TRY NOT TO ENTER THE WRONG PASSWORD."

In this part...

Wouldn't it have been nice, when forced to create a huge table of all the states and their flowers in grade school Geography, if you could have had an automatic table maker? Ami Pro has one, as you see here.

"Also," your teacher says, "prepare footnotes and a Table of Contents for your project, with accurate page references. And you know I'm going to make sure those page numbers are correct." Ami Pro has tools for these functions, too.

"And turn in your rough draft along with your final copy, so I can see that you did the work." Ami Pro enables you to compare two versions of an essay.

It might have been nice to have had all these things in grade school, huh? Well, now they are at your fingertips.

Chapter 14
Setting the Table

· ·

In This Chapter

▶ How to make a table with some simple tools

▶ How to enter information into a table

▶ How to move around in a table

▶ How to add and remove rows and columns to a table

▶ How to unite small cells into a big cell

▶ How to dress up a table

▶ How to reorganize a table

▶ How to add up figures in a table

· ·

*I*f information always came in lines of text across the page, life would be much simpler. But information often comes in tables. People who abhor rows and columns often go to great lengths to sidestep tables, even though the information in them often is easier to understand than in regular text. Because it is difficult to construct rows and columns using tab keys, learning how to construct a table is the way to go.

Fashioning a Table

Most people (except for nerds, of course) are intimidated by setting up tables in their documents. If they have to click their mouses more than twice to get a word on the page, they don't want to tackle the project. But tables can be easy and fun to do, and they make your documents look very professional. What a way to impress the boss!

Preparing the table

Before you begin to make a table in your document, be sure that you have some idea of how you want the table to look. It's helpful to know in advance, for example, how many columns you need and what you want to label your columns. The more work you do in advance to prepare your table, the less cleanup work you'll have to do later.

Remember, when working with special items such as tables, it is much easier to access the commands by changing the SmartIcon set. Before setting up your table, click the change SmartIcon set button (in the Status bar) and choose *Tables* (what else?). This way, you have immediate access to the myriad table icons.

A friend of mine is a sociologist who is always accumulating detailed information that cries out to be stored in a table. Believe it or not, she is doing a study on garbage and what garbage says about how we live. (I am restraining myself here — the opportunity for dirty garbage jokes is almost too much to pass up!) The example that you follow in the figures is based on her study of garbage.

To create a table, follow these steps:

1. **Put your cursor where you want the table to appear.**

2. **From the Tools menu, choose Tables or just click the Create a table SmartIcon (shown in the margin).**

   (The Create a table SmartIcon appears in both the Default and the Table icon sets.)

   The Create Table dialog box opens, as you can see in Figure 14-1. Here you can indicate how many rows and columns you want to have. (*Rows* go across the page. *Columns* go down the page — as in Greek temples.) Make whatever changes you feel are necessary to the number of columns and rows you need in your table. (For my example, I accept the default number of five columns and rows.)

   Before you choose OK, you can make some other changes by reviewing the planned layout of the table. You always can change the layout later, but the change is not always as easy as the books tell you it is. You are much better off making whatever changes you want at this point in the setup.

3. **In the Create Table dialog box, click the Layout button.**

   The Modify Table Layout dialog box opens, as shown in Figure 14-2. The recommended width of one inch is a good place to start, but you can experiment with the options, if you want. I explain the options later.

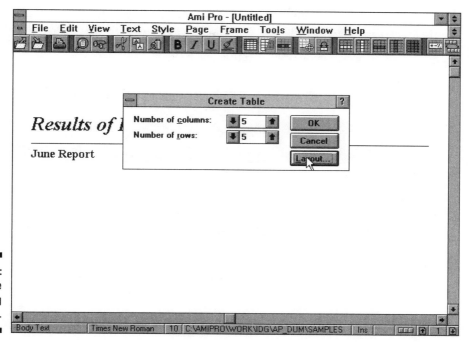

Figure 14-1:
The Create
Table dialog
box.

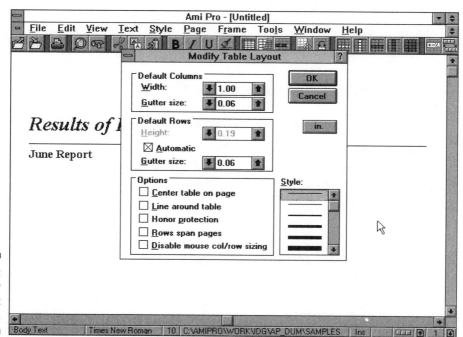

Figure 14-2:
The Modify
Table Layout
dialog box.

For the example table in Figure 14-3, I selected the Center table on page option and the Line around table option. In the Style box, I chose the third line down from the top. To choose the options, simply click whatever options you want and then click OK.

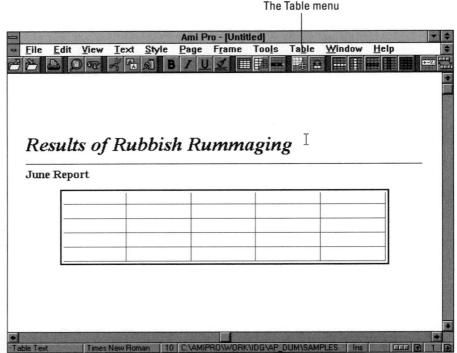

The Table menu

Figure 14-3:
The sample table, before adding any information to it.

4. **In the Modify Table Layout dialog box, choose OK.**

5. **In the Create Table dialog box, choose OK.**

A set of blank rows and columns appears on the page — centered and with a black border, because you selected those options. Also, note that when the cursor is located anywhere in the table, theTable menu appears in the Menu bar, next to the Tools menu.

Moving around inside the table

The rows and columns keep track of the information. You just have to get to the *cells* (the little squares) where you want to type in the information. To get to any cell, just click it or use the arrow keys to move the cursor to it. When you begin, the cursor is already in the top left cell, so you can just start typing.

You can follow the example in Figure 14-4, or you can create your own table.

To follow along, type **Dumpster Monitoring, Bay Area** in the top left cell. The cells automatically expand to fit the data they contain — a marvelous feature that is easy to take for granted. Did you ever make a table with a ruler and a pencil and then find that you had more to put into a little square than would fit there?

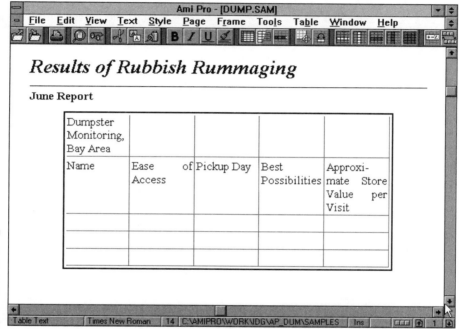

Figure 14-4:
A sample table for a Dumpster report.

You also can use the arrow keys, which actually may be easier to use than the mouse, to move around in the table. Table 14-1 lists the keyboard shortcuts that I have found most useful for moving around in a table. (Well, I don't use all the shortcuts — too many to remember. Mostly I use Tab and Shift+Tab.)

Table 14-1	Keyboard Shortcuts for Moving Around in a Table
Keystrokes	*Action*
Tab	Moves forward one cell
Shift+Tab	Moves the cursor to the left one cell
Ctrl+up arrow	Moves the cursor up one row
Ctrl+down arrow	Moves the cursor down one row

(continued)

Table 14-1 *(continued)*	
Keystrokes	**Action**
Home	Puts the cursor at the start of the cell you're in
Home, Home	Puts the cursor at the start of the first column of the row you're in
End	Puts the cursor at the end of the line in the same cell
End, End	Puts the cursor in the last column of the row you're in

Changing the Number of Rows or Columns

If you're making your own table (and not just doing the boring work of typing in a table some hotshot drew on the back of an envelope on the red-eye flight last night), you may find yourself needing more or less rows and columns at times. Life just isn't very predictable when it comes to tables. You may accept the default five columns and rows after the dialog box prompts you at the start of your table venture, but you may often change your mind after you get into your table a little.

Adding rows or columns

Adding a row to your table is easy, especially if you have the Table SmartIcon set showing. To add a row, first put the cursor in the row that you want the additional row to follow. Then click the Insert row in table SmartIcon, as illustrated in Figure 14-5.

In my example, I put the cursor in the Condos row and clicked the icon. The new row shoulders its way in after the Condos row and stands waiting for you to put in some solid information.

If you prefer to use the Menu bar to insert a table row, do the following:

1. **Put your cursor in the row that you want the new row to follow.**

2. **Choose the Insert Column/Row command from the Table menu, as you see in Figure 14-6.**

   The Insert Column/Row dialog box appears. Select the Rows radio button in the Insert box and select the After radio button in the Position box. Determine how many rows you want to add to your table in the Number to insert box.

The Insert row in the table SmartIcon

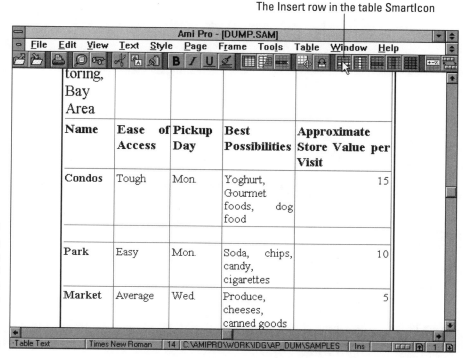

Figure 14-5:
Click the
Insert row
in table
SmartIcon
to add a
row.

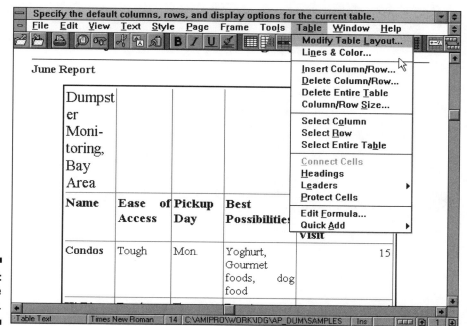

Figure 14-6:
The Table
menu.

3. Choose OK to close the dialog box.

The new row(s) appears on-screen. After you have the new row, you can enter research results into it, as shown in Figure 14-7.

```
┌─────────────────────────────────────────────────────────────┐
│ ─                    Ami Pro - [DUMP.SAM]              ▼ ▲   │
│ ─  File  Edit  View  Text  Style  Page  Frame  Tools  Table  Window  Help   ▲ │
│  [icons row]  B I U   [icons]                                │
```

Moni-toring, Bay Area				
Name	**Ease of Access**	**Pickup Day**	**Best Possibilities**	**Approximate Store Value per Visit**
Condos	Tough	Mon.	Yoghurt, Gourmet foods, dog food	15
Hi-rise	Tough	Thurs.	Doughnuts	4
Park	Easy	Mon.	Soda, chips, candy, cigarettes	10
Market	Average	Wed.	Produce, cheeses	5

```
│  Table Text       Times New Roman   14  C:\AMIPRO\WORK\IDG\AP_DUM\SAMPLES  Ins   [   ] 1  │
└─────────────────────────────────────────────────────────────┘
                                              The new row
```

Figure 14-7: The table with a new row added.

The technique for adding a new column is similar to that of adding a new row to your table. To add a column, put the cursor in the column just before the one you want to add. Then click the Insert column in table SmartIcon. In my example, I put the cursor in the Best Possibilities column and clicked the icon. The new column appears to the right of the Best Possibilities column, as you can see in Figure 14-8.

If you try to add a column and receive a message that says `Not enough room to insert a column,` you must resize your columns so you can fit another column on the page.

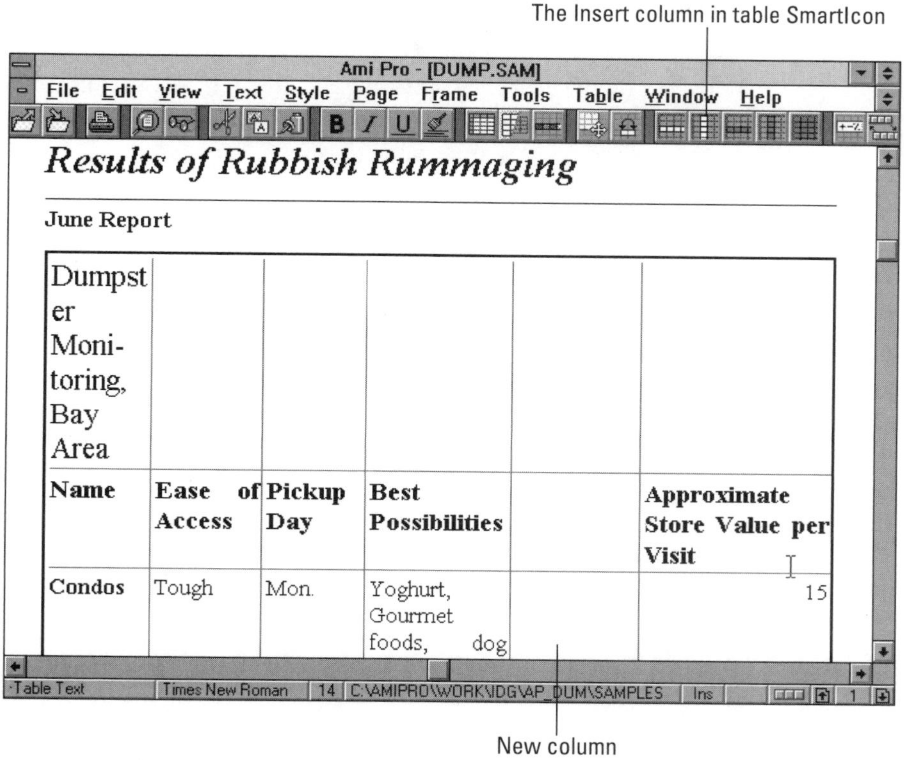

The Insert column in table SmartIcon

```
┌─────────────────────────────────────────────────────────────┐
│  Ami Pro - [DUMP.SAM]                                         │
│  File  Edit  View  Text  Style  Page  Frame  Tools  Table  Window  Help  │
│  [toolbar icons]                                              │
├─────────────────────────────────────────────────────────────┤
```

Results of Rubbish Rummaging

June Report

Dumpst er Moni- toring, Bay Area					
Name	**Ease of Access**	**Pickup Day**	**Best Possibilities**		**Approximate Store Value per Visit**
Condos	Tough	Mon.	Yoghurt, Gourmet foods, dog		15

Table Text   Times New Roman   14   C:\AMIPRO\WORK\IDG\AP_DUM\SAMPLES   Ins

New column

Figure 14-8:
The table with a new column added.

You can make the heading span across the table fairly easily by highlighting the first row in the table and choosing the Connect Cells command from the Table menu. This process is explained in detail in the section entitled "Turning several cells into one big cell."

To move to another row, just click the first cell of the new row and type the information in the cell. After you are finished typing, press Tab to move to the next cell in that row. If you are following my garbage example, your table should look something like Figure 14-4, with five column headings and a title for the table.

Again, if you prefer to use the Menu bar to insert a column, do the following:

1. **Put your cursor in the column that you want the new column to follow.**

2. **Choose the Insert Column/Row command from the Table menu (see Figure 14-6).**

The Insert Column/Row dialog box appears. Select the Columns radio button in the Insert box and select the After radio button in the Position box. Ami Pro enables you to select only the number of additional columns that fit on the size page you have selected for your document. In my example, I can add only one more column.

3. **Choose OK to close the dialog box.**

The new column appears on-screen. After you have the new column, you can type the new information into it, just as you did with the new row.

Deleting rows or columns

Deleting rows or columns from a table is not as easy as adding them, I'm afraid. You probably think that you can just select the row or column you want to remove and press the Delete key. Right? Sorry, but the process just isn't that simple.

You can drag the mouse over the column or row to select it, but the easiest way is to put the cursor in any cell in the column or row you want to delete and then click the Delete selected rows (or Delete selected columns) SmartIcon, both shown in Figure 14-9. Or you can choose the Delete Column/Row command from the Table menu. If you choose the second option, the Delete Column/Row dialog box appears, where you select whether to delete a column or a row and then choose OK.

The warning message in Figure 14-9 appears. Does this mean that you can't remove an extra column or row after you have added them to the table? No. This warning means that, technically speaking, you can't use the Undo command to get a column or row back after you have deleted it. So what? If you have deleted a column or row by mistake, just put it back in again. Choose Yes and watch the unwanted column or row go off to join the hordes of the long forgotten.

You can see the problem the makers of the program faced. If you select a row or column and press Delete, which do you want to delete — the row itself or just what's in it? The designers elected to have the Delete function delete only what's in the row, leaving the row itself fully intact. I'm willing to wager that many of you have resorted to all kinds of clever disguises to cover up the rows and columns that you just couldn't figure out how to delete from your tables. I mean, if Delete doesn't do it, what do you do? Time to punt.

Evaporating a whole table

Trying to delete an entire table can drive you bonkers, too. (Trust me — I speak from experience on this one.) Again, pressing Delete does not eliminate the table. You have to use a special command.

The Delete selected columns
in a table SmartIcon

The Delete selected rows
in a table SmartIcon

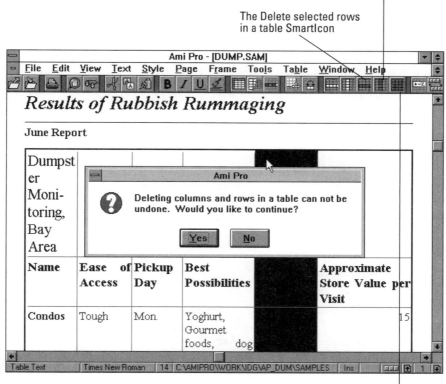

Figure 14-9:
Ami Pro
asks for a
true
commitment
before you
delete.

The Delete table SmartIcon

 To eliminate an entire table, first put the cursor anywhere in the table and then either click the Delete table SmartIcon (shown in the margin) or use the menu. To use the menu, choose the Delete Entire Table command from the Table menu. The table passes over to the great beyond.

 After you use the Delete table SmartIcon or the Delete Entire Table command, Ami Pro does *not* prompt you with a warning asking whether you are sure that you want to delete the table. The table simply vanishes. Be sure that you want to remove your entire table before you use this command.

The nice thing about deleting an entire table, however, is that you *can* get it back, unlike deleting a row or column. Simply click the Undo command in the Edit menu. Isn't it interesting that you can't get back a row or column when you delete it, but you can get back a whole table if you extinguish that? The lesson to be learned here is, "If you're going to mess up, mess up BIG. Then you can fix it." If you are following along with my example, be sure that you retrieve the table with the Undo command.

Adjusting the Table

All the stylistic commands you make to your table are made in basically the same manner as any other stylistic changes. You simply highlight the appropriate text in the cell and then choose the changes (for example, bold or Times font) from the menu or icon set.

Adding style to your table settings (linens on the table)

Figure 14-4 is rather boring as is, because it has the same font for the title, headings, and table text. You can make your tables much more interesting by simply adjusting the font styles for the various parts of your table (refer to Chapter 2) by using the Text and Style menus. Simply highlight the text you want to change and use these menus to experiment with different fonts and font options.

Figure 14-10 shows some adjustments I made to spice up the table. Now you easily can tell the difference between headings and table text.

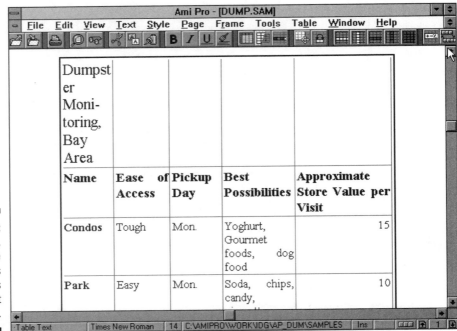

Figure 14-10: The table, after I made adjustments to the fonts and text style.

Turning several cells into one big cell

You may have noticed in the example that the cramped table title has made the table look amateurish. The time has come to stretch it out into a REAL title.

To convert several cells into one cell, do the following:

1. **Highlight the first row in the table.**

2. **Choose the Connect Cells command from the Table menu.**

   What a relief! The words spread out nicely as a title for the table.

3. **To center the title, highlight it, choose the Alignment command from the Text menu, and select the Center option.**

   Figure 14-11 shows the fused cells and the nicely centered title.

Figure 14-11:
The table finally has a REAL title.

Adjusting column widths (taffy-pulling the table)

Sometimes, after you choose an arbitrary column width to set up your columns, the result is not quite as good-looking as you had hoped. Some columns should be wider, for example, to accommodate a longer heading, while other columns should be narrower. You easily can adjust the width of your columns by using the mouse.

To adjust column width, just drag the mouse pointer over a column line until the pointer looks like an insignia on a medieval shield (known in Windows talk as a *four-headed arrow*). Figure 14-12 shows an example of this arrow. Then click and drag the column line to the position you want. Continue to click and drag various columns until the table looks right to you.

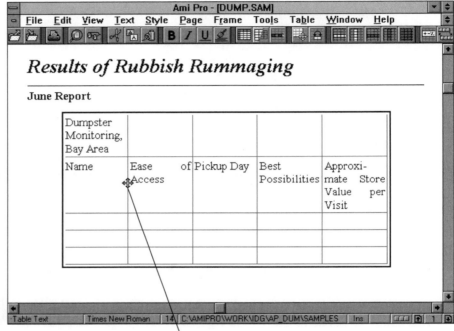

Figure 14-12:
The pointer
as a four-
headed
arrow,
meaning you
can drag in
four
directions.

Four-headed arrow

The I-beam doesn't change to a four-headed arrow unless the cursor is someplace in the table.

There are no particular rules for moving column lines. You don't have to go in any sequence or anything. Just keep pulling lines this way and that until you like the way the table looks. If you have been following along with the garbage example, try shrinking the first column a bit and stretching out the last column so that your results look like Figure 14-13. Then you can type in the rest of the information in the columns, too.

You cannot make the column wider if your table is already at maximum width. If this is the case, you may have to make another column skinnier first.

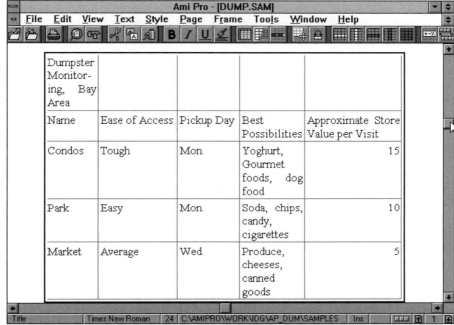

Ami Pro - [DUMP.SAM]

File   Edit   View   Text   Style   Page   Frame   Tools   Window   Help

Dumpster Monitor-ing, Bay Area				
Name	Ease of Access	Pickup Day	Best Possibilities	Approximate Store Value per Visit
Condos	Tough	Mon.	Yoghurt, Gourmet foods, dog food	15
Park	Easy	Mon.	Soda, chips, candy, cigarettes	10
Market	Average	Wed.	Produce, cheeses, canned goods	5

Title   Times New Roman   24   C:\AMIPRO\WORK\IDG\AP_DUM\SAMPLES   Ins   1

Figure 14-13:
The table, after you adjust the width of the columns.

Adding Finishing Touches

The following sections teach you how to add some pizzazz to your tables. Features that look professional and difficult are actually quite easy to implement.

Adding color to the table (boxing up and painting)

Occasionally, you may want to emphasize a row or column in a table by changing its color or shading. When you add shading to a table, you really impress the people looking at the table, because it looks like such a difficult thing to do. But adding shading to a table is really quite simple if you follow these steps:

1. Select the cells you want to add color to.

In my example, I selected the Approximate Store Value cells with the numbers in them. (See Figure 14-14.)

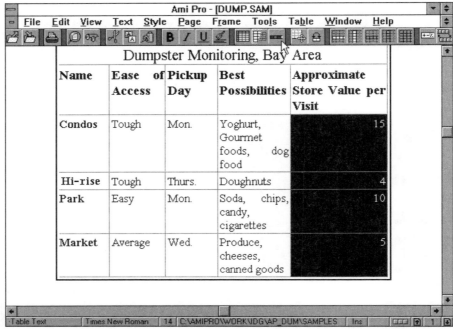

Ami Pro - [DUMP.SAM]

File Edit View Text Style Page Frame Tools Table Window Help

Dumpster Monitoring, Bay Area

Name	Ease of Access	Pickup Day	Best Possibilities	Approximate Store Value per Visit
Condos	Tough	Mon.	Yoghurt, Gourmet foods, dog food	15
Hi-rise	Tough	Thurs.	Doughnuts	4
Park	Easy	Mon.	Soda, chips, candy, cigarettes	10
Market	Average	Wed.	Produce, cheeses, canned goods	5

Table Text   Times New Roman   14   C:\AMIPRO\WORK\IDG\AP_DUM\SAMPLES   Ins   1

Figure 14-14:
Select your
cells before
you paint
them.

2. **Click the Modify lines & shades in a table SmartIcon or choose the Lines & Color command from the Table menu.**

   The Lines & Color dialog box appears, as in Figure 14-15.

3. **Click the Fill color option and select a color that suits your fancy from the choices next to the Fill color option.**

   Be sure to click the arrow to the right of color bar to get an entire spectrum of choices.

   As you choose your color choice, a sample of the color appears in the sample box above the color choices, as you can see in Figure 14-16.

   For my example, I chose a light gray color.

4. **Choose OK.**

   The table now has the color you have chosen for your selected cells. Figure 14-17 shows the table with some of the cells shaded gray.

The Modify lines & shades in a table SmartIcon

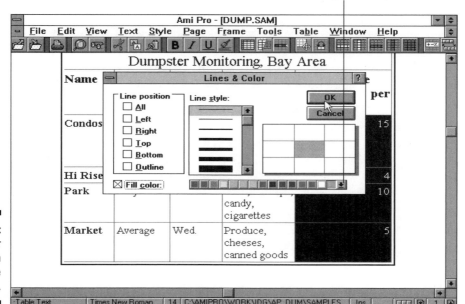

Figure 14-15:
The Lines &
Color dialog
box.

Click here to get the full palette.

Figure 14-16:
A color
selection
made in the
dialog box.

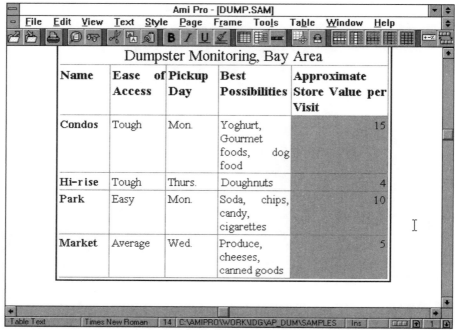

Dumpster Monitoring, Bay Area

Name	Ease of Access	Pickup Day	Best Possibilities	Approximate Store Value per Visit
Condos	Tough	Mon.	Yoghurt, Gourmet foods, dog food	15
Hi-rise	Tough	Thurs.	Doughnuts	4
Park	Easy	Mon.	Soda, chips, candy, cigarettes	10
Market	Average	Wed.	Produce, cheeses, canned goods	5

Table Text   Times New Roman   14   C:\AMIPRO\WORK\IDG\AP_DUM\SAMPLES   Ins   1

Figure 14-17:
The table with some of the cells shaded gray.

Rearranging your table

After you have set up your table, you may want to rearrange the entries. In my example, for instance, my sociologist friend organized her table by location. What if she wanted to organize it alphabetically, instead? This process is easy if you take the following steps:

1. **Select the rows or columns you want to rearrange alphabetically.**

   I chose to alphabetize the Name column.

2. **From the Tools menu, choose the Sort option.**

   The overwhelming-looking Sort dialog box appears, as in Figure 14-18. You can dizzy yourself trying to figure out what Level 1 and Level 2 are. If you don't change anything, though, Ami Pro sorts the selected cells in alphabetic order. That's good enough for me.

3. **Choose OK.**

   Ami Pro puts your selected cells in alphabetic order, as you can see in Figure 14-19.

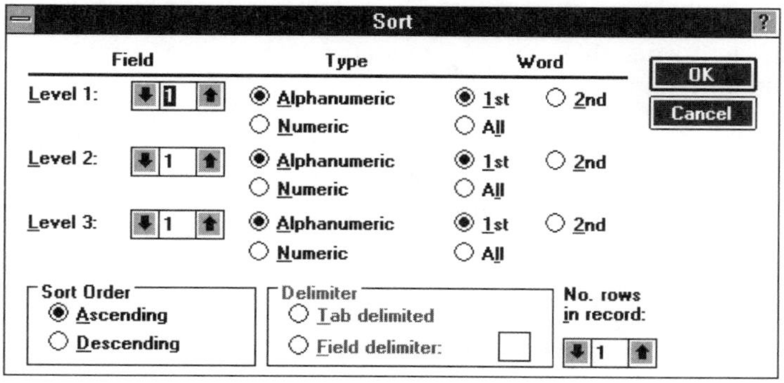

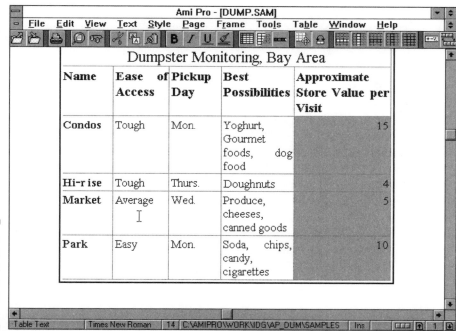

Figure 14-18:
The Sort
dialog box.

Figure 14-18:
The Sort
dialog box.

Figure 14-19:
The Name
column is
now in
alphabetic
order.

Seeing how things add up

The tables that you create with Ami Pro have spreadsheet power. (You can expect nothing less. After all, Ami Pro comes from Lotus.) You can import data from spreadsheets into a table and use Ami Pro's many features to dress up the data for presentation.

I'm not going to go into that much detail here; however, I am going to show you how to do the one thing that you are most likely to do in a table: add up a column of figures.

Be sure that you have an extra row at the bottom of the table if you are adding up a column of figures or an extra column to the right of the table if you are adding up a row of figures. This extra column or row provides the proper place to put the total for your figures.

To add up figures in your table, do the following:

1. **Insert the extra row or column into your table.**

   If you are following along with my example, you should create a new blank row at the end of the table and type **Total** in the cell on the left, as you can see in Figure 14-20.

2. **Now click the cell where you want to place the results of your addition.**

   For this example, click the cell in the bottom of the last column.

Ami Pro - [DUMP.SAM]

File Edit View Text Style Page Frame Tools Table Window Help

Dumpster Monitoring, Bay Area

Name	Ease of Access	Pickup Day	Best Possibilities	Approximate Store Value per Visit
Condos	Tough	Mon.	Yoghurt, Gourmet foods, dog food	15
Hi-r ise	Tough	Thurs.	Doughnuts	4
Market	Average	Wed.	Produce, cheeses, canned goods	5
Park	Easy	Mon.	Soda, chips, candy, cigarettes	10
Total				

Table Text   Times New Roman   14   C:\AMIPRO\WORK\IDG\AP_DUM\SAMPLES   Ins   1

Figure 14-20: Adding a new row in preparation for totaling up the figures.

The new row for totals

---

3. From the Table menu, choose the Quick Add command and select the Column option.

Ami Pro adds up the figures in the column and puts the total in the cell where you have the cursor, as you can see in Figure 14-21.

If you were to change any of the figures in the cells, Ami Pro automatically changes the total after you click the box that shows the total. Try changing some of the figures on your screen to see how this works.

Formula icon

Dumpster Monitoring, Bay Area				
Name	**Ease of Access**	**Pickup Day**	**Best Possibilities**	**Approximate Store Value per Visit**
Condos	Tough	Mon.	Yoghurt, Gourmet foods, dog food	15
Hi-rise	Tough	Thurs.	Doughnuts	4
Market	Average	Wed.	Produce, cheeses, canned goods	5
Park	Easy	Mon.	Soda, chips, candy, cigarettes	10
Total				34

Ami Pro - [DUMP.SAM]

File Edit View Text Style Page Frame Tools Table Window Help

Table Text   Times New Roman   14   C:\AMIPRO\WORK\IDG\AP_DUM\SAMPLES   Ins   1

Figure 14-21: Ami Pro knows how things add up.

The icon on the far right (shown in Figure 14-21 as the Formula icon) enables you to create more complicated formulas. If you are a spreadsheet type, this stuff will be very familiar.

You can put graphics right in the middle of a cell! Yes, I say again, you can import a picture into a table. Refer to Chapter 13 to see how to put a graphic on the page; you use the same method to insert the graphic into a cell.

Creating tables in your documents can really grow on you. Initially, using tables appears to be something strictly for nerds. I know that. But the more you experiment with tables, the more comfortable you will be with them. I know that, too. You will come across times in your life when the easiest way to keep track of something is by putting it in rows and columns. I like the way these tables help keep me organized.

In the next chapter, I write about something you will use less frequently than tables — reference tools, such as indexes and footnotes. Many people, I believe, go happily through life without needing them, but you never know when that situation may change.

Chapter 15
Serving on the Best China: Reference Tools

*M*ost people will probably never need to make a table of contents (TOC); even fewer people will ever need to put footnotes in a document; and nobody needs an index. However, if you are skimming through this chapter looking for cool features, check out the Notes features (in the section entitled "Sending Notes in Class"). It's something a novice might enjoy.

Most people into TOCs and footnotes, research suggests, are dust-covered scholars who have to highlight critical information quickly, or lawyers who add a TOC to a document because it adds more time to their $300-an-hour bill. If you have a short attention span, however — not unlike Beavis and Butt-Head on MTV — you may really get into TOCs, because you don't have to spend an eternity reading a complete work!

Creating a Table of Contents

Books and magazines always have a contents page in the front. Even newspapers have a little box that tells you which pages the movies, sports, and comics are on. (You can tell my priorities, right?) These tables are a necessity of life, but you probably take them for granted and never think about anyone actually making one. TOCs are just something, like road signs, to use and immediately forget about.

Creating a TOC with styles

If you are in the habit of using Ami Pro styles, you're in luck when it comes to making a table of contents. All you have to do is make sure that Ami Pro knows which styles to list as first heading, second heading, and so on. After you apply the heading styles, Ami Pro easily makes the TOC for you.

Try experimenting with a multipage document to see whether you can generate a TOC for it. If you don't have headings in the document already, put some sample headings in and attach the appropriate heading levels to them (see Chapter 3 to review attaching styles).

For the figures in this section, I use the Money Laundry business plan from Chapter 11, which I have turned into a sample multipage document by pasting blah, blah, blah into it a whole bunch of times. (OK, so my creative juices dried up! You'll be doing the same thing to get enough pages into your own sample document, too.)

If you use the SmartIcons to get your work done, you first have to get the correct set on-screen. Click the change SmartIcon set button in the Status bar and choose the Long Documents set, as shown in Figure 15-1. Watch your screen as Ami Pro puts the new set of SmartIcons on the icon bar for you to use.

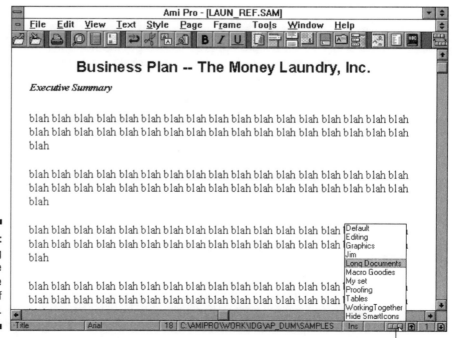

Figure 15-1: Choosing the appropriate set of SmartIcons.

Change SmartIcon set button

Now you are ready to generate a TOC for your document by following these steps:

1. Click the Generate TOC, Index SmartIcon (shown in the margin) or choose the TOC, Index command from the Tools menu.

The TOC, Index dialog box appears, as shown in Figure 15-2.

If you're in Outline or Draft mode when you click the SmartIcon, nothing happens. You try again: click. . . nothing. . .click. . . nothing. . . click. . . nothing. You have to switch to Layout mode.

The Generate TOC,
Index SmartIcon

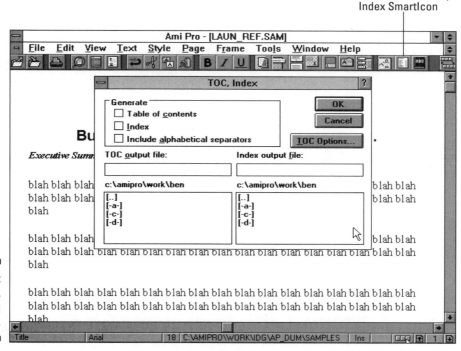

Figure 15-2:
The TOC,
Index dialog
box.

2. Click the Table of contents option in the Generate box.

3. To be sure that you have your styles set properly, click the TOC Options button.

The TOC options dialog box appears, as shown in Figure 15-3. I discuss how to use this dialog box next.

4. Choose OK to close this dialog box.

The moment of truth is here for you. You added headings and styles to your document. You chose the options you want in the TOC, Index and TOC Options dialog boxes. You hold your breath and hope.

5. Choose OK to close the TOC, Index dialog box.

Your TOC appears at the top of the document in all its glory. You did it!

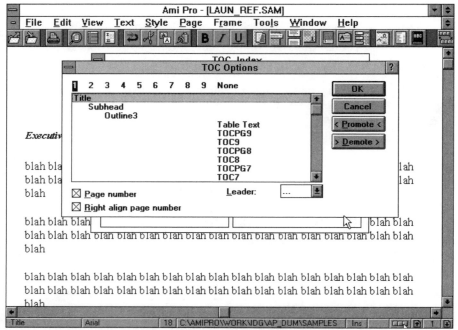

Figure 15-3:
The TOC
Options
dialog box.

The TOC is an Ami Pro table, as I discussed in Chapter 14. To delete the TOC, you have to open the Table menu and choose the Delete Entire Table command. Chances are good to excellent, in real life, that you'll have to delete your TOC again and again until it comes out the way you want it to look, so be prepared for this step in your writing process.

Creating a TOC from marked text

If you use styles and understand how to promote and demote them for a TOC, the method I described in the preceding section is the best way to make a TOC (in the unlikely event that you're going to make one at all). Realistically, however, if you create a TOC, you probably will make a quickie version of one by marking the text to appear in the TOC and then generating it.

Suppose, for example, that you show a document to Beavis and Butt-Head (you know, the ones with the short attention span), and they complain that it is much too long for them to read. You can create a short table of contents that simply highlights the important points of your document by going into the document and pointing to the text you want to appear in the TOC.

The options of your TOC

In the TOC Options box, you can promote and demote styles to have them appear as you want them in the final TOC. If you want to *promote* a style (advance the style to a higher level), for instance, you select the style and then click the Promote button. If you want to *demote* a style (put back the style to a lower level), you select the style and then click the Demote button.

You also can change such stuff as the Leader option. This option doesn't mean that you can change your leader (as in replace Bill Clinton). The Leader option does mean, however, that you can decide to have dots, dashes, or nothing on the line between the TOC entry and its page number.

In the TOC Options dialog box, you also decide whether to have page numbers in the TOC by selecting the Page number radio button. You also have the option of aligning the page numbers to the right of your TOC by selecting the Right align page number radio button. (Where else would you put the page numbers?)

You can put a TOC into its own file by putting a proper DOS filename into the TOC output file text box in the TOC, Index dialog box (see Figure 15-2). If you don't want to put a TOC into a separate file, however, Ami Pro puts the TOC at the top of the first page of the existing file, such as in the example in the accompanying figure. The TOC has the headings from the document on the left, the dot leaders in the middle, and the page numbers on the right.

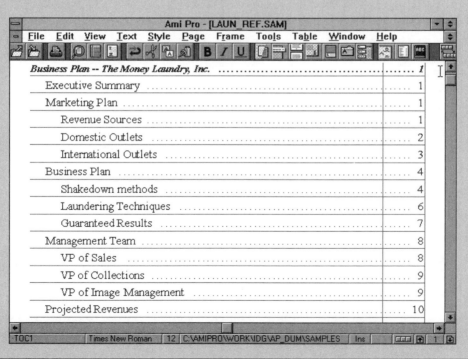

To create a TOC by marking the text in a document, do the following:

1. **Open the document for which you want to create the TOC.**

   Put your document in Outline mode so that it is easier for you to scan and mark the text.

2. **Select the first word or phrase for the TOC entry.**

3. **From the Edit menu, choose Mark Text and then select the TOC Entry.**

   Figure 15-4 shows the Mark Text submenu.

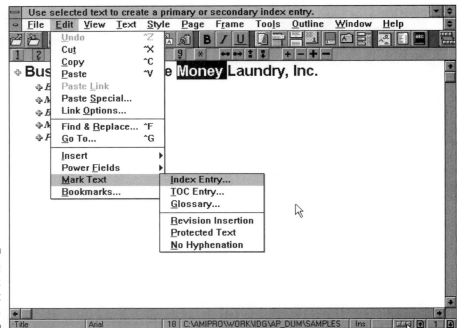

Figure 15-4:
The Mark
Text
submenu.

The TOC Entry dialog box appears, as shown in Figure 15-5.

4. **Make sure that the level is the one you want to appear in the TOC.**

5. **Choose OK.**

   Ami Pro puts a secret code — a *power field,* actually — into the document. The code can come back to haunt you and is very tough to delete. This power field stuff is heady material. Power fields are for nerds. Read on to find out how to delete them.

6. **Repeat Steps 2 through 5 for each additional word or phrase you want to include in your TOC.**

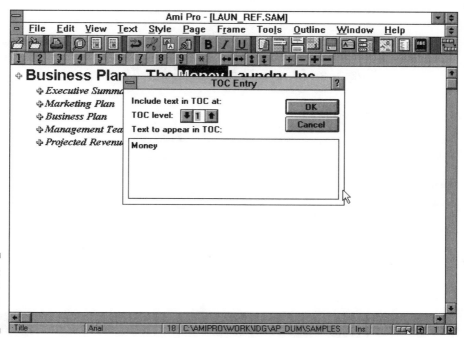

Figure 15-5:
The TOC
Entry dialog
box.

Do you want to know how to delete the code you put in the document without getting involved with power fields? Simply select the word you marked and the word right after it. Then press the Delete key. The warning message in Figure 15-6 appears to tell you that there's a power field in the word you're deleting. If you want to delete the code, choose Yes and then retype the words you deleted.

After you have marked the text, you are ready to create the TOC by following these steps:

1. **In Layout mode, choose TOC, Index from the Tools menu.**

2. **Choose TOC Options from the TOC, Index dialog box (see Figure 15-2).**

   I wish I could figure out a way around the next step, but I can't, so just plunge ahead.

3. **Adjust your TOC levels.**

   If you aren't using styles in your document, all the levels in the dialog box will be marked *None*. Promote the first style to level 1 and the second style to level 2, as in Figure 15-7. Do this for each level of words you have marked in your document and leave the rest at the None level. By going through this process, you assure the TOC of having indented levels and page numbers in it.

4. **Choose OK to close the TOC Options dialog box.**

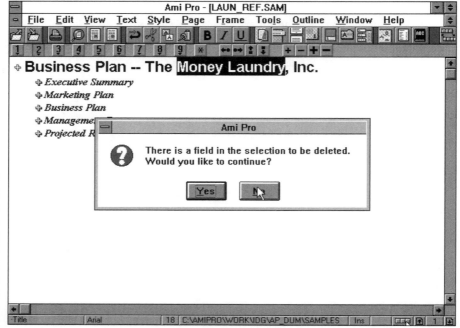

Figure 15-6:
You know
that you're
deleting a
power field
when you
see this
warning
message.

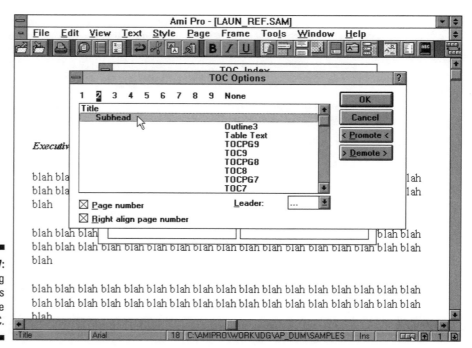

Figure 15-7:
Preparing
your levels
for the
marked TOC.

5. In the TOC, Index dialog box, be sure that you click the Table of con-tents option before you choose OK.

Ami Pro puts the nice, brief TOC — suitable for Beavis and Butt-Head — at the top of the file, as you can see in Figure 15-8.

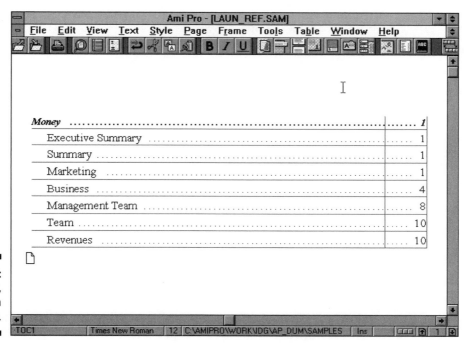

Figure 15-8:
A short TOC,
based on
marked text.

These power fields in the document are a nightmare. Everything's great if the TOC looks good the first time, but the chances of that are slim. You have to get the power fields in just right, with no extra spaces before or after the words, and you have to get the right outline styles showing in the TOC Options box. In other words, you can't afford to make any mistakes at all. If you do make mistakes and you start trying to fix things, you can end up in serious swamp conditions. Think seriously about making a TOC based on marking the text — at least back up your file on-disk before using this method. Make up any excuse not to do the TOC in this way.

Generating an Index

Creating an index works the same as creating a TOC, except that you don't have the option of using styles to simplify your task. You have to mark each entry that you want to include in the index. "What? I have to go through and mark each little word — all 500 entries on my 300 pages?" That's correct. Indexes are pretty much just for nerds — to *make*, that is. Dummies, like me, use them frequently and appreciate them.

Painstakingly preparing for the index

If you're really going to do an index for a document of any size (and only a document of any size needs one), set aside a month or two of your life. However, if you're a pro at indexing, then, fine, set aside just a week.

To create the index, you first mark the entries to appear in the index. You mark the entries in a very similar fashion to marking the words for a TOC, by doing the following:

1. **Open the document you want to index and select a word you want to appear in the index.**

2. **Choose the <u>M</u>ark Text command from the <u>E</u>dit menu (see Figure 15-5) and select <u>I</u>ndex Entry.**

   The Mark Index Entry dialog box appears, as in Figure 15-9.

    The Insert index mark SmartIcon (shown in the margin) is a particularly useful shortcut for this activity.

3. **Click the <u>M</u>ark button and then choose OK.**

   Ami Pro secretly puts a little code into the document next to the word you want in the index.

4. **Use the Find & <u>R</u>eplace command on the <u>E</u>dit menu to help you find and mark all occurrences of the word.**

5. **Repeat the steps until you have marked all the words you want to appear in the index.**

Giving birth to the index

Marking the text is the hard part of making an index. In comparison to that step, generating the index is a piece of cake. (Of course, that depends on how well you bake.)

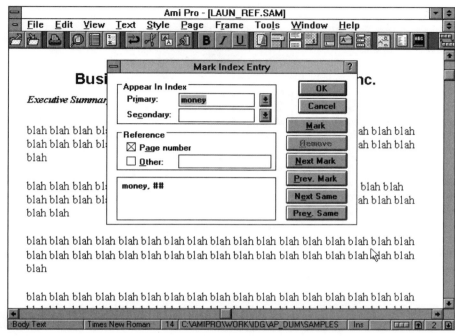

Figure 15-9:
The Mark
Index Entry
dialog box.

After the coding for your index is finished, follow these steps to produce the index:

1. **Click the Generate TOC, Index SmartIcon (see Figure 15-2) or choose the TOC, Index command on the Tools menu.**

   The TOC, Index dialog box appears.

2. **In the Index output file text box, type a name for the file to contain the index, such as INDEX.SAM.**

3. **In the Generate box, click the Index option and the Include alphabetical separators option, as shown in Figure 15-10.**

   The separators mean that a large letter *A*, for example, appears in the index list before the section of words that start with *a*, and so on.

4. **Choose OK.**

   Ami Pro creates an amazing, professional-looking index, as in Figure 15-11—one you've probably never dreamed of putting together in your life —and puts it into a separate file.

Indexes are one of those things that people who have never made one — or who sell word-processing programs — insist you can "generate automatically, with just a few keystrokes." Well, that statement is true: you *can* generate the index easily. (It's marking the text that's hard!) But it won't be right until you do it over and over and over again. After all, a chef with the right ingredients and years of experience can "throw a feast together in a day," too. What the chef fails to mention is that the preparation has taken all week.

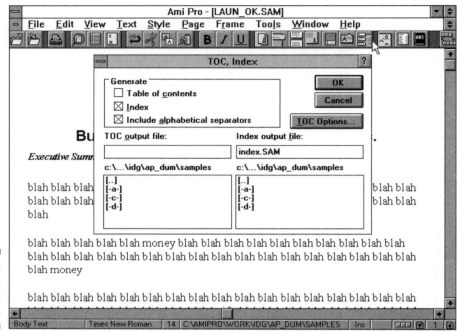

Figure 15-10:
Selecting
the index
options.

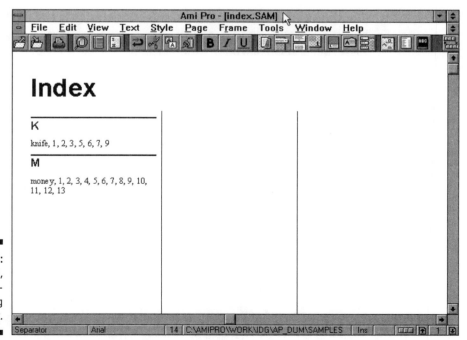

Figure 15-11:
An amazing,
professional-
looking
index.

Fooling Around with Footnotes

Maybe I shouldn't have been as disrespectful as I have been about tables of contents and indexes, because I'm going to be completely disrespectful about footnotes. Don't get me wrong: I'm not against the way that Ami Pro handles footnotes; I'm just against footnotes. I mean, you're reading along, and suddenly this little number floats before your eyes. Should you stop right then and read the footnote, which, incidentally, is way at the bottom of the page? If so, why not have the footnote right in the text?

Enough said. You probably can't wait to try it just to prove me wrong, so follow these steps to insert a footnote in your text:

1. **Open a document in which you would like to experiment with footnotes and put the cursor where you want the footnote reference to appear.**

2. **Click the Insert footnotes SmartIcon (shown in the margin). Or choose the Footnotes command on the Tools menu.**

   Ami Pro adds the number 1 above the word and puts the cursor next to the same number at the foot of the page, as you can see in Figure 15-12.

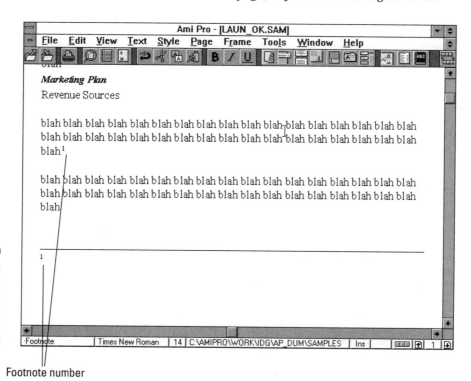

Figure 15-12:
Ami Pro sets you up to type the footnote.

Footnote number

3. Type in the text of the footnote.

Notice how Ami Pro automatically adds the correct indentation to your footnote if it is longer than one line. (See Figure 15-13).

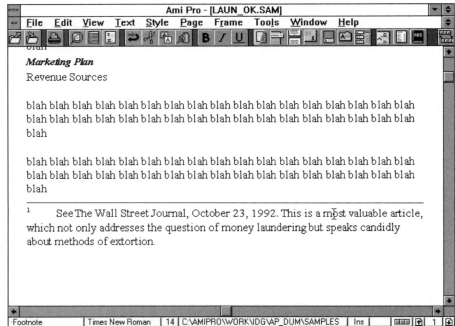

Figure 15-13:
A sample
completed
footnote.

If you use footnotes a great deal (which means that you work in some environment, such as a university, that requires them), you know that they are a major headache. It's hard to fit them on the page, and it's hard to renumber them if you put in an additional one or two. Ami Pro does solve these problems for you, however, which are great features. So I guess if you have to do footnotes, you are lucky to have Ami Pro to do them for you.

Sending Notes in Class

The only reason you may confuse notes with footnotes is that the names are decidedly similar. Notes, however, aren't like footnotes (in my opinion), because notes are actually *useful*. It took me a long time to figure out what notes were and how to use them. I was constantly scratching out little messages to myself on a memo pad about something in the text that I didn't want to forget. And then my wife came in and cleaned off my desk and I never saw those precious little messages again.

Notes are little messages that you embed directly in the document and that don't show up when you print the document (and are protected from the housekeeping instincts of a zealous spouse). Now that's a useful feature. Actually, the designers of Ami Pro liked the feature so much that they put notes in the style sheets that they created for the program so that they could give you some advice.

Why don't you check a note out for yourself by following these steps:

1. **Create a new document using the _LETTER1.STY style sheet or use your current document.**

2. **Near the end of the initial document, double-click the little colored box after the word *Sincerely*.**

   The note in Figure 15-14 opens with some helpful information in it.

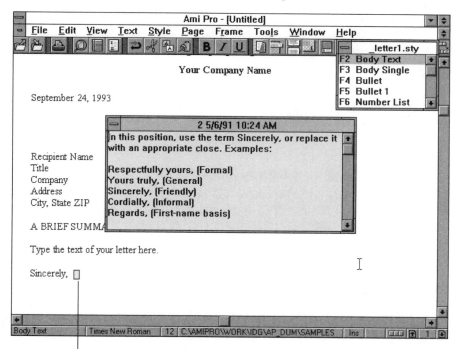

Figure 15-14:
A note from a style sheet.

Double-click here to open the note.

You also can insert your own note into a document with the following steps:

1. **Open a document in which you want to insert a note to yourself and put the insertion point where you want the note to appear.**

2. **From the Edit menu, choose the Insert command and then select the Note option, as you can see in Figure 15-15.**

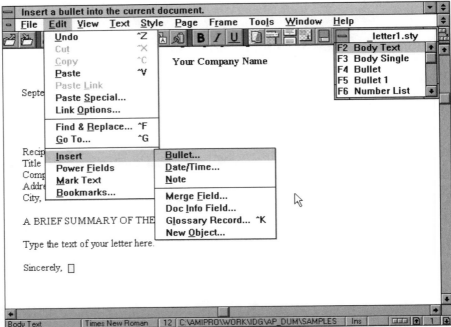

Figure 15-15:
The Insert
submenu.

Ami Pro puts the blank note box that you see in Figure 15-16 on-screen.

3. Type a reminder to yourself or a note to your group.

Depending on your situation, you can leave notes to yourself (FEED ROVER TONITE!) or leave comments in a document when working in a work-group atmosphere. The note doesn't appear in your document when you print it.

4. Click anywhere outside the note box to insert the note icon in your text.

If the Note icon does not show up in your document, you probably don't have this feature clicked to view it. Simply choose View Preferences from the View menu and check the Notes check box. The little box should now appear where you placed it.

To pull up the note on-screen, double-click the note icon in your document. As you can see in Figure 15-16, the note comes with its own window and its own control menu. Simply click the menu button in the top left corner to display the control menu, as shown in Figure 15-17.

You can move and size the note window as you can any other window in Ami Pro. You can choose also to remove this note or remove all notes in the document.

If you kept me company in this chapter, I do appreciate it. Sometimes you just

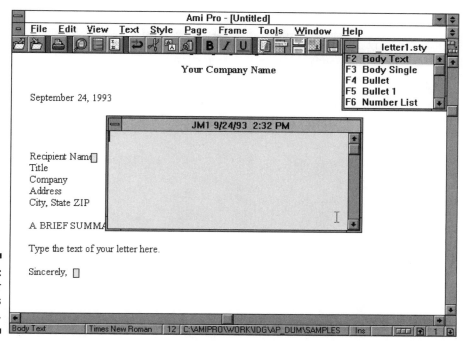

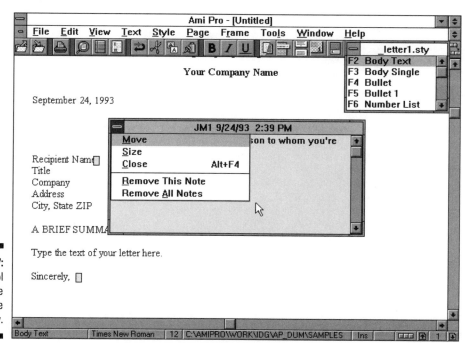

have to do a table of contents, an index, or footnotes. These unfortunate tasks can happen to anybody. Ami Pro doesn't force you to do them; it simply tries to help you out if you are faced with them. Ami Pro does a few more tasks to help you with long reference papers, too, and those tasks provide grist for the next chapter.

Chapter 16
Taking Care of the Leftovers

• •

In This Chapter
▶ How to create a master document
▶ When to use a master document
▶ How to use the Document Compare command
▶ How to use the Revision Marking command

• •

Who Uses These Features?

As you go along making your individual documents, it's natural to get caught up in the frenzy of completing the project you're working on. Suddenly, when you get to the end of your project, you may have to do some things that apply to all the documents, such as make a table of contents and index for them. Or — the worst, in my opinion — number all the pages.

Most people never run into this situation, of course. Using Ami Pro, they write short, irate letters to the editors, crank out memos bossing people around, or draw up fliers for the grade school picnic. They *don't* pull together complete tomes with fifty chapters. I think it's nice of Ami Pro, though, to give thought to people who do have to create long documents with several parts or chapters.

Even for short documents, however, you may have someone else review your work and gently offer advice to improve the text. (These people, as you must know, always know how to improve someone else's text.) You may want to be able to see their excellent suggestions and compare them with the puny offerings you had in the first place. You can benefit from their erudition and, well, just be sure that you do better the next time when you compare their suggestions with your original document.

Creating a Master Document with Slaves

I like the name *master document,* with its aura of strength, even invincibility. Hearing the name makes you think of a persuasive, beautifully constructed masterpiece that gives you hypnotic power over others.

Well, think again. A master document is nothing of the kind. It's basically an empty bookshelf that you pile chapters in to.

Usually, you don't create a table of contents (TOC) or index for a single chapter (in the unlikely event, that is, that you have to create one at all). Usually, you create a TOC or index for a collection of chapters in a book. You can, of course, combine all the chapters into one monstrous document when the time comes for creating the TOC or index or for putting in the page numbering for the whole project. Making the entire book one file does have some disadvantages, how-ever. You end up with a great deal of cutting and pasting, for one. Also, the individual files become outdated, and you have to work with the giant file forevermore.

Ami Pro thought about this situation and allows you to keep your documents as separate files but to treat them as a single file for the TOC, index, and page numbering. The concept is simple enough. Suppose, for example, that you wrote a guidebook to rabbit breeding and composed a number of chapters individually. To have Ami Pro treat these chapters as one document, do the following:

1. **Open one document (usually the first chapter), which becomes the** *source document.*

2. **From the File menu, choose Master Document, as shown in Figure 16-1.**

The Master Document dialog box opens, as you can see in Figure 16-2.

Figure 16-1: Choose Master Document from the File menu.

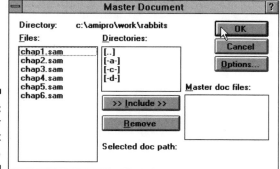

Figure 16-2: The Master Document dialog box.

3. **Make sure that you're in the directory you want.**

   The sample already shows the correct subdirectory, C:\AMIPRO\WORK\RABBITS.

4. **Select each document you want to have in the master document (in the order you want them to appear) and click the Include button.**

   The Master doc files box now displays all the chapters included in the master document, as illustrated in Figure 16-3.

5. **Choose OK.**

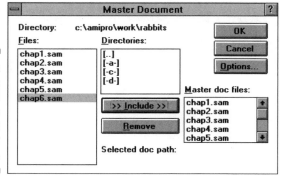

Figure 16-3: The dialog box, with all the chapters included in the master document.

To delete any document from the master document, choose Master Document from the File menu as before. Click the file you want to delete, then click the Remove button. Tada—it's gone!

When you work with the master document, you actually work with all the chapters inside it for purposes of page numbering, table of contents, and index.

Once you create the master document, you can print out a TOC or Index or add page numbers the same way you do for any document.

When you are numbering your pages for the master document, be sure that you did not specify a starting page number in the Page Numbering dialog box in any of the individual documents (accessed in the Page menu). I was in a hurry once and didn't check my individual documents. Sure enough, I had added page numbers to one of them, and those page numbers messed up my entire master document, which I had to abandon and start all over.

Using the Document Compare Command

No one — not Faulkner, not Dave Barry, not Alice Walker, and especially not *me* — gets published without someone else reading over the original manuscript and suggesting changes to it. You can keep track of changes that have been made to your original document with the Document Compare command.

To see how the Document Compare command can highlight the changes that are made in a document, you can experiment with a short document of your own or create the document you see in Figure 16-4, which is one of Shakespeare's sonnets. (Save the original sonnet as SUMMER.SAM.) Suppose, for instance, that you challenge a friend to update this sonnet and put it into more modern-day language.

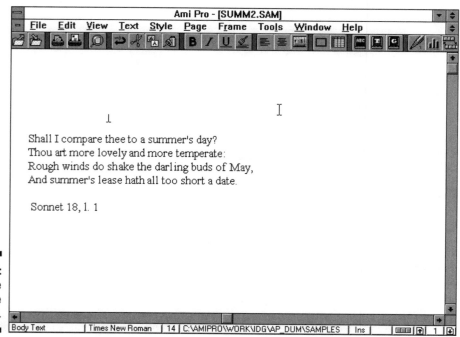

Figure 16-4:
Shakespeare in the original.

After a week of struggle, your friend finally gives you the rephrased sonnet that you see in Figure 16-5. (If you are following along with this example, you can create this document, too, so that you can have two documents to compare, or you can make some creative changes to another document of yours and save it as a new file.)

When your friend handed you the revised sonnet, you no doubt praised her developed ear and fine sense of the needs of the modern audience. But you were probably much more curious to see the specific changes she had made to the sonnet. To see those changes, you can do the following:

1. **Make one of the documents the current document by placing your cursor in it.**

   If you are following the sonnet example, make the updated sonnet the current document.

2. **From the Tools menu, shown in Figure 16-6, choose the Doc Compare command.**

   The Doc Compare dialog box, illustrated in Figure 16-7, appears.

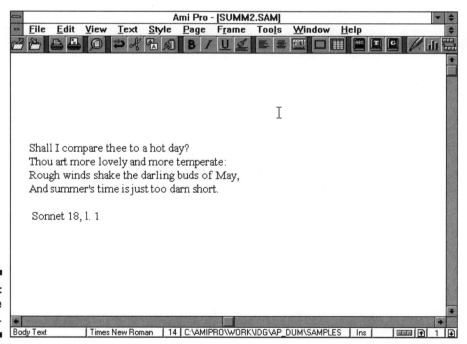

Figure 16-5:
Shakespeare
enhanced (?).

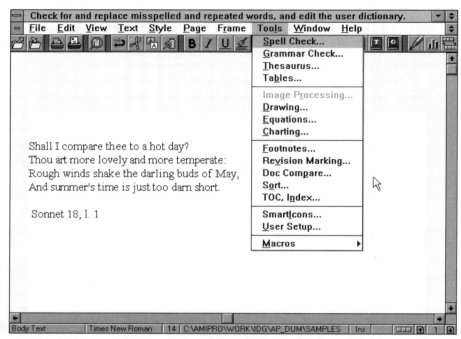

Figure 16-6:
The Tools
menu.

3. In the File name text box, type the filename of the document you want to compare with the current document.

The example uses SUMMER.SAM.

4. Choose OK.

Ami Pro shows you the updated, "improved" version of the document but also allows you to see Shakespeare's quaint, antiquated phrases with a line drawn through them, as you can see in Figure 16-8. The new version is in italic (in blue on my monitor), and the original version is in red (on my monitor) and has a line through the text.

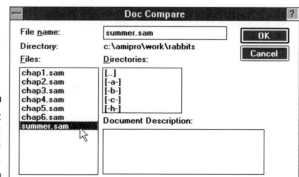

Figure 16-7:
The Doc
Compare
dialog box.

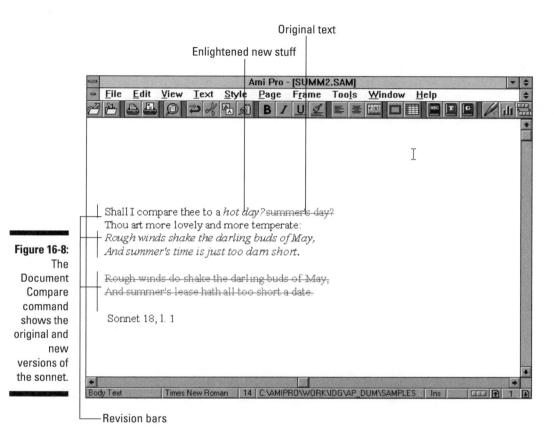

Figure 16-8: The Document Compare command shows the original and new versions of the sonnet.

A vertical line (the *revision bar*) in the left margin indicates each line of text that has some change in it. Revision bars are especially useful in long documents, where you quickly can flip through page after page of text to spot the revisions that have been made to the text. You also can choose Tools, Revision Marking and then click the Review Rev button to search and review all the revisions in a document.

When you use Compare, the current document shows the comparisons as well as the text. Before creating the final document, you may want to delete the portions of text that you no longer need.

Experimenting with the Revision Marking Command

You also can insert revision marks directly into the text of a document when you make changes to the text. English teachers love this capability and so do people in technical documentation departments.

Suppose, for instance, that a young aspirant to greatness named Frost submitted some lines of doggerel verse, as shown in Figure 16-9. A knowledgeable reader, such as yourself, can refine the young person's work and set him on the path to verbal competence by following these steps:

1. **Open the document you want to revise.**

2. **From the Tools menu, choose Revision Marking.**

   The Revision Marking dialog box appears, as in Figure 16-10.

3. **In the Revision Marking dialog box, select Mark revisions and then choose OK.**

   With the Revision Marking command in place, all the "deleted text" stays in place as the newly added text goes in to replace it.

4. **Type all the changes you want to make to the document text.**

   In Figure 16-11, I changed the word *world* to *planet* in the first line and the word *perish* to *cash in* in the fifth line. Notice the revision lines in the left margin.

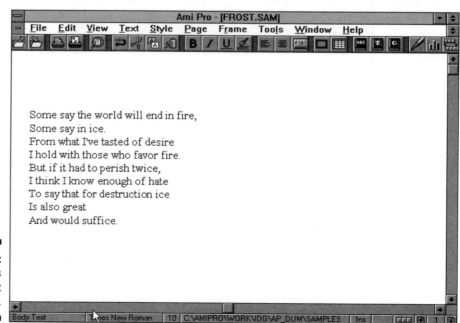

Figure 16-9:
Some lines
from Robert
Frost.

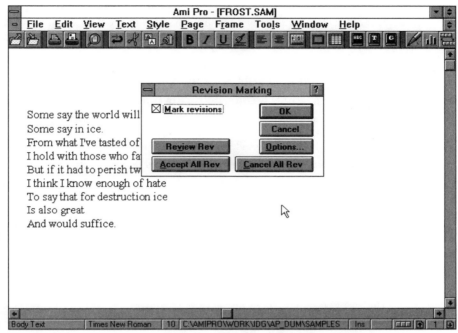

Figure 16-10:
The
Revision
Marking
dialog box

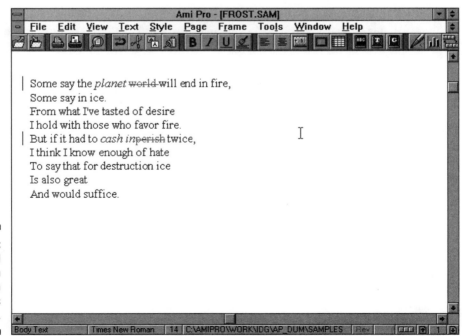

Figure 16-11:
The original
Frost poem
with
revisions
added.

Each time you change the text, the original text remains intact in red with a line through it. The replacement text appears in blue and italics, just as in the Document Compare command. A vertical line in the margin indicates a line with changes in it.

If you don't like the default colors of your original and revised text, you can change the appearance by doing the following:

1. **From the Tools menu, choose Revision Marking.**

2. **In the Revision Marking dialog box, click the Options button.**

   The Revision Marking Options dialog box appears, as in Figure 16-12.

3. **Make the changes to the insertions and deletions in your text that you want.**

   For example, instead of having the insertions in italic, you can make them bold or double-underlined. Rather than having your deletions in red, you can choose another color. You even can choose whether to have the revision bars and whether to have them in the left margin, the right margin, or both.

4. **Choose OK.**

Master documents and revision marking are advanced features of Ami Pro. Most users of Ami Pro probably don't use these features very often, and, therefore, these features see action very rarely — rather like the National Guard. However, should the time arise when you need these features, you'll be glad they're always at the ready.

If you think that master documents and revision marking are advanced, wait until you get to the next section! Macros and mail merges are sure to give you much food for thought.

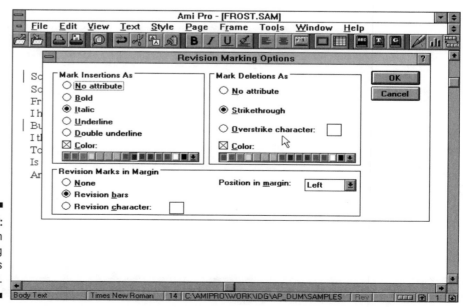

Figure 16-12:
The Revision
Marking
Options
dialog box.

Part VI
Stuff You Have No Business Touching (Stay Away!)

The 5th Wave
By Rich Tennant

"YO-I THINK WE'VE GOT A NEW KIND OF VIRUS HERE!"

In this part...

Mail merge — explained for those of you who have to learn it. Macros? Bad name, good idea. Don't be afraid of them, you'll be happy you learned a few. Don't say I said so, but you might want to check this part out.

Chapter 17

Using the Mix Master:
Mail Merge

- -

In This Chapter

▶ How to set up mail merge (and why you may not want to)

▶ How to establish data fields and records

▶ How to enter real names and addresses

▶ How to make your form letter and plug in the fields used in the merge

▶ How to push the button for the merge, stand back, and watch it happen

- -

All Hail the Mail Merge

I don't know what the big thing is about mail merge. But I do understand why
Ed McMahon likes it: He uses it to send "personal" letters to me, my wife, each
of my children, and my dog Michelangelo.

A *mail merge,* in essence, is a utility that draws information from a database (a
mailing list) to create multiple copies of a document (most likely, a form letter).

To see word-processing companies treat mail merge with such reverence, you'd
think that mail merge is what separates the true professional word-processing
user from, well, the dummies. You'd think that every time you turn around you
should be sending "personalized" mailings to long lists of people. If you write a
report of first quarter sales results, you should send it to everybody in the
Manhattan directory. When you make a chart of projected revenues for an
improved product, you're not done (supposedly) until you mail merge it into a
list of 5,000 employees, clients, and well-wishers.

The truth is that mail merges really aren't worth the trouble of creating unless
you have more than 25 addresses that you mail letters to on an ongoing basis.
For all you gluttons for punishment out there who want to impress your friends
with a professional Christmas card mailing, the information in this chapter will
make you mail-merge pros (or send you off the edge of the planet) in a short
period of time.

Creating the Data File

Ami Pro's mail merge feature does its best to help you in the frustrating, painstaking chore of going through all the steps of programming (that's right, and don't let anybody tell you otherwise) a mail merge from start to finish. But as bad as the process sounds, you can handle it if you take a step-by-step approach.

Beginning the merge process is easy. Simply choose the Merge command from the File menu. The Welcome to Merge dialog box appears, as you can see in Figure 17-1. This dialog box looks like a friendly chance for a little conversation with your computer. If you're smart (which you probably really are, in spite of the title of this book), you'll shut off your computer right now and run like heck for the nearest watering hole.

Still here? OK, let's go.

Figure 17-1:
The
Welcome to
Merge
dialog box.

Setting your fields

First, do the first of the three recommended steps: Set up a data file. A data file has in it the *fields* (codes that are converted into specified pieces of information) that you'll later use in your form letter. The data file not only contains data, such as names and addresses, but it also contains the fields for each type of data you're going to put in the file (fields such as NAME and ADDRESS). To create a data file, follow these steps:

1. Choose the Merge command from the File menu.

You receive the Welcome to Merge dialog box, shown in Figure 17-1.

2. Select Step 1 in the Welcome to Merge dialog box and choose OK.

The Select Merge Data File dialog box, shown in Figure 17-2, appears.

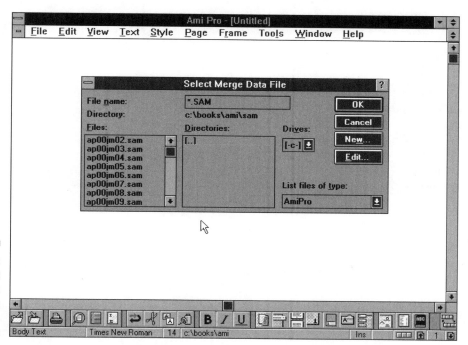

Figure 17-2:
The Select Merge Data File dialog box.

3. To create a new data file, click the New button.

The Create Data File dialog box appears, as shown in Figure 17-3.

4. In the Field Name text box, type the name of the first field (with no spaces) and click the Add button.

(An example field is NAME.) The field name appears in the Fields in data file box.

Continue to type in each field name in the order you want the fields to appear in each record. You can get an idea of field names from the sample data file in Figure 17-4.

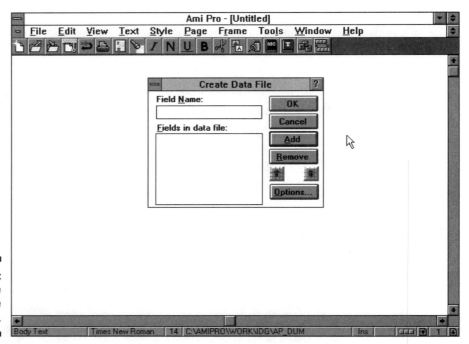

Figure 17-3:
The Create
Data File
dialog box.

Fields

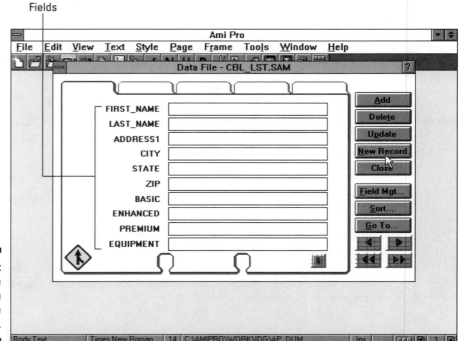

Figure 17-4:
A sample
data file in
the Data File
dialog box.

5. Click OK.

The field names appear briefly on-screen, as in Figure 17-5, before the Data File dialog box appears, ready for you to enter your first record.

At this point, it is a good idea to save your data file with a name that is appropriate for the information in the data fields. With your data fields safely stored, you can enter the records at any time.

6. Click the Close button and exit the file.

7. Save the file with a unique filename.

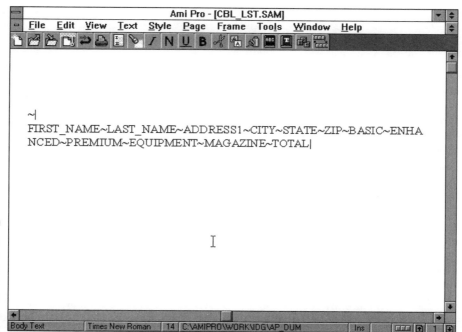

Figure 17-5:
The data file, ready to accept your data records.

Editing your fields

After you have created the data fields, you can edit them at any time. Simply open up the data file and follow these steps:

1. Choose the Merge command from the File menu.

2. Select Step 1 in the Welcome to Merge dialog box and choose OK.

3. In the Data File dialog box, click the Field Mgt button.

The Field Management dialog box appears, as you can see in Figure 17-6. You can add fields or rename them, but you cannot remove fields that you have already established.

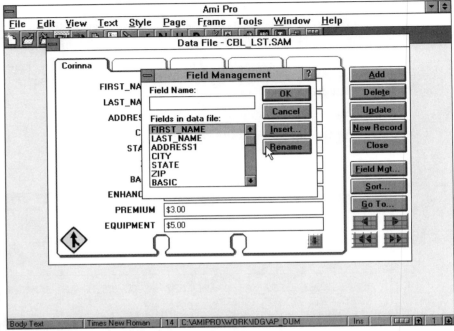

Figure 17-6:
The Field
Management
dialog box.

4. After you have edited your fields, choose OK.

You go back to the Data File dialog box, where any changes you made to your fields are now recorded.

You have to have your data file, with all its fields, created before you can merge them into a letter. I often find, however, that I have to write the letter first so that I know what fields I need. (Sort of like the chicken or the egg syndrome — which really *does* come first?). After I write the letter, I mark what I want the fields to be and then create the data fields as you did in this section. Then I create the actual form letter.

If you understand programming symbols, you can make the data file without using the Data File dialog box. Turn to the documentation or the Help files for a step-by-step guide to creating data files with programming symbols.

Entering the Data Records

After you have established your data fields, you can put in your *data records* (in this case, the specific names and addresses of the people). You can have as many data records as you need. The point of using the merge feature, however, is for you to have many address records. To create your data records, follow these steps:

1. **Open your data file and choose the Merge command from the File menu.**
2. **Select Step 1 in the Welcome to Merge dialog box and choose OK.**

   The Data File dialog box appears with the name of your data file on it.

3. **For each new record you want to create, first click the New Record button and then start to type the first field.**

   To move to the next field, use the Tab key. Your record will look something like the one in Figure 17-7.

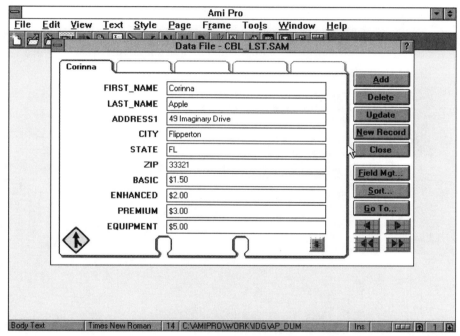

Figure 17-7:
A sample
data record.

4. **When you finish the first record, click the Add button.**

   Repeat Steps 3 and 4 for each record you want to put in the data file.

5. **When you've typed all your data records, choose Close.**

   You now have the data fields and your data records set up so that you can create a letter to go with the data file.

You can use the Data File dialog box to work with your data records. In Figure 17-7, notice that you can use the buttons to add and delete records, change the records (with the Update button), sort them numerically or alphabetically, and go to a specific record. Programmers and data entry people use a dialog box like this one all day long to do their work.

Creating the Merge Document

Creating your data file and entering all your records is the hardest part of the merge process. Now you need to create the *merge document,* which is usually the blank letter that receives the compiled data fields, by following these steps:

1. **In a new file, choose Merge from the File menu.**

2. **Select Step 2 from the Welcome to Merge dialog box and choose OK.**

   A dialog box appears asking whether you want to use the current document as the merge document.

3. **Choose Yes to use the current document.**

   The Select Merge Data File dialog box appears (review Figure 17-2).

4. **Find the data file you want to use and choose OK.**

   In this example, I used CBL_LST.SAM. The Insert Merge Field dialog box appears, as shown in Figure 17-8.

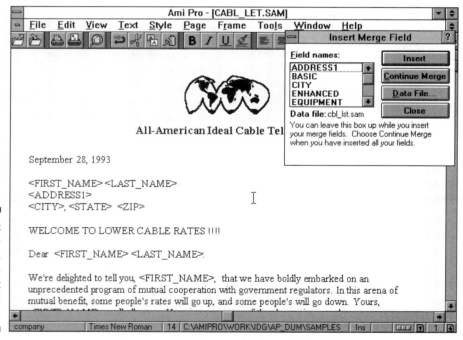

Figure 17-8: The merge document, with the Insert Merge Field dialog box.

5. **Now type your letter. Insert the field names by double-clicking them where you want them to appear.**

   Make sure your cursor is exactly where you want the field name to appear. (Now can you see why I usually type my letter first, before I create my data file? You simply must have the fields exactly as they appear in the style sheet you chose for your merge document.)

6. After finishing your letter, close the Insert Merge Field dialog box.

Putting in the merge fields takes a long time. If your finger slips, you may put one or more in the wrong place, and then you have to take the offenders out. You probably won't notice some of the mistakes you make until after you run your merge. So don't run the merge with 1,000 records right away. Try it with one or two records to make sure it really works the way you want.

The completed merge document in the example reads like Figure 17-9. (I had to hide all my menu bars and put the letter in 9 point to show the whole screen.)

Merge fields

All-American Ideal Cable Television

September 28, 1993

<FIRST_NAME> <LAST_NAME>
<ADDRESS1>
<CITY>, <STATE> <ZIP>

WELCOME TO LOWER CABLE RATES !!!!

Dear *<FIRST_NAME> <LAST_NAME>*:

We're delighted to tell you, <FIRST_NAME>, that we have boldly embarked on an unprecedented program of mutual cooperation with government regulators. In this arena of mutual benefit, some people's rates will go up, and some people's will go down. Yours, <FIRST_NAME>, will all go up. Here is a summary of the change in your charges:

Basic rate @md up by <BASIC>
Enhanced Rate @md up by <ENHANCED>
Premium channel @md up by <PREMIUM>
Equipment rental @md up by <EQUIPMENT>
Monthly Magazine @md up by <MAGAZINE>

Total monthly increase: <TOTAL>

As Americans, <FIRST_NAME>, all of us cherish the opportunity to do what is right. We're sure you'll agree that jacking up the rates every time you turn around is fair. We value your check each month and look forward to ripping you off for hundreds of unnecessary dollars in the near future. If you have any questions or complaints, please feel free to call our recently disconnected toll-free number. Thanking you for your money.

Guilelessly yours,

All your pals at All-American Ideal

Figure 17-9:
My
completed
merge
document.

Running the Merge

After you have created your data file and merge document, anyone can run the merge by following these steps:

1. In the merge document, choose Merge from the File menu.

2. In the Welcome to Merge dialog box, select Step 3 and choose OK.

The Merge dialog box appears, as in Figure 17-10, with the correct data file assigned to this merge document.

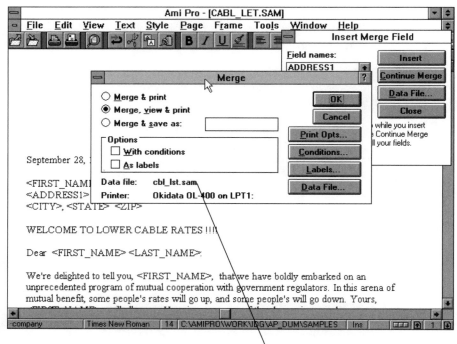

Figure 17-10:
The Merge
dialog box.

Name of data file

3. To see your letter on-screen before you print, select the Merge, view & print option and choose OK.

Ami Pro shows you a sample letter on-screen, as in Figure 17-11.

4. If you want to print all the letters, choose Print All in the Merge dialog box.

If you are printing addresses, you're probably printing them on labels. To print on labels, click the Labels button in the Merge dialog box (see Figure 17-10) and be sure that the Merge Labels dialog box, shown in Figure 17-12, describes the labels on your printer. Click OK to close the dialog box, and notice how the As labels option is now checked in the Options box of the Merge dialog box.

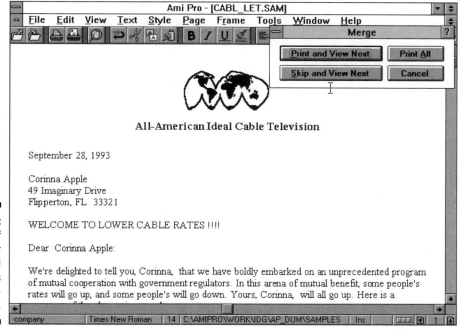

Figure 17-11:
The first of your personalized letters appears on-screen.

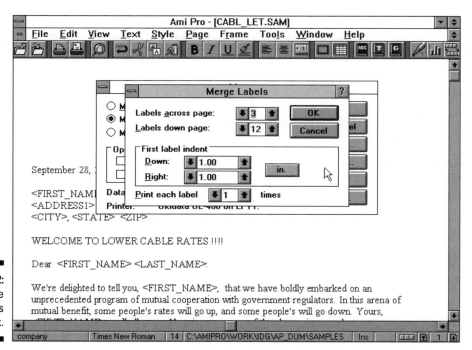

Figure 17-12:
The Merge Labels dialog box.

Figure 17-13 shows the complete, printed sample letter.

All-American Ideal Cable Television

September 28, 1993

Corinna Apple
49 Imaginary Drive
Flipperton, FL 33321

WELCOME TO LOWER CABLE RATES !!!!

Dear Corinna Apple:

We're delighted to tell you, Corinna, that we have boldly embarked on an unprecedented program of mutual cooperation with government regulators. In this arena of mutual benefit, some people's rates will go up, and some people's will go down. Yours, Corinna, will all go up. Here is a summary of the change in your charges:

Basic rate -- up by $1.50
Enhanced Rate -- up by $2.00
Premium channel -- up by $3.00
Equipment rental -- up by $5.00
Monthly Magazine -- up by $3.50

Total monthly increase: $15.00

As Americans, Corinna, all of us cherish the opportunity to do what is right. We're sure you'll agree that jacking up the rates every time you turn around is fair. We value your check each month and look forward to ripping you off for hundreds of unnecessary dollars in the near future. If you have any questions or complaints, please feel free to call our recently disconnected toll-free number. Thanking you for your money.

Guilelessly yours,

All your pals at All-American Ideal

Address • City, State ZIP • Phone • Fax

Figure 17-13:
Finally, the complete sample letter!

There's probably been more computer happy talk written about the merge function than about anything else. Everyone seems to be holding to the myth that you all have many occasions for merging data fields with form letters and that doing so is a trivial, intuitive matter. Neither myth can be further from the truth. You hardly ever have to do a merge, and if you do, it's a difficult process.

Macros, with their intimidating name and surly reputation, are actually just the opposite of merges. You will use macros often, and, despite the name, they're reasonably easy to use (up to a point). The next chapter tiptoes through the subject of macros.

Chapter 18

Automating Your Cooking with Macros

*W*hat is it that gives the word *macro* its chic? The first time I saw the word, it was in front of *economics,* I think, but I've also seen it used with *physics.* No matter how many times I see the word *macro,* I (being a dummy) never really know what it means. I think that it has something to do with big (as opposed to *micro,* which I do recognize and can remember, mainly because of *microscope*).

What is particularly big about a macro in Ami Pro more or less eludes me, however. A macro is big, I guess, because it always has some small stuff inside of it, such as steps. Maybe macros should be called ladders. Or staircases. I can visualize those terms better.

In any case, a *macro*, silly as the name might be, is a stored list of several commands or options, which, when played back, activates these commands in the order they were recorded. You can create macros to automate your tedious or frequent tasks, such as typing your company's name.

Examining the Macros in the Ami Pro Program

Macros, as previously stated, do the work of many keystrokes. The easiest way to see how a macro works is to run one that's already in the program. Didn't these Ami Pro programmers have anything to do but write macros? There are piles and piles of them — just like movie outtakes — pretty hot, but not hot enough to make the final cut. So, like outtakes, little programs that don't get in the Ami Pro menus end up in the collection of macros.

To run a macro that is already a part of the Ami Pro program, follow these steps:

1. **Put the cursor in the place in your document where you want to run the macro.**

2. **From the Tools menu, choose Macros and then Playback, as shown in Figure 18-1.**

   The Play Macro dialog box appears, as you can see in Figure 18-2, where you can look over the list of macros and decide which ones to run.

   Notice that all macros have an .SMM extension. Just as all document files have an .SAM extension and all style sheets have an .STY extension, macros can be identified by their extensions. Also, Ami Pro stores the macros in their own subdirectory, C:\AMIPRO\MACROS.

3. **Select the macro you want to run and choose OK (or double-click the macro).**

   Notice that as you select a macro, the Macro description box tells you what the macro does (if this option is checked). After you choose OK, you see the results of the macro in your document.

   How about a game? (You can play a game with a macro? YES!) GAME.SMM is the Mind Blaster game, Figure 18-3 (written on personal time, not on company time — NOT!). With a macro, you can do about anything. When you're finished playing, choose Quit.

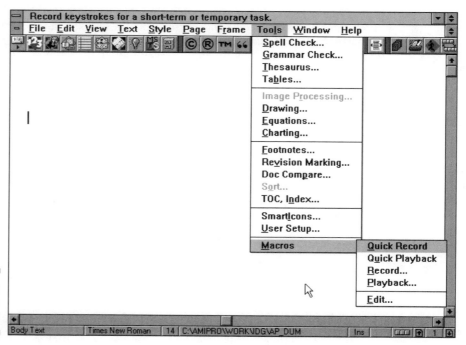

Figure 18-1:
The Macros
submenu.

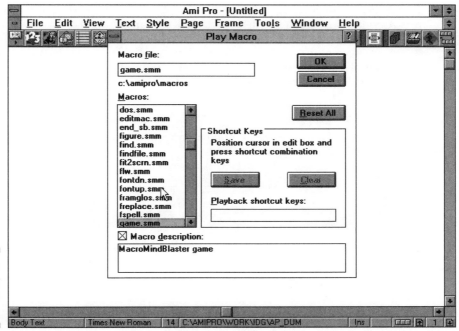

Figure 18-2:
The Play
Macro
dialog box.

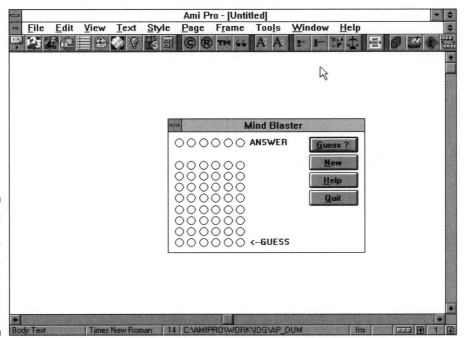

Figure 18-3:
The Mind
Blaster
game,
accessed
through the
GAME.SMM
macro.

Some of the best macros are the easiest to use if you bring up the Macro Goodies SmartIcon set on-screen. Click the change SmartIcon set icon in the status bar, as always, and choose *Macro Goodies*. Right-click any of these icons to read what they do (in the title bar, remember?). The MS-DOS icon, for example, moves you to DOS. A message comes up asking whether you want to exit to DOS and explaining how to get back to your document, as illustrated in Figure 18-4.

Table 18-1 lists some of the other macros (and their icons) that come with Ami Pro. I listed only the ones I thought you might find useful.

The MS-DOS SmartIcon   Macro Goodies SmartIcon set ─

Figure 18-4:
This macro
box means
you're on
your way to
DOS, if you
like.

Change SmartIcon set icon

Table 18-1 Some Macro Goodies SmartIcons

SmartIcon	What It Does
	Calls up the Play Macro dialog box so you can choose which macro to play
	Shells to DOS
	Starts Windows File Manager
	Inserts a copyright symbol
	Inserts a register mark
	Inserts a trademark symbol
	Changes quotations to typeset characters
	Fits your text within the screen
	Enables you to select pages to print
	Prints current document with default settings (you skip the Print dialog box)

Macros, then, are not-ready-for-prime-time programs that somebody worked awfully hard to make (all on company time, of course). Committees probably met for days over which programs would go on the menus and which ones would get relegated to the Play Macro dialog box. I'm sure that it was hard to break the news to the programmers about where their little programs ended up, but somebody had to do it.

Because the macros aren't quite ready for prime time, they're not always as robust as programs that are on the menus. I used to use the TILEHORZ.SMM macro, for example, which *tiled* (made windows smaller so both documents show on-screen) two open documents horizontally on-screen. Unfortunately, old TILEHORZ.SMM flakes out unexpectedly at awkward moments, and I had to go through the extra work of getting my documents back on-screen. I'll be blunt: The programmed macros do not provide the consistent results that the menus do for the same function. If the macros were good enough, they would be menu commands.

Making Your Own Holy Macros

The Ami Pro programmers have obviously dawdled away a great deal of time thinking up every conceivable function you can do with a macro. Why, then, would you want to make one of your own? Well, peculiarities can come up in your documents that the Ami Pro programmers didn't anticipate.

I like to make macros for a word or phrase that I type over and over again in a document (for example, a company's name). To make the figures for this chapter, for example, I would have had to type the phrase *Soup City Center* over and over again (that is the theme of the figures). Instead, I made a macro to insert this phrase anywhere in a document with just a few keystrokes.

To create your own macro, follow these steps:

1. **From the Tools menu, choose Macros and then Record (review Figure 18-1).**

   The Record Macro dialog box appears, as shown in Figure 18-5.

2. **Type a name for the macro, one that identifies the macro's function, in the Macro file text box.**

   (The extension is already there for you.) I chose the name SOUP.SMM for my macro.

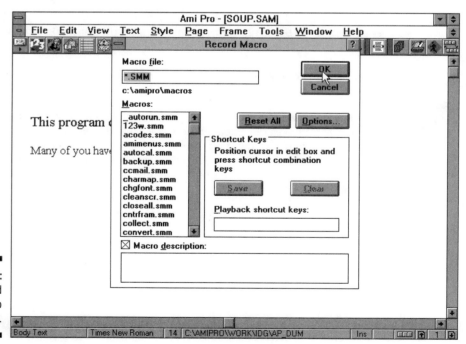

Figure 18-5:
The Record
Macro
dialog box.

3. **With the cursor in the <u>P</u>layback shortcut keys text box, press the
shortcut keys you want to use to activate the macro.**

The shortcut keys are automatically recorded for you in the text box. For
my macro, I chose Ctrl+Shift+S, as you can see in Figure 18-6. I always
assign keystrokes to my macros, usually with the Shift and Ctrl keys,
because the keyboard is the fastest way to play back a macro.

Be careful not to choose a shortcut sequence that is used by default by
Ami Pro (for example, Ctrl+P prints your document). Actually, if you never
use the shortcut keys on the menus, you can override them with no other
consequences. It's just good manners not to override the default settings,
though, just in case you forget that you did so later on. In general, just
avoid overriding any of the default settings that you use regularly.

Don't frustrate yourself trying to type in a Macro description. Heaven only
knows why, but you can't do it in the Macro <u>d</u>escription text box. The only
way I know to put in a description is to edit the .SMM file after you make it,
choose Save <u>A</u>s from the <u>F</u>ile menu, and put in the description then.

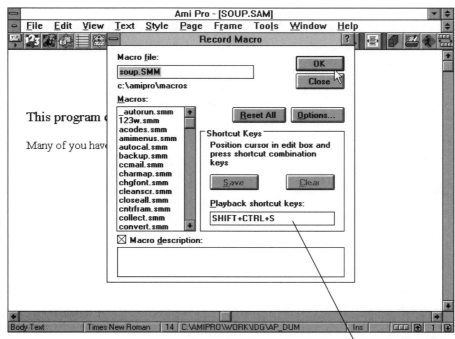

Figure 18-6:
The
completed
Record
Macro
Dialog box.

Pick a shortcut sequence that
hasn't been used before .

4. Choose OK.

The status bar displays a Recording Macro message in red, as in Figure 18-7. This message is the only sign that you're recording a macro and not just doing your work. You easily can forget that you're recording a macro, especially if you're interrupted by a phone call or your spouse starts hollering at you unreasonably. Then everything you do until you realize you're recording a macro goes into a GIGANTIC macro that you don't want. (It's like inadvertently having the answering machine record a two-hour phone conversation with your mother-in-law.)

5. Do the steps in your macro or type the phrase you want the macro to record.

For my example, I typed **Soup City Center**, highlighted it, then applied bold to the text. Yes, you simply type the text, choose the command, or do whatever it is you want to record, in the exact same manner you do if you were just working.

6. When you are done, choose <u>M</u>acros and then End <u>R</u>ecord from the Too<u>l</u>s menu.

The Recording Macro message disappears from the status bar, and the macro is ready for you to use it whenever you like.

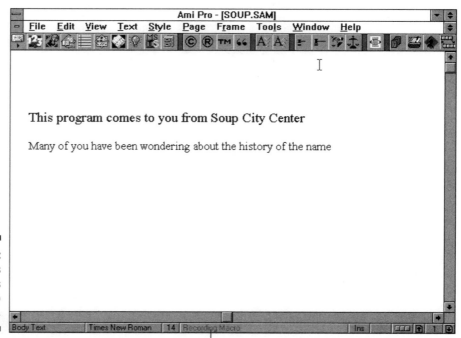

Figure 18-7:
The status bar displays a macro message.

Macro message

Sometimes, you can't put everything you want in a macro, such as the Find & Replace command from the Edit menu. Or, as in my Soup City Center macro, I tried to include the ™ symbol with the Soup macro, but I couldn't get the symbol to go in the macro (so I just pretended I didn't want it). To get something into a macro that won't go in the usual way when you record it, you have to put in the command by using the *macro language*. That's a nerd activity. Avoid macro language if at all possible, or hire someone to put it in a macro for you.

The next section tells you how to run your homemade macros.

Running Your Homemade Macros

After you have made your macro, you can run it the way you run any other macro by following these steps:

1. **Be sure that your cursor is in the place you want your macro to run.**

2. **From the Tools menu, choose Macros and then Playback, or click the Playback macro SmartIcon (shown in the margin).**

3. **In the Play Macro dialog box, select the name of the macro you want to run in your document and choose OK.**

   Ami Pro plays the macro. In my example in Figure 18-8, I used the macro to put *Soup City Center* in the document two more times.

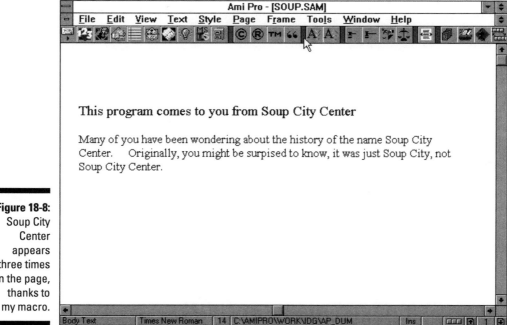

Figure 18-8:
Soup City
Center
appears
three times
on the page,
thanks to
my macro.

Remember that you can simply press the shortcut keys that you assigned to your macro, causing it to run immediately. This method is much faster than the three-step method mentioned previously.

When you press your shortcut keys and the macro runs, you'll see how much time macros can potentially save you. Another great thing about macros is that there's no chance of a typo, a spelling mistake, or an incorrect capitalization (assuming, of course, you got it right in the macro).

Assigning a SmartIcon to Your Macro

Macros are still not quick enough for you? Now you're getting into some pretty heady stuff — the territory of programmers, not dummies — but you can assign a SmartIcon to a macro you use a great deal. That way, you just click the SmartIcon (like you do any other) and the macro runs! I've assigned lots of macros to SmartIcons myself, and I'm a dummy.

To assign a macro to a SmartIcon, do the following:

1. **Make sure the set of icons that you want to change is showing in your icon bar.**

   Click the Change SmartIcon Set button to change to the desired set.

2. **From the Tools menu, choose SmartIcons.**

   The SmartIcons dialog box appears, as shown in Figure 18-9.

3. **Click the Edit Icon button.**

   The Edit SmartIcon dialog box appears, as you can see in Figure 18-10.

   In the Available icons listbox, you can find many icons to use for your macro. Choose an icon that you know you'll rarely use for its original purpose, such as the lightbulb icon, and turn it into your personal macro SmartIcon.

Be careful when choosing an available icon. Some icons are standard Ami Pro icons, such as the rainbow-colored *S* icon, and cannot be edited. You will get a warning box on-screen if you choose one of these icons, so you immediately can make another choice.

4. **In the Available icons box, click the lightbulb icon or another available icon of your choice.**

   The lightbulb icon, or the one of your choice, is highlighted in full color in the box at the center of your screen, as in Figure 18-11.

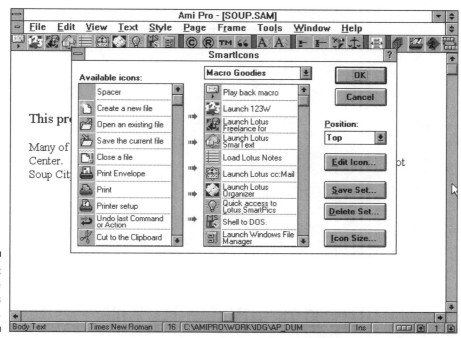

Figure 18-9:
The
SmartIcons
dialog box.

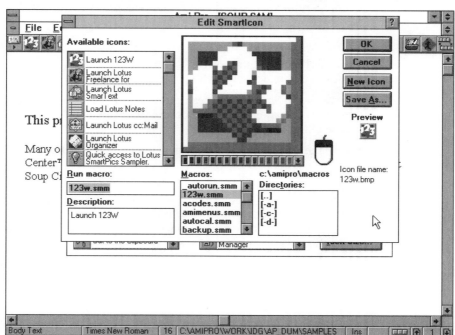

Figure 18-10:
The Edit
SmartIcon
dialog box.

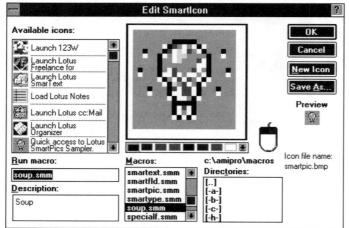

Figure 18-11:
The icon
that you
chose to be
your macro
SmartIcon.

5. **Highlight the name of your macro in the Macros listbox.**

   The name of the macro appears in the Run Macro box. In my example, I highlighted SOUP.SMM.

6. **In the Description text box, type in a brief description of your macro or the phrase that your macro represents.**

   Keep the phrase brief so that it can appear easily in the description box next to the icon. I used the word *Soup*.

7. **Click OK.**

   The SmartIcon with its new description appears in the Available Icons listbox in the SmartIcons dialog box.

8. **If your macro SmartIcon doesn't normally appear in the icon bar you are currently using, simply click and drag the icon to the listbox in the center of the dialog box.**

   Your SmartIcon now appears in the icon bar of your document.

9. **Click OK.**

Creating your own macro SmartIcon may seem time-consuming; however, this technique does produce the fastest way to generate your macros in a document. With the cursor in the proper place in your text, you simply click the macro SmartIcon, and the macro runs — one easy step.

Making a quick macro

If I'm going to go to the trouble of making a macro, I want to be able to keep it; therefore, I hardly ever use Ami Pro's Quick Record command, which lets you make a macro that's only for your current session. As soon as you close Ami Pro — or in the unlikely event that Ami Pro crashes — you lose the macro.

Also, if you make more than one quick macro at a time, you only can use Quick Playback for the most recent macro. (And if you're going to use any other kind of playback, why use a quick macro?)

To make a quick macro for a document, follow these steps.

1. **Put the pointer where you want to run the macro the first time.**

2. **From the Tools menu, choose Macros and then Quick Record (review Figure 18-1).**

As in recording a regular macro, the status bar reads Recording Macro.

3. **Type the keystrokes for the macro.**

4. **From the Macros menu, choose End Quick Record.**

If you're going to use the menus, there's not much quick about playing back the quick macro. With your cursor in the proper place in the document, choose Macros and then Quick Playback from the Tools menu. The macro inserts the phrase where it should be in the text.

Ami Pro has a SmartIcon for quick playback. Refer to Chapter 5 to see how to put the SmartIcon in the icon bar you're currently using. After you have the SmartIcon for quick playback, you can play back your quick macro fast enough to justify making it in the first place.

Fixing a Macro's Code

If you need to change a spelling in a macro or add a word or two to a phrase, you don't have to create a new macro — you simply edit the existing one. To edit a macro, do the following:

1. **From the Tools menu, choose Macros and then Edit.**

   The Edit Macro dialog box appears, as shown in Figure 18-12.

2. **Double-click the name of the macro you want to edit.**

   Your macro document appears on-screen, looking something like the one in Figure 18-13. Suppose I wanted to edit my SOUP.SMM macro and change the word *Center* to the British spelling *Centre*.

3. **Very carefully, make the changes to your macro.**

   In my case, I simply change *Center* to *Centre*.

4. **From the File menu, choose Close to close the file.**

5. **Choose Yes to accept the changes to the file.**

The next time you run the macro, the changes will appear in it. Editing the macro does not change any of the words in the macros you have already run.

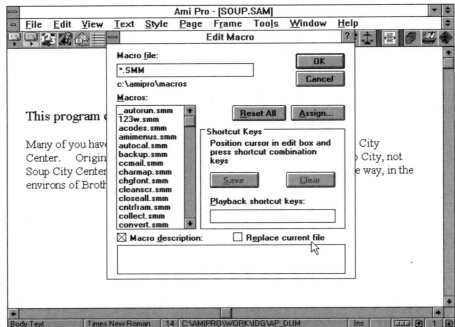

Figure 18-12:
The Edit
Macro
dialog box.

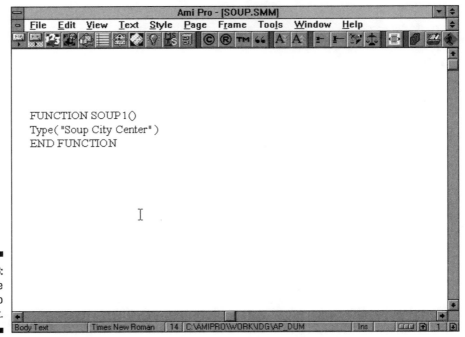

Figure 18-13:
A sample
macro
document.

Notice in Figure 18-13 the words in all capital letters, such as (FUNCTION). These words are programming commands, and the parentheses are programming symbols. If you change one of these commands even slightly, your macros may not work any more. Programmers type macros in directly. Non-programmers have to think twice about editing any macro. If you mess up the syntax in the macro, you'll either have to do it over or go begging, hat in hand, to some programmer who may help you. (I recommend redoing the macro in that case.)

Now that all is said and done about macros, I hope I've made my point that macros can be easy to use once you get the hang of them. Macros really aren't that difficult to use, even if they do have a pretentious, pseudotechnical name. You can live without them, though. People have for centuries. The chapter concludes the instructional part of the book. The next part has a few lists that will help you remember the important (and not-so-important) features of Ami Pro.

Part VII
The Part of Tens

The 5th Wave   **By Rich Tennant**

"WHY DON'T YOU TAKE THAT OUTSIDE, HUMPTY, AND PLAY WITH IT ON THE WALL?"

In this part...

Making a list of ten has great organizing power. This part looks at Ami Pro one last time and allows those lists of ten to have their organizing effect. You may have seen this stuff before, but not in this way. Oh, and there's a few funny ones too.

Chapter 19
Ten Great Ami Pro Capabilities I Frequently Use

If you happen to have read those sections, you may have detected my enthusiasm for some of these things in Ami Pro as I talked about them. All users develop little pets as they go along, just as teachers and coaches do. Obviously, you're free to develop your own personal biases, and you'll probably hate some of the things that I like the most. That's OK. I'll most likely never know about it anyway.

Outliner

I'm working in the Outliner right now, as you read. (Well, I'll be done by the time you read this.) You may remember the benefits of outlining, discussed in Chapter 11.

Here are a few reasons I like the Outliner:

1. **You can collapse your text and see all your headings at once, without any text getting in the way.**

   I like to keep my headings parallel, but I just can't do it without the Outliner. I can't remember what one of them looked like if I have to go down a few pages to see the next one. Besides, I forget to compare them. With the Outliner, I compare all the headings at the end, covering all the bases.

   Figure 19-1 (top screen) shows a complete outline — too much stuff to digest all at once. The bottom screen shows the same outline collapsed so that you just see the main subheadings.

2. **You can move whole sections around easily.**

   Being organized isn't that easy for me. I get distracted and fill in whole parts of my chapter and then realize that what I wrote in the beginning goes better at the end. It's easy to make the move using the Outliner.

3. **You can see your heading as you move it.**

   One of the things I don't like about cut and paste is that, once you cut something to the Clipboard, you can't see it. Well, I hate to admit it, but many's the time that in the instant after I put something in there . . . I forget what the heck it was. With the Outliner, I can look right at a section head as I slide it up and down through the other heads until I find the right place for it.

4. **Clicking the little buttons — the fat expand button and all those — is fun.**

   I love clicking a certain level, such as 3, and having just that level and no other lower ones stay on-screen. That's cool.

5. **You might get an ego rush out of knowing that you work in a hot way that most people don't.**

Style sheets

When I used other word processors, where style sheets were usually called templates, I just basically didn't have any. Maybe one or two came with the word processor, but I did my best to stay away from them. My page was always an ordinary page with some words on it. If my words didn't carry any weight, my document didn't either, because there was sure nothing special about how it looked.

Now I make fancy fax sheets, such as the one in Figure 19-2.

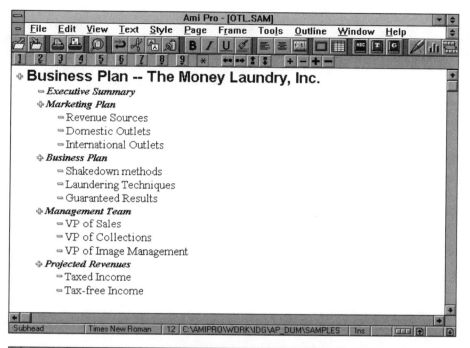

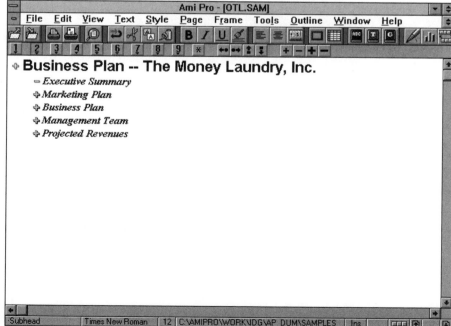

Figure 19-1:
How
Outliner can
organize
your work.

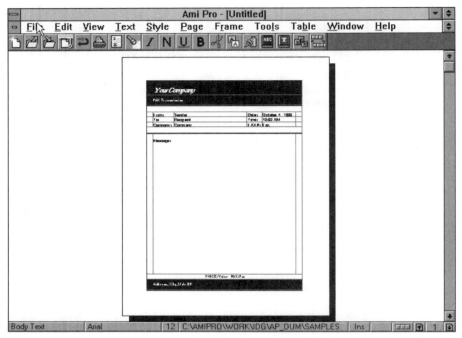

Figure 19-2:
A hot-
looking fax
sheet I
didn't have
to format.

I can make neat cover sheets, fancy overheads, elaborate looking newsletters —
and I really do make all those things. (They aren't just unused horsepower
sitting under the hood of my computer.) I don't just look like a word processing
nobody any more, even though I am. Chapter 3 discusses style sheets in detail.

Styles

Styles are good if you keep changing your mind about the way the document
looks. If you use the select and shoot technique to change all the typefaces, for
example, you've got a headache. You change some you didn't mean to. You
think you've selected some when you really haven't, so you don't change them.
You can waste days doing the little change that nobody ever notices or con-
gratulates you for.

With styles, you simply modify the style in one place, and Ami Pro changes it
every place for you.

Also, when you design one style for a level one heading, for example, you don't
have to remember each time what type of formatting you used to create that
heading. You simply attach that style to the text. This helps you remain consistent in your document, so you don't end up with three different types of level-
one headings. That way, when someone else reads your document, they won't
be muttering unflattering things about you.

SmartIcons

Picking something from the menu takes at least two clicks — one to open the menu and one to start the command you want. And when you click a menu, sometimes you click the command above or below the one you want, which sometimes spawns some whole process that you have no interest in doing. Also, lettered commands are frequently harder to remember than visual cues.

SmartIcons are a single click away, hard to misclick because they're so big, and harder to forget because they are visual cues.

And besides, you can set up your own personal set of SmartIcons including only the ones you frequently use and listing first the ones you use all the time. Also, I love the surge of power of clicking a tiny little drawing and having it do some elaborate series of steps. See Chapter 5 for more information on SmartIcons.

For those of you who are keyboard-oriented, the hot keys are a real time-saver as well. Hot keys are beneficial because you don't have to take your hands off the keyboard in order to use them (a few seconds saved there!). Hot keys, indicated by underlined letters on the menu, take awhile to learn and they aren't always the first word of the command, but if the keyboard is your preference, they are definitely time-savers. And most of the Windows products use the same hot keys for their commands, meaning you have to learn fewer hot keys.

Frames

Suppose you're working with a newsletter and you decide you want to put a clever little factoid inside a box on the page — "Last year 425,000 people with no interest attended ball games in New York to please a partner."

So, you click the Frame SmartIcon, type in your words, and drag the frame to whatever size and position you want on the page. It works great and it looks good most of the time even if you never studied art and don't get it within the exact number of millimeters on the page. (Read more about frames in Chapter 12.)

One time I was having a heck of a time getting the page number to print on my page. Something cute that Ami Pro was doing put the number too far up in the margin, and I was getting sick of trying things to get it where I wanted it. So I just put it inside an invisible frame, dragged the frame to just where I wanted it, and had the last laugh on Ami Pro without having to figure out the real cause of the problem. Frames can come in handy at the most unexpected times!

Status bar

The Styles box seems to be in the way no matter where you slide it on-screen. But when you do want it, you want it so fast that you don't want to take time to figure out how to get it back on the page. Thanks to the Status bar, you can click the same information you would have clicked in the Styles box, without having to show the Styles box. The Status bar is always there, it is easy to click to see all your formatting options (you can even find out what time it is), and it doesn't get in the way. Figure 19-3 shows the Status bar, marked with all the options you can change.

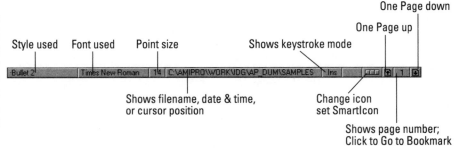

Figure 19-3:
The Status bar is likely to become your best friend.

Sample boxes

One of the horrible things about using word processing before (though nobody was ever supposed to say so) was how long it took to do anything other than type in text. If you were going to put in a graphic or even change your typeface, you had to follow an elaborate series of steps, including printing your project several times to see whether it matched your expectations, and praying to a higher power.

Very few people ever complained about this lost time, but there was a great deal of guilt because of that secretly misused time. Job stress increased. People ended up having to take unexplained leaves of absence. Maybe some of them even died, though I doubt it.

Suppose you had the picture inside a frame, and you wanted to have a frame that looked different. Get ready to end up on the analyst's couch. It would take much longer to get it right than you could ever admit to your boss (or to yourself if you're self-employed).

With the *sample box,* though, you can immediately see what your change will look like. Figure 19-4 shows an example of a sample box (aka: *idiot box*) that shows a possible frame. I have used these extensively throughout this book to show you your possible changes. Nerds claim that they know what a deep shadow is without having to view it in a sample box. Well, aren't they hot! Most of us don't. This box is a life-saver (well, maybe nobody died, like I said).

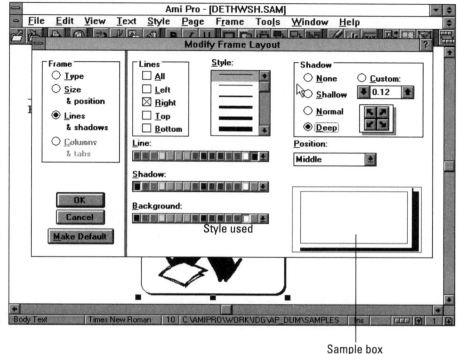

Figure 19-4:
The sample box can save you hours of tedious changing and pounds of precious paper.

Sample box

Drag and drop editing

To drag and drop, as you might recall, you double-click the word (or words) you want to move, hold down the mouse button, drag the cursor to the new location, and then release the button. Your words are magically placed in the new location.

Drag and drop is a rather new feature to word processing and I'm trying to assimilate this one as fast as I can because it's great! The great benefit to drag and drop is that it is much faster than cutting and pasting, even with the icons.

Remember Undo, particularly if you do much of dragging and dropping, because many times you drag from the wrong place or drop in the wrong place and create such an incomprehensible mess that it's easier just to forget about what you did and try again.

Tables

It's really tough to get data into columns. I hate to admit it, but I even use *spreadsheets* sometimes, because they make it so much easier to keep track of information in columns.

Because you can change the cursor into a Ninja-weapon-looking pointer and move the sides of the table (shown in Figure 19-5), it's easy to change the size of the table (one of the main reasons dummies don't ordinarily want to work with one — a rigid table is an awful table.) Besides, the cells grow when you type into them — another form of flexibility that's a great boon to dummies.

It's also easy to get around in the table. The Tab key moves you about anywhere, and if you're stuck, you can just click where you want to be.

I don't put stuff into logical categories every day. That's for nerds. When somebody forces me to do it (because I'm hungry and need to make the money to buy food), I'll use a table to help me out. That way, it can keep track of the logic (much as an Outliner does). Refer to Chapter 14 for more information on tables.

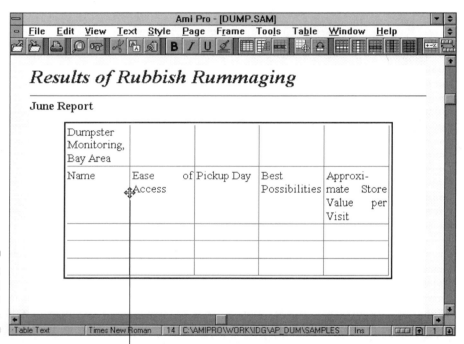

Figure 19-5:
You can
stretch a
table easily.

Ninja pointer

Macros

I bet you're surprised to see this in the list. *"He uses macros. A dummy like him! Come on!"* I can hear you from here, the disbelief hanging in your voice.

I don't use them for hard stuff very much. I would, but as I mentioned in the chapter, some of the menu commands don't go into macros. To get them in, you'd have to write code, which I avoid. When you try to put them in using the Macro Recorder, Ami Pro doesn't tell you anything is wrong, but the macro just doesn't work correctly. You might get some incomprehensible, bozo message, or the macro might just not do all that it's supposed to. That's annoying.

I find myself using macros for certain stock phrases — like the names of products. They're always so cute that they're hard to type — MegAlumps, SuperInFlataBulls, NomencLatures. So I just have to get them right once — when I type the macro — and then I can use them forevermore. This way, when I get them wrong, hey, no problem. I just go in and edit the macro, get it right, and then use it forevermore. And I use the keyboard shortcut to play back the macro, so it's quick to do. (Refer to Chapter 18 for a complete description of macros.)

Chapter 20

Ten Great Ami Pro Capabilities I Almost Never Use

. . . .

In This Chapter

▶ Power fields

▶ Nonsense equations

▶ Footnotes

▶ The Grammar Checker

▶ Bookmarks

▶ Clean screen

▶ The ruler

▶ The Styles box

▶ Fast Format

▶ Initial Caps command

. . . .

Some of these aversions are purely irrational. Who can say why someone doesn't like something? Some of them have to do with my own overweening sense of laziness. And some of them are to fill up the list, so I can reach ten. (Actually, I had to pare this list down from 14, and I apologize to those who didn't make it — Master document, WordPerfect translator, footnote, and mail merge. I want all you near-misses to know that you fully deserved to survive the cut.)

Power fields

These are too hard. I don't even like to think about them. I don't even like to say the word. Mere mortals don't use power fields, only mortals who want to appear as if they are supermortals, or people who worked real hard at programming when you were learning something worthwhile in school. Power fields are hard. That's all you need to know about them. Ignore them and feel no guilt.

Equations

I never use equations, that's all. You can use Ami Pro to rattle off an equation quickly, but you have to have some reason to put the mathematical characters into your text. One equation says omega plus or minus the square root of upside down A equals 14 kappa as an integral of N to the thirty third-power, but, of course, that doesn't mean anything unless you know the value of upside down A.

If somebody has been trying to do equations in WordPerfect, this is probably a whole lot easier way to do them. But someone who stumbles into them unaware should know just one thing — beat feet. This feature is for nerds.

Footnotes

If something is important enough to be in a footnote, it's good enough to go into the regular text. I forget who taught me that (or which 500 or so people, because I've heard it many times), but it pretty much applies to all the writing I ever do.

I hate footnotes on principle, that's all. I rather like the way Ami Pro handles them, but footnotes in general are phony and pretentious. If you have to use footnotes, Ami Pro is the way to go.

No, a footnote is a cryptic way of saying, "Don't read what I've put into this note, and as a matter of fact, don't even bother to read what you're reading right now either." So, I don't use Ami Pro's footnoting myself, but maybe you'll want to.

Grammar Checker

I loved this when I first got it. I always dreamed about knowing the Flesch Reading Ease Score for any piece that I wrote. Seriously. I was kind of curious about that. Well, OK, I wasn't. But I did want to know my Gunning's Fog Index. Guess not.

Basically, I found that the hit rate on these grammar suggestions wasn't that high for me. I don't want to go around touting my own background in grammar (a little like touting one's background in Medieval Latin or something. I mean, who cares?), but I do know enough to know that the Grammar Checker has set me down the wrong path a few times.

I made an honest attempt to use the Grammar Checker, but it kept flagging dumb stuff. If I had all year to train the Grammar Checker just so, maybe it would be a great thing. Maybe I just didn't give it a fair chance. I gave it an unfair one, though, and I stopped using it, for whatever that may be worth.

Bookmarks

When you use a book, how many bookmarks do you put into it? Does the term *one* ring a bell? And what do you name your bookmark? Does the name nothing make sense to you? You put a scrap of the *New York Times* at your place in the book. Later, you pick up the book, open to the scrap of paper, put the scrap into the back of the book for later use, and resume reading.

Now, suppose you had two bookmarks? Would you turn first to one place, and then to the second, and try to remember which was the place where you really were? And wouldn't you find that annoying? What if you put in four bookmarks? Let's take this to its logical limit. Suppose you have a scrap of the *New York Times* between every set of pages in perhaps a 1,000-page Norman Mailer book — the short life and hard times of Gary Gilmore or something. Would those little insertions be helpful, even if they had names?

I don't think so.

Once in awhile I put in a single bookmark, which I usually name *Mark* (and that tells me nothing about where it is). In general, though, I find them confusing.

Clean screen

If you want, you can get all the menus, SmartIcons, scroll bars, restore buttons, and everything off your screen, kind of like going in and putting masking tape over everything on the dashboard of the car and then, for good measure, taking out the steering wheel.

Figure 20-1 shows the screen with everything gone except the little icon in the bottom right that lets you get everything back (if you know what that icon does). This is a great feature if you want to sit and stare at your screen all day without being able to accomplish anything. It's also a great way to set up coworkers (on April Fool's Day) so that they return to the desk and feel scared to death because they have broken Ami Pro.

You can even set up your clean screen options so that there is no icon you can click to get everything back. Then you're completely unable to do anything and unable to get back the missing stuff. Well, that's just ducky. I need something like that all the time.

Press Alt+V to get the View menu and, from there, work your way back to having a dirty, helpful screen again. See Chapter 9 if you've completely forgotten (or never knew) how to get back the stuff you scrubbed off your screen.

All-American Ideal Cable Television

September 28, 1993

<FIRST_NAME> <LAST_NAME>
<ADDRESS1>
<CITY>, <STATE> <ZIP>

WELCOME TO LOWER CABLE RATES !!!!

Dear <FIRST_NAME> <LAST_NAME>:

We're delighted to tell you, <FIRST_NAME>, that we have boldly embarked on an unprecedented program of mutual cooperation with government regulators. In this arena of mutual benefit, some people's rates will go up, and some people's will go down. Yours, <FIRST_NAME>, will all go up. Here is a summary of the change in your charges:

Basic rate @md up by <BASIC>
Enhanced Rate @md up by <ENHANCED>
Premium channel @md up by <PREMIUM>
Equipment rental @md up by <EQUIPMENT>
Monthly Magazine @md up by <MAGAZINE>

Total monthly increase: <TOTAL>

As Americans, <FIRST_NAME>, all of us cherish the opportunity to do what is right. We're sure you'll agree that jacking up the rates every time you turn around is fair. We value your check each month and look forward to ripping you off for hundreds of unnecessary dollars in the near future. If you have any questions or complaints, please feel free to call our recently disconnected toll-free number. Thanking you for your money.

Guilelessly yours,

All your pals at All-American Ideal

Figure 20-1:
You can set up the screen like this, but why would you want to?

Ruler

Rulers stick in my craw. I think it goes back to some previous life (or maybe it was this life) when teachers used rulers to whack me on the hands. Also, rulers were a convenient thing to lose, or just not have when the time came to use them in class. Also, rulers are for doing painstaking things that never come out right, like measuring the page and putting boxes on it in just the right place.

It's easy enough to put a ruler on-screen. Once it's in there, though, you either have to ignore something that's there taking up so much of your usable space or actually put it to use. And putting it to use implies manually lining things up in just the right place. It implies eyestrain.

I think in older word processors and on typewriters people got used to looking up and seeing right there on a ruler where their margins and tabs were and everything. I suppose that's good, but, because I don't do it myself, I don't want rulers in my text and almost never put them there.

Styles box

The poor Styles box has suffered a rapid and almost total fall from prominence. Before the pop-up Status bar came along, anybody who worked with styles (which was probably a minority of the Ami Pro population to begin with) no doubt worked with the Styles box, too. It even had its own toggle switch. Ami Pro is just being polite and a little bit sentimental to still have it.

It has gone the way of the corner grocery, the TV repairer, the honest automobile mechanic. You might find one, but it'll just never be the way it was.

It's best to get into the habit of using the Status bar for whatever you'd use the Styles box. Then, near as I can tell, you don't need the Styles box at all.

Fast format

I don't use this. I guess it's redundant for me to say that, because this is the theme of this chapter. So shoot me.

You can put your pointer in one paragraph, extract the formatting you have there, and then go around painting it in all over your screen. The pointer is even in the shape of a paint brush. Doing this pretty much amounts to handing a paint brush to your dog and letting her do whatever she wants.

For my part, I like to use styles to format my paragraphs. Then, if I change the styles, I change all the paragraphs in that style. Although this method is fast to apply initially, it's more difficult to change.

The Initial Caps command

Nobody I know of ever wants me to capitalize every word in a title or subtitle. They all want a person to capitalize the important words and put the other ones in small caps — you know, the *ofs*, the *thes* and the *ins*.

Suppose you have a subhead and want to capitalize it. You'd select it; then, from the Text menu, you'd choose Caps and then Initial Caps. It sounds great in theory.

However, this command caps all the words, not only the important ones. It's also much faster to simply type the words in initial caps in the first place. That way, you have more control over what's capped and what's not.

Chapter 21

The Top Ten Reasons to Stay with WordPerfect

Reason ten

Somebody handed you WordPerfect macros a long time ago. They're useful and hard to make. The person now refuses to hand you any Ami Pro macros. You're trapped, and you know it.

Reason nine

Your dog ate your wallet.

Reason eight

On your way to install Ami Pro, you fell into a time warp and landed in Elizabethan England. You forgot to come back.

Reason seven

You thought your Ami Pro disks were bologna, accidentally put them between two slices of bread, and ate them.

Reason six

You think that frames belong on beds, once in a while on a wall, maybe around someone falsely accused of murder, but never on your screen.

Reason five

You don't see what the big thing is about style sheets anyway.

Reason four

You hate having your documents look on-screen the way they will when they're printed. It's distracting.

Reason three

You've finally learned whether or not the *P* in the middle of WordPerfect is a capital and whether WordPerfect is one word or two. You feel you're entitled to some mileage out of this knowledge.

Reason two

You are stubborn and don't want to increase your productivity. Or, you forgot.

Reason one

Your boss says flat out, "We're a WordPerfect shop. It's very simple. It's my way or the highway."

The 5th Wave   By Rich Tennant

Poet e.e. cummings makes his last service call.

Appendix A
Installing the Great Beast

*H*ere's where I'm supposed to give you all kinds of reassurances about how easy this is to do and everything. Well, if you're doing it for the first time, nothing's that easy. Maybe disks are new to you. Maybe floppy drives on the computer are new. Maybe a hard drive, to you, is a long car trip through the Rockies. Swallow hard. Do whatever you do to give yourself courage, and let's go.

The Easiest Way

Most people start Windows, type one command, and then follow the instructions on-screen. If this method works, you are in luck!

Starting your computer

First, be sure your computer and monitor are running (well, you know, not running around or anything like that, but going. I don't mean going away or anything like that. Just turned on. Not turned on in the sense of enthusiastic, just switched on. Oh, I give up.)

Starting (or opening) Windows (or windows)

You might or might not want to open a few windows before you get into this. If you do want to, make sure the window is unlocked, grasp it firmly by the base, and pull up.

But I was mainly referring to Microsoft Windows.

To start Windows, find the DOS prompt, which looks something like this:

```
C:\
```

Type **win** and press the Enter key. The Windows Program Manager comes up, which bears some kind of resemblance to Figure A-1.

Some computers are set up to start Windows automatically, which means all you have to do is turn your computer on. If this happens (you turn on your computer and get a screen similar to the one in Figure A-1), consider yourself very lucky and skip to the next section.

If your Program Manager starts out as just a little icon, as shown in Figure A-2, double-click the icon to get it to open up.

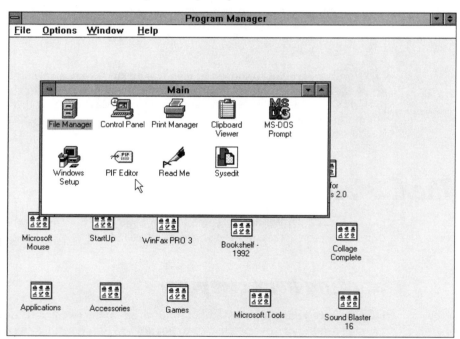

Figure A-1:
The
Windows
Program
Manager.

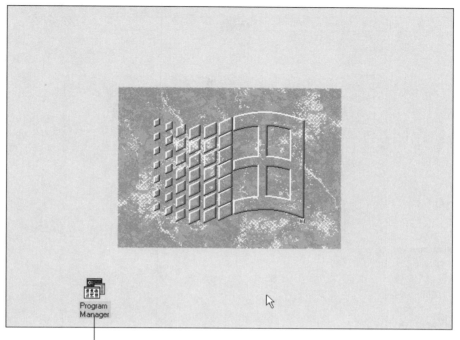

Figure A-2:
The
Program
Manager is
minimized.

Double-click the icon to open it.

Sliding your disks into the floppy drive

Follow these steps; they are the key ones:

1. **Find the Ami Pro disk that reads** *Install (Disk 1)*.

   You may have two sets of disks: bigger, more bendable ones (5¼") and smaller, more rigid ones (3½"). Slide in the one that fits your floppy disk drive.

2. **In the Program Manager, open the <u>F</u>ile menu (see Figure A-3).**

3. **Choose <u>R</u>un.**

   The Run dialog box opens, as shown in Figure A-4.

4. **In the Run dialog box, type** A:INSTALL **or** B:INSTALL.

   Whether you type **a:** or **b:** depends on which drive you put your disks in. If you have only one drive, it's called *A*. If you have two, try one and then the other (trial-and-error — don't worry, nothing bad will happen).

   You have to type the A, then a colon (:), and then INSTALL. It doesn't matter if you use capital letters, small ones, or a mixture. Figure A-4 shows the box with the command in it.

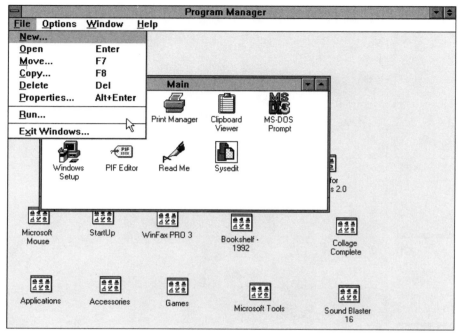

Figure A-3:
The Windows File menu.

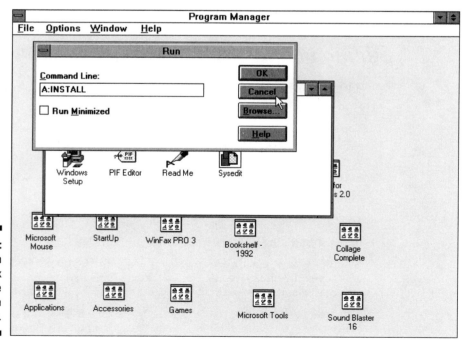

Figure A-4:
The Run dialog box with the command in it.

5. **Choose OK.**

   A *Please Wait* box shows for awhile; then the Ami Pro Install Program appears, as shown in Figure A-5.

6. **Unless you are installing on a server (you'll know if you are), click Install Ami Pro.**

7. **In the Install Choices box, Figure A-6, choose Complete Ami Pro Install.**

   From here on out, follow the instructions on-screen the best you can.

Ami Pro tells you which disks it wants, copies each disk into the computer, and lets you know its progress as it goes. It beeps when it finishes a disk and tells you which one to put in next. Simply put in the disks as it asks for them, and press Enter or choose OK.

When you've finished all the disks, Ami tells you what to do next. You get the chance to try out the QuickStart Tutorial if you like; then you're ready for this book.

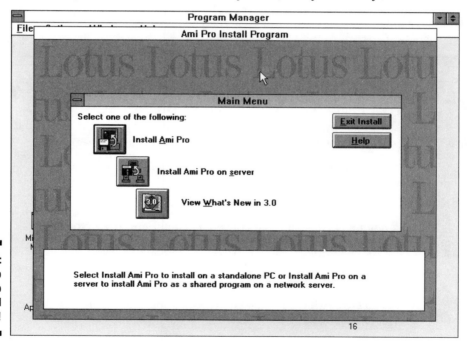

Figure A-5:
Welcome to
the Ami Pro
Install
Program!

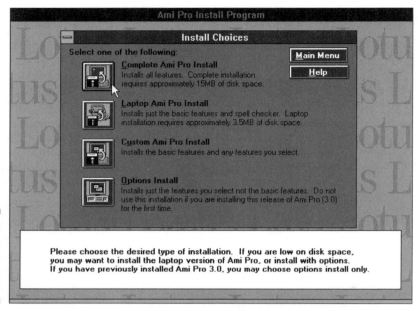

Figure A-6:
Choose
Complete
Ami Pro
Install here.

Equipment You Need to Install Ami Pro

Normal chapters on installation start out with an incomprehensible list of stuff you need to run Ami Pro. What nearly everybody I know does, though — and especially engineers I've seen work — is first try to get it to run. If it goes, you've got what you need. Whoever is responsible for setting you up has already seen to that.

If it doesn't work, though, you have to look back and see why not. Maybe you don't have the bare essential equipment. Here's what you need.

Your computer

You have to have at least an IBM-compatible 286 computer. It can also be a 386, 486, or Pentium. But an older model XT or below won't hack it.

Your monitor

A monitor with some kind of graphics capability — EGA, VGA, Super VGA, or Hercules, which, despite its epic name, is black-and-white.

Your mouse

You don't, *technically,* need a mouse to install Ami Pro. You can ski, technically, on one ski, too. But that style of operating isn't for most of us. Get a Microsoft-compatible mouse and save yourself much frustration, heartache, and wasted time. Mieces are the wave of the present and future — and you'll love them to pieces.

Your memory

If you have Windows running, you probably have enough memory already. Ami formally requires 2M (megabytes) of memory. 4M is even better, because it's a drag if the Spell Checker can't run or you can't open all the documents you need or you can't open the Ami File Manager or whatever type of problem might possibly come up if you don't have enough memory.

Memory is hardware. It's little chips you install on a board. Get your dealer to do it for you, preferably when you buy the computer.

Your disk space

You have to have a *hard disk,* (A *hard disk* is inside the computer. Ask your dealer how big your hard disk is.) You have to have at least 5M available to install Ami Pro. More is better, probably much more, but you need at least the 5M to get out of the starting gates. To do a full installation, you need 15M.

Just because a 3½" floppy disk is actually quite stiff and unyielding, it's not a hard disk. You don't have to check in advance to see how much room is available on your hard disk. Ami Pro checks when you install and, if it doesn't see the room there, it doesn't proceed.

Your Windows software

You have to have Microsoft Windows Version 3.0 or 3.1 (or, if something else higher than 3.1 has come out when you get this book, that will do). You can't use anything below 3.0.

Getting Someone Else to Install It

Most people who are installing software for the first time get someone else to help them. You have to use your personality for this. All of us have our little strategies, based on how we generally function in life. These are just a few suggestions, which you can adapt to your own style.

If all this bribing or sucking up fails, call the Lotus technical support line at 1-404-399-5505 (hours are 8:00 a.m. to 8:00 p.m. EST).

Bribing with whammy burgers, and so on

Take a programmer or other computer whiz to lunch — a nice lunch, maybe a quiche or some nice soup and bread in one of those Crock Pot deal type of restaurants. Burgers are always popular with technical folks. Go for the big stuff — Big Macs, Quarter Pounders, Whoppers, big things with tons of cheese and fries. Spring for a milk shake and a sundae. Maybe do this more than once. It's worth the investment.

Not all programmers will come across for you even after this treatment. They don't always believe in normal quid pro quo. This person may think you just like to be with him or her. Tell these computer nerds that you like them so much that you want to be with them while they install your Ami Pro.

Fumbling around and looking helpless

Make sure a programmer is around where he or she can see your struggles; then try to do the installation yourself. Fumble around. Try a few groans. Maybe start to cry if you feel comfortable with that. And look like you're nobly giving it your best shot.

Don't get too carried away trying to do it yourself and get your computer all fouled up. Remember, you're just faking this to get somebody to do it for you.

Going prostrate and begging

There comes a time to abandon your pride. It's better than installing some software program yourself if that's not your shtick. Use the direct approach. Beg. Say "please" and "pretty please." Offer to provide pizza, popcorn, cookies, or movie tickets.

Index

Title	Author	ISBN	Price
INTERNET / COMMUNICATIONS / NETWORKING			12/20/94
CompuServe For Dummies™	by Wallace Wang	1-56884-181-7	$19.95 USA/$26.95 Canada
Modems For Dummies™, 2nd Edition	by Tina Rathbone	1-56884-223-6	$19.99 USA/$26.99 Canada
Modems For Dummies™	by Tina Rathbone	1-56884-001-2	$19.95 USA/$26.95 Canada
MORE Internet For Dummies™	by John R. Levine & Margaret Levine Young	1-56884-164-7	$19.95 USA/$26.95 Canada
NetWare For Dummies™	by Ed Tittel & Deni Connor	1-56884-003-9	$19.95 USA/$26.95 Canada
Networking For Dummies™	by Doug Lowe	1-56884-079-9	$19.95 USA/$26.95 Canada
ProComm Plus 2 For Windows For Dummies™	by Wallace Wang	1-56884-219-8	$19.99 USA/$26.99 Canada
The Internet For Dummies™, 2nd Edition	by John R. Levine & Carol Baroudi	1-56884-222-8	$19.99 USA/$26.99 Canada
The Internet For Macs For Dummies™	by Charles Seiter	1-56884-184-1	$19.95 USA/$26.95 Canada
MACINTOSH			
Macs For Dummies®	by David Pogue	1-56884-173-6	$19.95 USA/$26.95 Canada
Macintosh System 7.5 For Dummies™	by Bob LeVitus	1-56884-197-3	$19.95 USA/$26.95 Canada
MORE Macs For Dummies™	by David Pogue	1-56884-087-X	$19.95 USA/$26.95 Canada
PageMaker 5 For Macs For Dummies™	by Galen Gruman	1-56884-178-7	$19.95 USA/$26.95 Canada
QuarkXPress 3.3 For Dummies™	by Galen Gruman & Barbara Assadi	1-56884-217-1	$19.99 USA/$26.99 Canada
Upgrading and Fixing Macs For Dummies™	by Kearney Rietmann & Frank Higgins	1-56884-189-2	$19.95 USA/$26.95 Canada
MULTIMEDIA			
Multimedia & CD-ROMs For Dummies™, Interactive Multimedia Value Pack	by Andy Rathbone	1-56884-225-2	$29.95 USA/$39.95 Canada
Multimedia & CD-ROMs For Dummies™	by Andy Rathbone	1-56884-089-6	$19.95 USA/$26.95 Canada
OPERATING SYSTEMS / DOS			
MORE DOS For Dummies™	by Dan Gookin	1-56884-046-2	$19.95 USA/$26.95 Canada
S.O.S. For DOS™	by Katherine Murray	1-56884-043-8	$12.95 USA/$16.95 Canada
OS/2 For Dummies™	by Andy Rathbone	1-878058-76-2	$19.95 USA/$26.95 Canada
UNIX			
UNIX For Dummies™	by John R. Levine & Margaret Levine Young	1-878058-58-4	$19.95 USA/$26.95 Canada
WINDOWS			
S.O.S. For Windows™	by Katherine Murray	1-56884-045-4	$12.95 USA/$16.95 Canada
MORE Windows 3.1 For Dummies™, 3rd Edition	by Andy Rathbone	1-56884-240-6	$19.99 USA/$26.99 Canada
PCs / HARDWARE			
Illustrated Computer Dictionary For Dummies™	by Dan Gookin, Wally Wang, & Chris Van Buren	1-56884-004-7	$12.95 USA/$16.95 Canada
Upgrading and Fixing PCs For Dummies™	by Andy Rathbone	1-56884-002-0	$19.95 USA/$26.95 Canada
PRESENTATION / AUTOCAD			
AutoCAD For Dummies™	by Bud Smith	1-56884-191-4	$19.95 USA/$26.95 Canada
PowerPoint 4 For Windows For Dummies™	by Doug Lowe	1-56884-161-2	$16.95 USA/$22.95 Canada
PROGRAMMING			
Borland C++ For Dummies™	by Michael Hyman	1-56884-162-0	$19.95 USA/$26.95 Canada
"Borland's New Language Product" For Dummies™	by Neil Rubenking	1-56884-200-7	$19.95 USA/$26.95 Canada
C For Dummies™	by Dan Gookin	1-878058-78-9	$19.95 USA/$26.95 Canada
C++ For Dummies™	by Stephen R. Davis	1-56884-163-9	$19.95 USA/$26.95 Canada
Mac Programming For Dummies™	by Dan Parks Sydow	1-56884-173-6	$19.95 USA/$26.95 Canada
QBasic Programming For Dummies™	by Douglas Hergert	1-56884-093-4	$19.95 USA/$26.95 Canada
Visual Basic "X" For Dummies™, 2nd Edition	by Wallace Wang	1-56884-230-9	$19.99 USA/$26.99 Canada
Visual Basic 3 For Dummies™	by Wallace Wang	1-56884-076-4	$19.95 USA/$26.95 Canada
SPREADSHEET			
1-2-3 For Dummies™	by Greg Harvey	1-878058-60-6	$16.95 USA/$21.95 Canada
1-2-3 For Windows 5 For Dummies™, 2nd Edition	by John Walkenbach	1-56884-216-3	$16.95 USA/$21.95 Canada
1-2-3 For Windows For Dummies™	by John Walkenbach	1-56884-052-7	$16.95 USA/$21.95 Canada
Excel 5 For Macs For Dummies™	by Greg Harvey	1-56884-186-8	$19.95 USA/$26.95 Canada
Excel For Dummies™, 2nd Edition	by Greg Harvey	1-56884-050-0	$16.95 USA/$21.95 Canada
MORE Excel 5 For Windows For Dummies™	by Greg Harvey	1-56884-207-4	$19.95 USA/$26.95 Canada
Quattro Pro 6 For Windows For Dummies™	by John Walkenbach	1-56884-174-4	$19.95 USA/$26.95 Canada
Quattro Pro For DOS For Dummies™	by John Walkenbach	1-56884-023-3	$16.95 USA/$21.95 Canada
UTILITIES / VCRs & CAMCORDERS			
Norton Utilities 8 For Dummies™	by Beth Slick	1-56884-166-3	$19.95 USA/$26.95 Canada
VCRs & Camcorders For Dummies™	by Andy Rathbone & Gordon McComb	1-56884-229-5	$14.99 USA/$20.99 Canada
WORD PROCESSING			
Ami Pro For Dummies™	by Jim Meade	1-56884-049-7	$19.95 USA/$26.95 Canada
MORE Word For Windows 6 For Dummies™	by Doug Lowe	1-56884-165-5	$19.95 USA/$26.95 Canada
MORE WordPerfect 6 For Windows For Dummies™	by Margaret Levine Young & David C. Kay	1-56884-206-6	$19.95 USA/$26.95 Canada
MORE WordPerfect 6 For DOS For Dummies™	by Wallace Wang, edited by Dan Gookin	1-56884-047-0	$19.95 USA/$26.95 Canada
S.O.S. For WordPerfect™	by Katherine Murray	1-56884-053-5	$12.95 USA/$16.95 Canada
Word 6 For Macs For Dummies™	by Dan Gookin	1-56884-190-6	$19.95 USA/$26.95 Canada
Word For Windows 6 For Dummies™	by Dan Gookin	1-56884-075-6	$16.95 USA/$21.95 Canada
Word For Windows For Dummies™	by Dan Gookin	1-878058-86-X	$16.95 USA/$21.95 Canada
WordPerfect 6 For Dummies™	by Dan Gookin	1-878058-77-0	$16.95 USA/$21.95 Canada
WordPerfect For Dummies™	by Dan Gookin	1-878058-52-5	$16.95 USA/$21.95 Canada
WordPerfect For Windows For Dummies™	by Margaret Levine Young & David C. Kay	1-56884-032-2	$16.95 USA/$21.95 Canada

FOR MORE INFORMATION OR TO ORDER, PLEASE CALL ▶ 800. 762. 2974

For volume discounts & special orders please call
Tony Real, Special Sales, at 415. 655. 3048

IDG BOOKS

Order Center: **(800) 762-2974** *(8 a.m.–6 p.m., EST, weekdays)*

12/20/94

Quantity	ISBN	Title	Price	Total

Shipping & Handling Charges

	Description	First book	Each additional book	Total
Domestic	Normal	$4.50	$1.50	$
	Two Day Air	$8.50	$2.50	$
	Overnight	$18.00	$3.00	$
International	Surface	$8.00	$8.00	$
	Airmail	$16.00	$16.00	$
	DHL Air	$17.00	$17.00	$

*For large quantities call for shipping & handling charges.
**Prices are subject to change without notice.

Ship to:

Name _____

Company _____

Address _____

City/State/Zip _____

Daytime Phone _____

Payment: ☐ Check to IDG Books (US Funds Only)

☐ VISA   ☐ MasterCard   ☐ American Express

Card # _____ Expires _____

Signature _____

Subtotal _____

CA residents add applicable sales tax _____

IN, MA, and MD residents add 5% sales tax _____

IL residents add 6.25% sales tax _____

RI residents add 7% sales tax _____

TX residents add 8.25% sales tax _____

Shipping _____

Total _____

Please send this order form to:

**IDG Books Worldwide
7260 Shadeland Station, Suite 100
Indianapolis, IN 46256**

*Allow up to 3 weeks for delivery.
Thank you!*

IDG BOOKS WORLDWIDE REGISTRATION CARD

RETURN THIS REGISTRATION CARD FOR FREE CATALOG

Title of this book: Ami Pro For Dummies

My overall rating of this book: ❏ Very good [1] ❏ Good [2] ❏ Satisfactory [3] ❏ Fair [4] ❏ Poor [5]

How I first heard about this book:

❏ Found in bookstore; name: [6]   ❏ Book review: [7]

❏ Advertisement: [8]   ❏ Catalog: [9]

❏ Word of mouth; heard about book from friend, co-worker, etc.: [10]   ❏ Other: [11]

What I liked most about this book:

What I would change, add, delete, etc., in future editions of this book:

Other comments:

Number of computer books I purchase in a year: ❏ 1 [12] ❏ 2-5 [13] ❏ 6-10 [14] ❏ More than 10 [15]

I would characterize my computer skills as: ❏ Beginner [16] ❏ Intermediate [17] ❏ Advanced [18] ❏ Professional [19]

I use ❏ DOS [20] ❏ Windows [21] ❏ OS/2 [22] ❏ Unix [23] ❏ Macintosh [24] ❏ Other: [25]_____
                                                              (please specify)

I would be interested in new books on the following subjects:

(please check all that apply, and use the spaces provided to identify specific software)

❏ Word processing: [26]   ❏ Spreadsheets: [27]

❏ Data bases: [28]   ❏ Desktop publishing: [29]

❏ File Utilities: [30]   ❏ Money management: [31]

❏ Networking: [32]   ❏ Programming languages: [33]

❏ Other: [34]

I use a PC at (please check all that apply): ❏ home [35] ❏ work [36] ❏ school [37] ❏ other: [38] _____

The disks I prefer to use are ❏ 5.25 [39] ❏ 3.5 [40] ❏ other: [41]_____

I have a CD ROM: ❏ yes [42] ❏ no [43]

I plan to buy or upgrade computer hardware this year: ❏ yes [44] ❏ no [45]

I plan to buy or upgrade computer software this year: ❏ yes [46] ❏ no [47]

Name: Business title: [48]   Type of Business: [49]

Address (❏ home [50] ❏ work [51]/Company name: _____)

Street/Suite#

City [52]/State [53]/Zipcode [54]:   Country [55]

❏ **I liked this book!** You may quote me by name in future
IDG Books Worldwide promotional materials.

My daytime phone number is _____

IDG BOOKS

THE WORLD OF
COMPUTER
KNOWLEDGE